IN JULIA'S KITCHEN *WITH* MASTER CHEFS

■

IN JULIA'S KITCHEN
WITH MASTER CHEFS

Julia Child

with Nancy Verde Barr
Photographs by Micheal McLaughlin

Alfred A. Knopf

New York

2000

This Is a Borzoi Book Published by Alfred A. Knopf, Inc.

Library of Congress Cataloging-in-Publication Data

Child, Julia
    In Julia's kitchen with master chefs/by Julia Child; with Nancy Verde
    Barr; photographs by Micheal McLaughlin.—1st ed.
        p. cm.
    Includes index.
    ISBN 0-679-43896-3—ISBN 0-679-76005-9 (pbk.)
    1. Cookery, American. 2. Cooks—United States—Biography.
    I. Barr, Nancy Verde. II. Title.
    TX715.C54542 1995
    641.5973—dc20   97-39380
                                                                          CIP

Manufactured in the United States of America
Published April 12, 1995
Reprinted Twice
Fourth Printing, July 2000

CONTENTS

INTRODUCTION

This book is a celebration of food in America today, and we have come a remarkably long way in the last thirty-five years. When my first book, *Mastering the Art of French Cooking,* was published in 1961, many cooks had never heard of a leek, had never seen or used a shallot, hardly knew that the word "braise" existed, and most salads were made with iceberg lettuce. Good wine was French wine. Period. There were fine restaurants, mostly in New York, mostly French, and one expected chefs in those restaurants to be French. Notable foods and great cuisine were not demanded by the general public, since we were still, on the whole, a meat-and-potatoes culture.

Although World War II brought some enlightenment, I think the great revolution came through the airplane. Before that the only way to go abroad was by boat, and few but the leisure classes and students on summer vacations had the time to spend five or six days to get to Europe, and five or six days to come back. By the early sixties, however, all kinds of people were flying abroad (the Far East had yet to open up), where for the first time they began to take a discriminating interest in what they ate; they sampled fine wines, experimented with fine foods, and began to hope for the same quality when they came home. The Kennedys in the White House also had a significant effect, I believe, with their talented French chef, René Verdon, and their obvious interest in the good life. Stories about their banquets and menus abounded in the press. Suddenly fine dining was not only fascinating, but acceptable in the highest places.

For years he (but very rarely she), the chef, was considered an artisan, not an artist. Professional cooking was a career, but it was not looked upon by the public as an honored profession. The great chef Escoffier, the exception to the rule, tried his best in the early 1900s to raise the standing of his cooks. "When you go out on the street," he said to them, "wear a hat and a coat and a tie. You want to look like a somebody!" But it was not until the early 1970s in France, with the coming of "nouvelle cuisine," that breakaway from the old classical harness, that chefs got any real recognition. It ushered in the era of the superstar chefs, led by Paul Bocuse, and featuring Michel Guérard, Roger Vergé, the Troisgros brothers, and others. It caught the fancy of the American press, who always need an exciting topic to write about, and suddenly chefs were news.

Now, some twenty years later, chefs and cooks and American cuisine are indeed news. We have fine professional culinary schools, we can find excellent produce in our markets, American wines are in the world-class category, and we can be proud indeed of our gastronomic achievements. That is what this volume, which accompanies our television series, is about—an in-depth look at contemporary American cooking through twenty-six of our nationally recognized and newsworthy chefs. We want to know how they got where they are, we want to learn their special ways with food, and, above all, we want to be well aware of what is going on in this country's top kitchens today.

It is exciting to see how all of them, each in his or her special way, are proud of the profession. All of them passionately love their work, and, more important from our point of view as home cooks, all of them have been delighted to share their knowledge with us. Jasper White gives us his famous Pan-Roasted Lobster, one of his restaurant's signature dishes. Gordon Hamersley describes the way he makes his most popular Roast Chicken with Garlic and Lemon, and George Germon of Al Forno reveals the secret of his famous Dirty Steak. Jacques Torres's chocolate constructions are the pride of Le Cirque in New York, where his spectacular works are displayed and enjoyed, and he teaches us how to make them. Zarela Martínez's tamales are famous, as are Leah Chase's fabulous baking-powder biscuits, and we have their recipes here. We also have Charlie Trotter's Smoked Salmon Napoleons, Jean-Georges Vongerichten's Crab Spring Rolls, and Daniel Boulud's Roasted Veal Chops and Sweetbreads, to say nothing of his Warm Chocolate Upside-Down Soufflés, and Jim Dodge's great all-American Chocolate Buttermilk Fudge Cake.

Although these dishes are the creations of professionals, and you can see the pros cooking them on the television screen, every recipe in this book has been carefully worked out for the home cook—the cook who really loves to cook. I make no apologies for the length of some of the recipes—I seem to be known for my long recipes! I want them to work for you whether or not you see them demonstrated on the screen. If you wish to cook them and have them turn out the way they should, you need all the details. You want to know, for instance, exactly how to form and twirl Roberto Donna's pizza dough, and how to cut and stretch out onto the baking sheet Carol Field's breadsticks, as well as the technique for preparing Julian Serrano's Oven-Roasted Figs.

In their creative enthusiasm a goodly number of our chefs call for multiple sauces and numerous garnishes, all of which are dutifully included here, but many of which you may decide to omit, or will want to use separately for another dish or occasion. A fine example of this is Dean Fearing's Mansion Shrimp Diablo "Tamale," one of the specialties in his restaurant at The Mansion on Turtle Creek in Dallas. In addition to the shrimp, he calls for Red Jalapeño "Caesar Salad" Dressing, Spicy Red Salsa, Diablo Sauce, and his Fresh Corn Puree. To put directions for these four recipes within the shrimp recipe itself would have been not only cumbersome but ridiculous. Besides it would effectively have taken them out of circulation when they need to stand by themselves so that they may be referred to easily in the index. Wherever sensible, therefore, we have included such examples as separate recipes, with page references to them in the main dish.

Of course it is ideal if you can see the dishes on television as they are being made, and then have this book as reference. But Nancy Barr and I have written this to be a cookbook that stands alone, like any cookbook, making it possible for you, the cook, to read, visualize through the accompanying photographs, and then (for example) roast Reed Hearon's cod in its crust of salt—another good reason for writing the recipes out in great detail. We want the same for Christopher Gross's Alder-Smoked Loin of Beef, Madhur Jaffrey's Basmati Rice, and Jody Adams's Stuffed Braised Breast of Veal.

It's useful also to have an appendix in addition to what we call "boxes"—tidbits of information boxed off throughout the pages, such as how to produce salted almonds or herb-toasted pecans, or a discussion of deep-fats to use for frying. Can you make your own self-rising flour, for instance, and what is it used for? Another topic is the earthshaking difference between sweet potatoes and yams, another tapioca versus arrowroot, and still another fresh versus dried herbs and their equivalents. There are bits of lore on pureeing garlic, on olive oils, anchovies, which duck to use for what, and how to make a quick curry butter. Some of the longer boxes and appendix entries are short recipes, such as those for chicken stock, custard sauce, and the cooking of green beans.

If you happen to be following both the book and the TV recipes, you will see some minor differences now and then in sequences, timing, or even proportions. For instance, the chef will start the sauce after the fish is done while the book starts it earlier, or 3 egg yolks will be used rather than the 2 in the book, and so forth. These differences, usually noted in the text, are sometimes to cut down a chef's restaurant proportions to family size, or at other times to make the sequence of events more relevant to the way we cook at home. In any case, both versions work, but the book recipes always have the home cook in mind.

As for nutrition (always one of my favorite subjects!), certainly enough has been written in the last few years so that we all know the litany: moderation, small helpings, weight watching, moderate exercise, and a great variety of foods. I would add to that: Take an adult point of view! We all know that we should eat lots of fresh fruits, vegetables, and whole grains, that we should watch our intake of fats, and if we indulge one day we must pay for it the next. Most important of all, food is a family affair and every meal (including breakfast) should be a joyous occasion. While we are here on this earth we should not only be nourished by our food, we should also enjoy the infinite pleasures of the table—as well as enjoying the cooking of what goes upon it.

Many of the dishes are teeming with exciting new ideas from Spain, Mexico, the Orient, and from right here in America. They are a stimulating look into what is going on in the professional kitchens of today, and should inspire all of us who enjoy our own cooking to get out into our markets and see what's new, and to get into our own kitchens and try them out. One can never master it all since some new machine, or vegetable, salad ingredient, exotic fish, or technique is always around the corner. The culinary arts make a wonderfully exhilarating profession and an always satisfyingly creative hobby.

With all good wishes and—*toujours bon appétit.*

ACKNOWLEDGMENTS

This book was written to accompany our "Master Chefs" television series, as was the previous book, *Cooking with Master Chefs* (1993). I speak in the plural because we are always a close-knit team, a family unit, as those who take part in a television series so often are. Our father figure, Geoffrey Drummond, president of our production company, A La Carte Communications, had the idea in the first place. He wanted to produce a carefully constructed and beautifully filmed television series showcasing the best we have to offer in contemporary American cuisine—the chefs and cooks, the foods, the techniques. The programs would be directed to the serious home cook as well as to aspiring young cooks, in an understandable, doable, as well as lively manner. In our last series, "Cooking with Master Chefs," we visited chefs and cooks in their home kitchens. In this series they came to visit us here, in my kitchen.

Fortunately I live in a large gray Cantabridgian mansion, built in the late 1880s during the period of multiple maids and domestic help. The house therefore includes a wonderfully roomy kitchen, not one but two pantries, and a vast cellar with a separate laundry room. Geof and his crew rearranged the first floor and basement so that all twenty or more of our team plus the visiting chef managed to fit themselves into the various spaces. The kitchen became the studio filming area, and our Norwegian kitchen table gave way to a practical cooktop-worktop island with shelves and drawers underneath. My wall oven with its squeaking door remained, as did the sink. Steel pipes for hanging TV lights ran the length of the ceiling, and there was room facing the island for our three cameramen—a tremendously important advantage, having three of them, so that one camera could always be focused closely upon the action.

The dining room table was carted up to the attic, and the dining room itself became the control center where the director sat with his bank of TV monitors, audio controls, switches, and his various engineers. The visiting chef and his assistants did their preparatory work in the laundry room while an immense array of props took over the rest of the cellar, the domain of our culinary producer, Susie Heller, who had also interviewed all the chefs and planned out their menus.

Since we were taping the shows in July and August, some kind of air-conditioning was essential, and an ingenious system was worked out by Geof's associate producer, Kimberly Nolan. A large, flexible plastic pipe two feet in diameter and forty feet long was inserted into the window frame of the living room. Snaking its cumbersome way across the hallway, its mouth was dragged to the edge of the kitchen door, where it blew in a most welcome stream of cool air. At the same time warm air was sucked noiselessly out of the kitchen through the mouth of another immense pipe inserted in the pantry window. I doubt that we could have survived otherwise, but a weird-looking house it was from the outside. Trucks, cars, and miscellaneous equipment lined the street, a big Dumpster was parked in the driveway next to the strange orange-colored air-conditioning pumper, and wires of all sorts were running in every direction. The inside was even more peculiar, beginning with the bulky air-conditioning pipe laid from hall to kitchen, and all those people wearing headsets wandering around or crouched over monitors, all those lights and machines, and our own company television chefs, Charlie Saccardi and Bernard Giordano, constantly running up and down from cellar to kitchen carrying platters of food. A strange and busy household indeed, but the smell of good cooking was always in the air.

On most days one chef was in the kitchen performing while another was in the laundry room prepping for the next day's taping. My role was to be with the performing chef, as though he or she were giving me a private lesson—which indeed was the case. I saw myself as representing the audience with such questions as: "Was that a 375-degree oven?" or "Did you say 3 cups?" or "Would you please do that again, so I can see it from this angle?" and so forth. While I was in the kitchen, my colleague and co-writer, Nancy Barr, was down in the cellar, in the laundry prep room, with her laptop computer, television monitor, and next day's chef, taking down what was going on in both kitchen and laundry. She was responsible not only for recipe information but for the chefs' biographies that appear at the beginning of each chapter. When I was not in the kitchen with the chef, I was upstairs, whacking away at my own computer, turning Nancy's drafts into what we came to call "Julia language," and organizing the formal text for this book.

We finished on schedule, August 15th (my birthday), and our team had my big old house back in order two days later. We had a wonderful, happy, hardworking, intense, and unforgettable time together. Such a pleasure and privilege it was to be with people who care deeply about what they are doing, whether it be adjusting a light, recording the right squish and slap of an *aïoli* sauce being made in a giant mortar and pestle, or turning a dish this way and that and rearranging the food countless times to get just the right angle to satisfy our photographer, Micheal McLaughlin, or our directors, Bruce Franchini and Herb Sevush—Herb also had the awesome task of editing the thirty-nine episodes in the series. I thank them all, and everyone on our television team.

As always, my administrative assistant, Stephanie Hersh, has been invaluable in keeping the house and office and mail going, all the while helping with the manuscript, and constantly ready to assist anyone at any time. "A cookbook is only as good as its index," and our Pat Kelly, charter member of The Culinary Historians of New England, has done it again—as she so ably has done for my last three books. Kathleen

Annino, our able and affable chief recipe tester, fried innumerable chickens and crab rolls, yet still made time to develop the unique Common Crackers (page 225) for Chef Jasper's fish chowder. My makeup artist, Louise Miller, and I have been together since the early "French Chef" television days, in the 1960s; she struggled mightily with face and hair, and always with good humor, during our humid summer taping days.

Of course there would be no book at all without Alfred A. Knopf, Inc., who have always been my publisher, and I have always been grateful indeed to be with them; I love the look of their books and the care they take in their production and distribution. I know how fortunate we are to be in the hands of Knopf's distinguished editor, Judith Jones. I have been with Judith since my first book, *Mastering the Art of French Cooking;* I have tremendous admiration for her and confidence in her judgment. She knows how to get a book through the maze of steps it must negotiate to get out on time! She is a wonder, as well as dear friend.

Williams-Sonoma and Wilton Industries/Rowoco provided us with an endless supply of essential props, platters, kitchenware, and gadgets, while Schreibmen Jewelers of Cleveland sent us all the dinner, dessert, and other handsome plates you see here in the photographs. Bourgeat and Le Creuset provided special pots to simmer in, while New Hearth Products/Viking stoves installed and maintained our cooktop to simmer upon. The Charles Hotel in Cambridge graciously provided a home to our visiting chefs, while Olgo Russo of A. Russo and Sons delivered their fresh-produce demands—no matter what esoterica they needed, he found it.

Of course, four of the most serious and important "without whoms" to whom we are all eternally grateful are PBS for their continuing support of our series, and especially to Maryland Public Television, A La Carte's caring and enthusiastic co-producer/presenting station. Lastly we give most resounding and heartfelt thanks to our generous underwriters, Farberware Millennium cookware, and The Wineries of E. and J. Gallo/Gallo Sonoma Wines.

In Julia's Kitchen *with* Master Chefs

ROBERTO DONNA

Watching the exuberant Roberto Donna spin his pizza and roll his pasta, it is easy to imagine him as a jubilant three-year-old boy watching the chefs in the restaurant near his parents' grocery store in Torino, Italy. "The kitchen was my playground. I was always there. As soon as my eyes were at table level, the chefs let me stuff ravioli." Chef Roberto has never lost the sense of joy and playfulness he found in that kitchen; he names his delicate, giant puffed pizza "a pizza in the form of a child's large ball."

At thirteen, with eyes well above table level, Roberto enrolled in professional cooking school and graduated first in his class. He arrived in Washington, D.C., when he was nineteen, and although he might not have intended to build a culinary dynasty, it certainly seems as though he has. His restaurants, Galileo, Il Radicchio, I Matti, and Osteria del Arucula, are all flourishing. Customers and critics have come to expect from him innovative Italian specialties; they are not disappointed. He learned as a child that the emphasis must be on the ingredients, and his passion for the best led him to open two other culinary establishments—with Jean-Louis Palladin, Pesce, a retail fish store with a small café, and Il Pane, a bakery that offers breads and confections as well as pasta and cheese.

"Chef Roberto Donna has practically become a national treasure," wrote Phyllis Richman in *The Washington Post*. Italy, however, did not relinquish its young chef easily and in 1991 awarded him the Caterina de' Medici Award, naming him the "Ambassador of Food outside of Italy." Either way, we are very lucky to have Roberto Donna on our soil and luckier still that he took the time to "play" in the Master Chefs' kitchen.

ALL-PURPOSE DOUGH FOR PIZZAS, PALLONES, PANINOS, BREADS, AND ROLLS

Chef Roberto's pizza dough is a simple classic bread dough—no frills, no olive oil, just fresh yeast, water, flour, and salt. He prefers that his doughs be made with a starter—that is, the yeast dissolved in a little water, then left to bubble with a small portion of the flour. When it is ready, in half an hour or so, he then completes the dough. He likes to knead his doughs either in a heavy-duty electric mixer with dough hook or by hand.

Manufacturing Note: Roberto's TV recipe makes 8 pizzas. You may wish to cut his proportions in half; but note that extra dough may be cut into portion sizes and frozen.

Technique: More details on working with yeast doughs are on page 6.

Preparing the Yeast Starter: Stir the yeast and ½ cup of the water in the mixer bowl, blending for several minutes with your fingers to dissolve the yeast completely. Then, still using your fingers, blend in 1 cup of the flour, mixing well to form a smooth batter. Cover the bowl with a towel and set in a warm (about 72° F), draft-free place for half an hour or more, until the starter is full of big bubbles.

Ahead-of-Time Note: May be prepared in advance and left in the refrigerator for several hours or overnight.

Mixing and Kneading the Dough: Stir the salt into the remaining flour, mix together well, and add it to the starter. Pour in all but ¼ cup of the remaining water and attach the bowl to the machine. Start beating at slow speed and gradually increase to medium, adding droplets of water if the dough seems stiff and dry. Knead for a good 5 minutes, until the dough is smooth. It is ready when it forms a ball that cleans all the flour from the sides of the bowl. Transfer the dough to a floured counter and knead it several minutes by hand—until it is smooth and elastic, and holds its shape when bent back and forth between your two hands.

Rising: Briefly knead the dough into a smooth, round ball. Dust the bowl with a sprinkling of flour and flour the ball of dough lightly before turning it about in the bowl. Cut a cross 3 inches long and ½ inch deep in the top of the dough, and sprinkle with a dusting of flour. Cover the bowl with a

INGREDIENTS FOR ABOUT 3 POUNDS OF DOUGH (ENOUGH FOR EIGHT 9-INCH PIZZAS)

2 packages (1.2 ounces) fresh yeast or 2 packages (.5 ounce, 3½ teaspoons) dry-active yeast

2 cups warm water (at body temperature— not over 100° F)

7 cups (2 pounds) unbleached all-purpose flour

1 teaspoon salt

SPECIAL EQUIPMENT SUGGESTED

A freestanding electric mixer with dough hook attachment (useful but not essential)

A 6-quart, fairly straight-sided bowl (for rising the dough)

towel. Let rise to double its volume, again in a warm, draft-free spot (about 72° F)—2 hours or so.

Finishing the Dough: Turn the dough out onto a floured counter and knead for 2 minutes. The dough is now ready to use in any way you wish. For pizzas, cut it into 8 pieces, as described in the next step.

Ahead-of-Time Note: At this point, the dough may be returned to its bowl, covered with plastic, and left overnight in the refrigerator—punch and weight it down occasionally until it has chilled.

Preparing the Pizza Shape: Working on a lightly floured counter and keeping your hands lightly floured so the dough will not stick, cut the dough into 8 even pieces. Work on one piece at a time, leaving the others covered with a towel. Roll a piece in a circular motion under the palm of your hand to form a tennis ball shape, then pick it up in both hands, with your thumbs on top, and gently stretch and fold the dough, always maintaining its round ball shape. Once you start forming the dough, a kind of skin forms on the surface, as though it were very fine rubber—you can't see it, but you can feel it. By stretching the top surface down to the bottom of the ball and turning and repeating that motion, you create a surface tension that will hold the ball in shape. After 5 to 6 folds and turns, you should have a smooth surface with a rough bottom; now either roll the dough in your hands or rotate it on the counter to smooth the bottom. Repeat with the remaining pieces of dough, setting the balls, smooth side down, on a floured baking sheet. Dust the tops with flour, cover with a towel, and place in a warm (72° to 75° F), draft-free place until they have doubled in volume—about 2 hours.

Ahead-of-time Note: The dough may be kept overnight in the refrigerator, in which case set the balls on an oiled pan, brush the top surface of each ball with olive oil, and cover with plastic wrap, to prevent a crust from forming on the surface. Or you may freeze the balls of dough, wrapping each separately.

JULIA'S NOTES ON THE RISING AND CHILLING AND THE FREEZING AND THAWING OF DOUGHS

The normal rising temperature for yeast doughs is between 70° F and 75° F. At higher temperatures the dough rises too quickly and does not develop the flavors and texture that yeast offers the dough. At colder temperatures, particularly in the low 60s, the dough takes much longer to rise, and, depending on other factors in its makeup, it can develop a rougher, country-type texture. A dough may be left in the refrigerator to slow its rise for a few hours or overnight, and a risen dough may be frozen, as suggested for Chef Roberto's formed pizza-dough pieces.

PIZZA MARGHERITA

When your pizza dough is having its final rise, it's time to prepare whatever topping you have chosen. Chef Roberto particularly likes this simple, straightforward Margherita formula, a Neapolitan classic with its excellently crafted crust, perfectly seasoned tomatoes, and its always appealing topping of mozzarella and fresh leaves of basil.

Preparing the Tomato Topping: Slice the drained tomatoes open, and use your fingers to scrape away the seeds. Drop the pulp into a bowl and crush with a fork into bite-size pieces. Stir in the garlic, basil, salt, pepper, and oil. Taste, correct seasoning, and set aside.

Readying the Oven: Thirty minutes before you plan to bake, set the pizza stone or tiles on the middle rack of the oven and preheat to at least 500° F—550° F if your oven will go that high. It is essential that the baking surface be very hot.

Manufacturing Note: The next step describes Roberto's pizza technique. The dough is to be treated gently so that the pizza itself will have a crisp rather than hard crust. "Never use a rolling pin," he says. "Only the balls of your fingers." If you are not up to the final twirling over the back of your hand, continue to stretch the dough with your fingers. But you'll soon master a serviceable, if not professional, twirl with a little courage and not too much practice. Eventually you can hope to twirl like a Neapolitan master. Suppose a piece of dough falls on the floor—pick it up and use it to practice.

INGREDIENTS FOR FOUR
9-INCH PIZZAS

*1½-pound can (2½ cups) of
    peeled Italian plum tomatoes,
    drained*

*1 to 2 garlic cloves, peeled and
    finely chopped*

*8 large fresh basil leaves, torn
    into rough ½-inch pieces*

Salt to taste

*½ teaspoon freshly ground black
    pepper*

(continued)

Stretching the Dough into Its Pizza Shape: When the oven is well heated (and/or between pizzas), sprinkle the peel liberally with flour and set aside. Form a ball of dough into the pizza shape as follows: Set it on your lightly floured work surface, keeping the rest of the dough covered with a towel. Gently flatten the ball into a disk shape, then, using the balls of your floured fingers, starting from the center, press and dimple the dough rapidly down and then up around your previous track, down again, and so forth, coming to within ⅜ inch of the circumference—with your fingers you are making a gentle pushing-out movement. When the circle is about 6 inches across, turn the dough over and continue on the other side. Finally, to enlarge it even more, scoop it up onto the back of one hand, give that hand a little jerk to start the dough moving, and rotate it as you gently pull at the rim all around—being careful not to tear it. Spread the circle of dough on your floured peel. Don't be too concerned if its shape is not perfect—you can correct it to some degree with the finger-ball-push. Proceed at once to the topping.

On Goes the Topping: Leaving ½ inch of the circumference free all around, spread 2 to 3 tablespoons of the tomato topping over the pizza—it is not supposed to be a deep layer, only a rough but thorough covering. Scatter ⅓ to ½ cup of the mozzarella over the surface—again, this is not a heavy coating, just a scattering. End with 2 tablespoons of Parmesan sprinkled over all,

The cheese and basil

8 ounces (2 cups) mozzarella cheese, cut into ⅜-inch dice

½ cup grated Parmesan cheese

4 tablespoons excellent olive oil (optional)

8 or more large fresh whole basil leaves for decoration (optional)

The pizza crusts

4 risen and ready-to-form balls of pizza dough (see page 4)

SPECIAL EQUIPMENT
SUGGESTED

A pizza paddle (peel), or a cookie sheet with an open end

A pizza baking stone, or unglazed floor tiles to line your oven rack

JULIA'S NOTES ON USING THE MICROWAVE FOR WARMING CHILLED DOUGH AND THAWING FROZEN DOUGH

We have found the following methods to be safe and successful, though conservative: if you go a few seconds too long, you've cooked the dough. (I am indebted to Linda Eckhardt and Diana Butts and their *Bread in Half the Time* [Crown] for introducing me to yeast doughs and the microwave.)

Preparations for microwaving: Place the dough in a microwave-safe glass container, cover the container closely with microwave plastic wrap, and pierce several pin holes in the surface. Fill a 1-cup glass measure with water and set in a far corner of the oven.

Warming chilled dough: For 1 full recipe of Roberto's dough, packed in its container as described, microwave on "defrost" exactly 2 minutes. Let rest 5 minutes. This warms the dough enough so that it can rise again, or so that you can deflate and form it.

Defrosting a whole recipe of Roberto's frozen dough: Packed in its container as previously described, microwave at "defrost" for 2 minutes; let rest 5 minutes, then microwave another 2 minutes at "defrost." Let rest 5 minutes more and knead, to soften any frozen lumps. Let the dough come to room temperature.

Defrosting formed balls of frozen dough: Defrost only 1 piece of dough at a time, and pack in its container as previously described. Microwave at "defrost" for 1 to 2 minutes, let rest 5 minutes, and microwave at "defrost" 1 minute more. Let rest 5 minutes, then knead and squeeze to soften any lumps; let come to room temperature.

and a dribble of olive oil if you wish. Bake at once, to prevent the dough from sticking to the peel.

Baking—5 to 6 minutes at 500° to 550°F: Place the far tip of the peel near the far end of the baking surface; slowly and gently shuffle the pizza off the peel with small jerks, hoping the circle of dough has retained its shape— with practice, it will!

When Is It Done? The cheese topping should be bubbling, and the crust golden. Lift up an edge to see if it has browned lightly underneath.

Slide the paddle under the pizza and remove it to a cutting board. Place a few basil leaves in the center if you wish and cut it into wedges for serving. The sign of a good pizza crust, says Roberto, is that the tip of the wedge will droop just a little, but the wedge will hold its shape.

Manufacturing Note: Allow a wait of 3 to 4 minutes between baking pizzas so the stone has time to reheat.

OTHER USES FOR ROBERTO'S PIZZA DOUGH

The same dough and general method for pizza yields two more of Chef Roberto's specialties, the *panino* and the *pallone.* First he forms a ball of dough into a thickish disk, and it puffs up into a crisp ball on the hot baking surface. For the *panino,* he turns the crisp ball into a salad sandwich, rather like the *pan bagna* of Nice, which is filled with a *salade niçoise.* For the *pallone,* he simply drapes mortadella or prosciutto and cheese over it. They are easy to do, easy to serve, and always a big hit with young and old.

CHESTNUT FLOUR

Most chestnut flour—*farina di castagne*—comes from Italy or France and it is not always easy to find. Look for it in ethnic neighborhoods, especially where there are Italian markets. Smell and taste the flour carefully before buying since it can turn bad. It should have a sweet, nutty scent and flavor; if it is old it will taste bitter. Store it well sealed in a cool spot.

PANINO A FORMA DI PALLONE
PUFF PIZZA FILLED WITH MOZZARELLA,
MORTADELLA, AND LETTUCE

Preliminaries: Have your filling at the ready, along with a serrated knife. Then start out as you would when making a pizza, with the hot baking surface, a 500° to 550° F oven, and a floured peel. Form the ball of dough, using the balls of your fingers, into a disk 8 to 9 inches in diameter.

Baking: Transfer the disk of dough to the peel and slide it onto the hot baking surface. If you have an oven window, you will see the disk gradually begin to puff up in parts, then balloon into a good-size round ball. In 4 to 5 minutes it will be a fine golden brown and crisp all over. Transfer it from oven to cutting board, and at once cut it in half horizontally. Remove the top and set aside.

Preparing the Filling: Rapidly toss the salad greens with the oil, then the vinegar, and season nicely with salt and pepper. Arrange the greens on the bottom half of the *panino,* drape the cheese and meat over the salad, and cover with the top.

Serving: Serve at once, while still hot. Break the crusty top down into the salad with an outstretched hand, and then cut in quarters.

Manufacturing Note: If you are making more than one *panino,* wait 3 to 4 minutes before putting in a second dough so the stone has time to reheat.

INGREDIENTS FOR ONE 8-INCH
"BIG-BALL SANDWICH"
(SERVING 1 OR 2 FOR LUNCH,
OR 4 AS AN APPETIZER)

For the dough
*1 risen ball of pizza dough
(see page 4)*

For the filling (per *panino*)
*A handful (1½ cups loosely
packed) of mesclun or mixed
salad greens, in a mixing bowl*
2 tablespoons excellent olive oil
*2 teaspoons balsamic vinegar,
or to taste*
Salt
Freshly ground black pepper
5 or 6 thin slices of mozzarella
*3 or 4 thin slices of mortadella
or prosciutto*

ROBERTO'S PALLONE DI PIZZA
(PIZZA BALL)

Remove the puffed brown ball from the oven and immediately drape the prosciutto on top, covering the entire surface. Scatter the cheese over the prosciutto and press down on the top with the flat side of a chef's knife, deflating the ball. Cut into wedges and serve as an appetizer for 4 to 6 people.

*The pizza ball, baked as in the
preceding* panino *recipe*
*6 or more paper-thin slices of
prosciutto*
*1 ounce Parmesan cheese slivers
(8 or more shaved off with a
vegetable peeler)*

TROFFIE DI FARINA DI CASTAGNE
CHESTNUT PASTA SAUCED WITH PESTO, AND SERVED
WITH A POTATO AND GREEN BEAN GARNISH

Troffie *are small pastas made principally from chestnut flour in the shape of baby pig tails or curly worms—a specialty of Genoa on the Ligurian coast of the Mediterranean. Chestnut flour gives a very special nutty, slightly sweet taste quite unlike the usual wheat-flour pastas. These are hand-formed shapes, and their preparation gives you an opportunity to have a friendly family pasta-rolling get-together in the kitchen, with conversation and giggles. Chef Roberto serves his* troffie *with a fragrant basil and garlic sauce—pesto—and garnishes them in the traditional regional manner, with a sprinkling of finely diced potatoes and green beans.*

Manufacturing Note: The white flour called for in the recipe is bleached all-purpose, since bleached flour produces that certain gummy quality which chestnut flour needs if the *troffie* are to hold their shape. You should find chestnut flour in Italian markets and some health food stores. Be sure it smells fresh and fine since it can turn rancid; store it in your freezer. You can, of course, make pasta in the *troffie* shape using bleached white flour only.

Preparing the Dough: If you are using a mixer, stir the two flours and the salt together in the bowl. Start running the machine at moderate speed and add just enough water to make a somewhat stiff but pliable dough; remove the dough to the counter and knead briefly. (Or mix and knead by hand.) The dough will be quite firm and rather rubbery. Wrap in plastic and refrigerate for 2 hours.

Ahead-of-Time Note: You may make the dough a day in advance.

Readying the Beans and Potatoes: Although these vegetables could be added to the pasta while it is boiling (for the last few minutes of its cooking), Chef Roberto prefers to do them separately to be sure they are perfectly cooked. An hour or so before serving, wash the beans, trim off the two ends, and drop the beans into a large saucepan of rapidly boiling, lightly salted water. Let boil uncovered for several minutes, until just tender—taste to make sure. Scoop them out and plunge them into a large bowl of cold water to stop the cooking and preserve their beautiful green color. Drain in a moment, cut crosswise into ⅛-inch dice, and set aside. Bring the water in the

INGREDIENTS FOR ABOUT 8 DOZEN *TROFFIE* (SERVING 4 AS A MAIN COURSE, OR 6 AS AN APPETIZER)

For the pasta
2 cups chestnut flour
1 cup plain bleached all-purpose flour
1 teaspoon salt
½ cup or more cold water

For serving
¼ pound very thin green beans (haricots verts, *ideally*)
1 large baking potato (9 to 10 ounces)
½ to ¾ cup Pesto Sauce (see page 14)
Freshly grated Parmesan cheese (optional)

(continued)

Troffie di Farina di Castagne (continued)

saucepan back to the boil. Meanwhile, peel the potato and cut into dice the same size as the beans. Drop them into the boiling water and boil for 4 to 5 minutes, just until cooked through—taste to be sure. Drain, run cold water over them to stop the cooking, and set aside with the beans.

Forming the Troffie:

Manufacturing Note: After a number of trials, the following system differs slightly from the television version in that we find it best to let the dough come to room temperature before forming, and we prefer working on a non-floured surface, since flour dries out the dough. Before forming the shapes, we first like to break off all the requisite number of dough bits, and store them under a sheet of plastic; then the forming may proceed without interruption.

Break off ½-teaspoon bits of dough—about the size of a raspberry. The classic forming technique is to set the piece of dough on your work surface, then roll it into a pig tail: Start rolling each piece under the palm of your hand at the thumb joint, and, pressing it against the surface, roll it firmly under your hand as you draw your hand diagonally down toward you, ending at the tip of your fourth finger. You must feel the dough forming under your hand— a somewhat curled shape with pointy ends and a thicker middle. It is a guided *tour de main,* as you will realize after several formings. (This is the classic movement, but you may prefer rolling each piece into shape between the palms of your hands.) Whichever way you roll, you have done it right when all the pieces are about 2½ inches long, and the same shape and size. Drop each formed piece onto the floured pan.

Ahead-of-Time Note: The pasta may be shaped a day ahead to this point. Toss in the flour, cover with plastic, and refrigerate. Don't forget to make the pesto sauce before you cook the pasta!

Cooking the Pasta: Bring at least 5 quarts of water to the rolling boil, adding 1½ teaspoons of salt per quart of water. Stir in the pasta, letting it boil slowly for 8 to 10 minutes, until cooked through—the *troffie* are done when a little darkened in color and slippery when handled; they will have the somewhat firm texture of gnocchi or ravioli. Then drop in the beans and potatoes just to let them warm through a moment.

Serving: Scrape the pesto sauce into the warm serving bowl. Drain the pasta and vegetables in a colander, and immediately turn them into the serving bowl, tossing gently to combine pasta, pesto, and vegetables. Sprinkle on the optional Parmesan, and serve at once.

SPECIAL EQUIPMENT SUGGESTED

A freestanding electric mixer with dough hook (useful but not essential)

A baking sheet generously coated with flour

A 6-quart kettle (a pasta insert for straining is useful but not essential)

A Chinese wire-mesh strainer or a large slotted scoop, or a regular medium-size strainer

A large saucepan of rapidly boiling water (for the beans and potatoes)

A colander

A large warm serving bowl

PESTO SAUCE

Basil, garlic, and olive oil are all pounded together for this heady, fragrant, and typically Mediterranean sauce. Pesto means something that is pounded to a paste, but if you haven't an ancient stone mortar and a hefty olive-wood pestle to pound in, feel free to use your electric blender or processor. Chef Roberto adds toasted pine nuts to his—a Ligurian touch that gives the sauce a special body and fullness. Serve it with all sorts of pasta dishes which, when tossed with pesto, need nothing else except perhaps a little more olive oil and Parmesan. Stir a big dollop into a minestrone and you have transformed the soup. Serve it with fish and fish soups, too, or with beans, boiled potatoes, egg dishes, and so forth.

Either pound the basil, pine nuts, and garlic in your mortar to make a fragrant, somewhat grainy paste, then gradually whisk in the olive oil, fold in the cheese, and season highly to taste; or, if you are using a machine, puree the garlic by hand into a smooth paste, then scrape it into the machine with the basil and pine nuts; puree rather roughly and pulse in the oil; fold in the cheese and seasonings after you have transferred the sauce to a bowl.

Ahead-of-Time Note: The pesto is at its best and most colorful served soon after you make it, but you can refrigerate it for a few days in a bowl if you film the top of the sauce with olive oil and cover with plastic.

INGREDIENTS FOR ¾ TO 1 CUP

2 cups (loosely packed) fine fresh basil leaves

2 tablespoons pine nuts, toasted in a 350° F oven 3 to 5 minutes until golden

1 or more large garlic cloves, to taste

¼ cup good fruity olive oil

1 tablespoon grated Parmesan cheese

Salt and freshly ground black pepper to taste

SPECIAL EQUIPMENT SUGGESTED

A large mortar and pestle, or an electric blender or food processor

cook's notes

....

....

....

....

....

....

....

....

....

BUNET—CARAMEL CUSTARD GARNISHED WITH WINE-POACHED PEARS AND CHILLED ZABAGLIONE

Bunet is a Piemontese dialect word for baked custard. It not only sounds very French, but in fact is French in origin, since Piemonte was once part of France. This is Chef Roberto Donna's grandmother's recipe for caramel custard, which he lovingly serves in his restaurant, Galileo, with his favorite garnishes. All dressed up or served as is, Grandmother's bunet, *with its caramel, almond cookies, cocoa, Marsala, and Cognac, takes an already splendid custard to heavenly heights.*

Technique: Full details on making caramel are in the appendix.

Caramelizing the Baking Dish: Blend the sugar and water in the saucepan and bring to the boil, swirling the pan rather slowly by its handle until the sugar has dissolved completely. Cover the pan closely and boil without stirring for several minutes, until the sugar syrup has turned a light caramel-brown. Immediately pour it into the bottom of the baking dish or loaf pan, turning it in all directions to cover the bottom completely. Set aside. Meanwhile, preheat the oven to 300° F and bring a kettle of water to the boil.

Preparing the Custard Mixture: Heat the milk just to the boil. Whisk the eggs and sugar in the mixing bowl to blend thoroughly, but do not create bubbles or foam. Blend in the cocoa and crumbled amaretti, then, gradually at first, stir in the hot milk—again, be careful to stir rather than beat, thus preventing bubbles and foam, which could remain in the cooked custard. Stir in the Marsala and Cognac.

Baking—1 hour to 1 hour and 10 minutes at 300°F: Strain the custard through a fine-meshed sieve into the caramelized dish, and set the dish in the roasting pan. Place the oven rack on the lower middle position, pull it out, and arrange the roasting pan upon it. Pour boiling water into the roasting pan around the custard dish to a point halfway up, then very carefully slide the rack back into place. Keep your eye on the water in the roasting pan; it should never come to the boil but should just remain at the barest simmer throughout the cooking.

When Is It Done? The custard is done when a skewer or small sharp knife comes out clean when plunged into the custard an inch from the edges; the center should still tremble slightly. Remove from the roasting pan and set aside to cool.

INGREDIENTS FOR 8 SERVINGS

For the custard
1 quart milk
6 "large" eggs
1¼ cups sugar
2 ounces (¾ cup) cocoa powder
10 amaretti (Italian store-bought almond cookies), crumbled (1 cup)
1 cup dry Marsala wine
¼ cup Cognac

For the caramel
⅓ cup sugar
3 tablespoons water

For serving (optional)
4 Moscato-Wine Caramelized Pears (see page 16)
Chilled Zabaglione (see page 17)
Fresh mint leaves

(continued)

Bunet (continued)

Ahead-of-Time Note: When cool, cover with plastic and store in the refrigerator, where it will hold 2 to 3 days.

Serving: Unmold the custard onto a platter, and spoon the collected caramel juices around it. Or, for the full treatment on individual plates, combine the pears (recipe follows) and the custard caramel sauces. Spoon a little pool of the sauce off-center on each dessert plate. Lay a serving of custard off-center on the caramel. Cut the pears in half lengthwise, then fan them out by slicing lengthwise up to ½ inch of the stem to keep the slices attached. Lean a pear half against each serving of custard, and baste with caramel sauce. Plop a nice dollop of the chilled zabaglione in a strategic location, and serve—to shouts of joy!

SPECIAL EQUIPMENT
SUGGESTED

A 2-quart mixing bowl

A 6-cup heavy-bottomed saucepan with tight-fitting cover (for the caramel)

A fine-meshed sieve (for straining the custard mixture)

An 8-cup baking dish or pan, such as a 13- by 4½-inch loaf pan 2½ inches deep

A roasting pan large enough to hold the above dish or pan comfortably

MOSCATO-WINE CARAMELIZED PEARS

Chef Roberto made these lovely pears as a garnish for his baked custard, bunet, *on page 15, but they make a sumptuous dessert on their own with a dollop of his chilled zabaglione.*

Baking: Preheat the oven to 350° F. Wash the pears and trim the bottoms so they will stand up. Butter the pan well and stand the pears in it. Blend the sugar and wine in a saucepan and stir over heat until the sugar has dissolved, then pour it around the pears. Bake in the lower third of the preheated oven for 30 to 40 minutes, basting the pears with the cooking juices several times.

When Are They Done? A skewer will pierce several of them with relative ease—do not overcook, but make sure they are cooked through.

Finishing the Dish: Very carefully remove the pears to dessert plates or a platter. Pour the cooking liquid into a saucepan and boil it down until a thick syrup, almost a caramel, forms. Spoon it over the pears just before serving.

Ahead-of-Time Note: May be prepared a day or two in advance. Keep the pears in their baking dish, cover with plastic wrap, and refrigerate. Liquefy the pear syrup over heat before serving.

INGREDIENTS FOR 8 SERVINGS

8 fine ripe firm unblemished pears, such as Bosc, with their stems on

2 tablespoons softened unsalted butter

1 cup sugar

2 cups Moscato wine (sweet Italian dessert wine from muscat grapes)

SPECIAL EQUIPMENT
SUGGESTED

A baking pan just large enough to hold the pears comfortably when standing upright

CHILLED ZABAGLIONE

Zabaglione is best known as that ethereal Italian egg dessert that is served warm, usually in your favorite Italian restaurant, and usually made table-side with effusive drama by your very own waiter. It is indeed a divine and warm and frothy ambrosia. Chef Roberto likes his ambrosia chilled. He folds whipped cream into it and serves it alongside his grandmother's baked custard. It is great, too, with his caramelized pears (see opposite) or with any other poached fruit.

INGREDIENTS FOR 4 SERVINGS

4 egg yolks

*4 eggshell halves of sugar
(6 tablespoons)*

*4 eggshell halves of dry Marsala
wine (6 tablespoons)*

*½ cup chilled heavy cream,
whipped to light peaks*

SPECIAL EQUIPMENT SUGGESTED

*A 6- to 8-cup stainless steel
double boiler (or a 6- to 8-cup
stainless steel saucepan set over
a flame tamer or simmer
plaque)*

*A hand-held electric mixer or a
wire whip*

Manufacturing Note: The traditional Italian manner of measuring ingredients for zabaglione is to count the egg yolks and use that many half-eggshells of sugar and Marsala—1 "large" egg yields 3 tablespoons, thus ½ shell makes 1½ tablespoons.

Bring an inch or so of water to the simmer in the bottom of the double boiler. Off heat, blend the egg yolks, sugar, and Marsala in the top, then set the top over the bottom, being sure the bottom of the top pan is over, but not in, the simmering water. (Or blend the ingredients in the saucepan, then set on the flame tamer or simmer plaque over low heat.) Beat the ingredients until just warm to your finger, foamy, and almost tripled in volume. Remove from heat and chill until cold, then fold in the whipped cream.

Ahead-of-Time Note: The zabaglione will keep for a day or two in the refrigerator.

cook's notes

MADHUR JAFFREY

"**I**ndian food uses spices in the most magical way," declares Madhur Jaffrey with obvious appreciation. As she toasts, blends, and grinds an array of aromatic seeds and leaves, she makes it clear that she is borrowing from the vast culinary palette that centuries of Indian culture have nurtured. She shared that tradition with us as she expertly wound her way through the techniques of handling fragrant Basmati rice, preparing spicy red pepper paste, and blending her own curry. The aromas and tastes were indeed magical.

Born in Old Delhi to a very old Delhi family, Madhur studied acting at London's Royal Academy. Undoubtedly, this training has much to do with her ease and confidence in demonstrating exotic cuisines on her BBC cooking programs. She has a number of fine films to her credit and it was because of her acting that she became a cooking personality. After she won a film award, Craig Claiborne wrote about her as an actress known for giving great, grand Indian dinner parties. The award did not bring the hoped-for plethora of film work but it did bring an offer to publish a cookbook. "The publisher asked how long it would take. I had all these recipes lying around and I said it couldn't take much more than three months. It took me five years!" Since then she has written more books as well as acted in more movies. As of this writing, she is about to direct her first film in India.

Madhur seems to manage both the kitchen and the stage effortlessly. And her passion is to know all about whatever role she is playing or what foods she is using. "I keep learning. It is an endless saga of learning."

ROASTED CURRY POWDER

Curry powders are mixtures of various spices, Madhur Jaffrey explains. There is no one curry powder; different combinations are used to flavor different dishes. So good Indian cooks make their own as the occasion demands. This one, Madhur is quick to point out, is a roasted curry—the spices are toasted or roasted before grinding, since there is a distinct difference in taste.

Toasting and Grinding the Spices: Set the skillet over moderate heat, and when hot, pour in the coriander seeds, peppercorns, and fenugreek seeds. Stir them around until the coriander is a shade darker and emits a roasted aroma, about a minute. Pour these spices onto a paper towel and let them cool 30 seconds, then empty them into the container of the grinder and pulverize into a powder. (If using an electric blender, shake up the contents several times to get a powder grind.) Pour into a bowl and stir in the paprika, cayenne, and turmeric. Set aside.

Ahead-of-Time Note: The curry powder will keep for a week or so in an airtight screw-top jar, but the fresh flavors gradually fade.

INGREDIENTS FOR ABOUT ¼ CUP

The spices for the curry

2 tablespoons whole coriander seeds

1 teaspoon whole black peppercorns

¼ teaspoon whole fenugreek seeds

1 tablespoon bright red paprika

¼ to 1 teaspoon cayenne pepper, depending on how spicy you like it

½ teaspoon ground turmeric

SPECIAL EQUIPMENT SUGGESTED

A heavy 6-inch skillet, preferably cast-iron

A spice grinder or coffee grinder, preferably, or an electric blender

Clockwise from the top: a plate of shrimp; a lump of tamarind; fenugreek; a bowl of basmati rice; some fresh curry leaves; a small bowl of black pepper; a bowl of mustard seeds; a bowl of coriander seeds; a bowl of chopped red peppers; 3 shallots; garlic; ginger; 2 red peppers; a bowl of raw cashews; tamarind beans; and a package of tamarind beans. *Center:* a plate with ground paprika (the largest amount), tamarind, and cayenne; a plate with chopped shallots, garlic, and ginger.

SHRIMP IN A SPICY COCONUT SAUCE

"The aromas rising from this dish clearly proclaim that it is from southern India," Madhur Jaffrey explains. "Roasting black peppercorns, coriander seeds, and fenugreek seeds together and then grinding them is very southern. So is the use of shallots, which are the onions of the south. All these, combined with the use of mustard seeds and fresh curry leaves, help to place the dish as nothing else would." Madhur makes a spicy sauce with a special spicy paste, thins it out with coconut milk, and the result becomes the poaching medium for her fresh shrimp. She serves it over basmati rice with dill—a very special treat.

Preparing the Paste: Put the red pepper, shallots, garlic, and ginger root into the blender in the listed order so that the moister ingredients will be on the bottom and produce a liquid. Blend and pulse until you have a paste, adding 1 to 3 tablespoons water, if necessary, to make a smooth puree. Add the cashews and the curry powder, and puree again to a paste. Scrape out of the blender into a bowl and set aside.

Preparing the Sauce: Set the pan over moderately high heat, add the oil, and heat until very hot and almost smoking, then pour in the mustard seeds—the oil must be hot enough for the seeds to pop so you might want to test with one or two before proceeding. As soon as the seeds pop, in a matter of seconds, stir in the curry leaves. Stir once quickly and then scrape in the paste. Fry, stirring constantly, until the paste is reduced, turns reddish brown, and begins to separate from the oil—8 to 10 minutes. Stir in the water, salt, and tamarind paste, and bring to the boil. Reduce the heat to moderately low and boil slowly for 5 minutes. Strain through the sieve into a bowl, pushing out every last bit of the sauce. Return the sauce to the pan.

Ahead-of-Time Note: The sauce may be made to this point in the morning of the day it is to be served. Too long a wait and the aromas will be lost.

Preparing and Then Poaching the Shrimp: Peel and devein the shrimp, wash well in cold water, and pat dry. (Cover and refrigerate if you are not ready to cook immediately.) Bring the sauce to a gentle boil, stir up the coconut milk in its can to blend thoroughly before mixing it into the sauce; add the chiles. Return the sauce to the boil, reduce the heat, and stir in the shrimp. Poach them gently, stirring and folding them in the sauce, until they are opaque and just cooked through—2 to 3 minutes only.

INGREDIENTS FOR 6 SERVINGS

For the red pepper paste

½ medium red bell pepper, seeded and coarsely chopped

5 medium shallots, peeled and coarsely chopped

5 medium garlic cloves, peeled and coarsely chopped

1-inch piece of fresh ginger root, peeled and coarsely chopped

8 raw cashew nuts, coarsely chopped

¼ cup Madhur Jaffrey's Roasted Curry Powder (see page 19)

Water, as needed

For the sauce

5 tablespoons corn or peanut oil

1 teaspoon whole black (brown) or yellow mustard seeds

15 to 20 fresh curry leaves (available in Indian markets)

Red pepper paste (see above)

1¾ cups water

¾ to 1 teaspoon salt, or to taste

1 tablespoon thick Tamarind Paste (see page 22)

(continued)

Serving: Spoon the hot rice onto dinner plates and ladle the shrimp with its sauce next to it. Garnish the shrimp with a red and a green chile and place a sprig of dill on the plate. Spoon a little more sauce over the shrimp and serve immediately.

Note: The chiles are small but very aggressive, Madhur warns us; they are in the dish as a garnish, and should be eaten only by the brave.

For finishing the dish
2 pounds medium-size shrimp
14-ounce can (1¾ cups) of
  coconut milk (see page 24)
3 whole fresh hot green chiles
  (optional)

For serving
Basmati Rice with Dill
  (see page 22)

For the garnish
Tiny red and green chiles
Sprigs of dill

SPECIAL EQUIPMENT
SUGGESTED

A 12-inch straight-sided no-stick
  sauté pan or a wide saucepan
A coarse-meshed sieve
Warm dinner plates

TAMARIND PASTE

Although the lovely tamarind tree grows in many warm climates, it is associated with India to such a degree that its fruit is often referred to as "Indian dates." However, rather than being a fruit, the tamarind is a legume with a large brown pod and many seeds surrounded by a pulpy mass. Only the pulp is used, but tamarind is most often sold in a sticky, fibrous lump from which you must extract the pulp, as described here. Although there are other sources, Madhur Jaffrey always prefers Indian tamarind because she feels it is less bitter. Tamarind adds a fruity, sour taste to food and is a staple ingredient in Indian cuisine. It is also used by Jean-Georges Vongerichten, who calls for it in his dipping sauce (see page 90), and Mark Militello, who makes his own (see page 235).

Softening the Tamarind Block: Break the tamarind into ½-teaspoon pieces. *Either* cover with very hot water in a mixing bowl and let soften for several hours or overnight, *or* place in a glass bowl, cover with plastic wrap, poke a steam hole in its surface, and microwave on "low" or "defrost" until softened—about 10 minutes.

Sieving the Pulp: Mash the softened tamarind with your fingers to release the pulp. Turn it into a sieve set over a glass or stainless steel bowl, and push the pulp through the sieve with your fingers or a rubber spatula. The resulting thick paste is now ready to use.

Ahead-of-Time Note: Store the paste in a closed container, where it will keep for several weeks under refrigeration, or for several months in the freezer.

A block of tamarind, about 7 ounces (available in some gourmet shops and all Indian groceries)

SPECIAL EQUIPMENT
SUGGESTED

A sieve
A rubber spatula
An 8-ounce glass or plastic container with fitted lid

BASMATI RICE WITH DILL

Grown in the foothills of the Himalayan Mountains, basmati is a long-grain rice—slender, delicate, and naturally perfumed. It is aged a year before being sold, to intensify the aroma; the color then takes on a yellowish cast. A very white basmati probably has not been aged.

In India they say about rice that the grains should be like brothers—very close but not stuck together. During cooking the grains of basmati rice expand to become a little longer as well as a little fatter. Madhur Jaffrey keeps them well separated by following three important preliminary steps:

1. Washing *the rice to remove the excess starch*
2. Soaking *the rice to begin the swelling of the grains*
3. Sautéing *the rice to control the release of the starch*

(continued)

Washing and Soaking the Rice: Pour the rice into a bowl, cover it with cold water, swish it around, then tip the bowl to drain most of the water out. Repeat this 5 or 6 times, until the water is almost clear—it won't be one hundred percent clear, but almost. Finally, pour in enough cold water to cover the rice by an inch and leave to soak for 30 minutes. Drain through the sieve, leaving the rice in the sieve set over a bowl.

Preheat the oven to 325° F if you are using it in the next step.

Cooking the Rice: Set the saucepan over moderately high heat, add the oil, and when it is hot, stir in the cardamom and cinnamon. After a few seconds, stir in the shallots and let them brown nicely, stirring to prevent them from burning. Pour in the rice, lower the heat, add the dill and salt, and sauté for 2 minutes, stirring gently so as not to break the grains—if the rice begins to stick, reduce the heat. Pour in the stock and bring to the boil. Cover tightly, first with foil pressed down all around the rim, then with the lid. *Either* set in the middle level of the preheated oven for 30 minutes, *or* cook on top of the stove over very, very low heat for 25 to 30 minutes (watch carefully that it does not grab on the bottom).

When Is It Done? The liquid should be absorbed, and the rice should be tender with no bite at the center.

Remove the rice from the heat, fluff carefully with a fork, and serve warm. You can remove the cinnamon stick if you wish.

Ahead-of-Time Note: Our team finds that you can cook it a good half hour ahead if you keep it covered and set the pan over very low heat upon a flame-taming mat—it should just stay warm.

INGREDIENTS FOR ABOUT 6 CUPS OF COOKED RICE

2 cups Indian basmati rice (available in some gourmet shops and all Indian groceries)
2 tablespoons vegetable oil
3 whole green cardamom pods
2-inch cinnamon stick
1 large shallot, peeled and cut into fine slivers
1 cup (firmly packed) chopped fresh dill
1 teaspoon salt
2⅔ cups chicken stock

SPECIAL EQUIPMENT SUGGESTED

A fine-meshed sieve
A 2½- to 3-quart heavy-bottomed ovenproof saucepan or casserole
A well-fitting lid for the pan
Aluminum foil

cook's notes

MINTY SWEET-AND-SOUR EGGPLANT

Eggplant is very much a part of Indian cooking, and this recipe, with its fine spiciness and minty flavor, both serves as a splendid appetizer and goes beautifully with main-course lamb and fish dishes.

A Note on Eggplants: Madhur Jaffrey's first choice is the slim, long, pinkish mauve Japanese eggplant. Second would be the smaller, purple Italian one. If you can find only the larger, purple, oval eggplants, you may want to halve them lengthwise, then cut the halves into crosswise slices. Whichever type of eggplant you choose, be sure that it is firm, shiny, and unblemished—bruised and dull-skinned examples will be bitter and disappointing.

Readying the Broiler: Turn the broiler on to high and position a rack on the top level.

Preparing the Eggplant: Brush the baking sheet with oil. Cut the eggplants crosswise at a slight diagonal into oval slices ⅓ inch thick, and lay as many as will fit in one layer on the baking sheet—you will probably have to broil in two or even three batches. Brush generously with oil, sprinkle lightly with salt, and grind the pepper over all. Broil until golden brown on one side. Repeat for the other side. The slices should be cooked all the way through to the center. When all the slices are browned, turn off the broiler and preheat the oven to 350° F.

Ahead-of-Time Note: The eggplant may be broiled several hours in advance.

Preparing the Seasonings: Pour the cumin seeds into the small pan and toast, shaking and stirring over moderate heat for about 1 minute, until the seeds have darkened and released their aroma. Pour into a small bowl and let cool a moment, then stir in the rest of the seasoning ingredients.

Assembling the Dish: Lay the eggplant slices in the baking dish in slightly overlapping rows or concentric circles. When the bottom is filled, dribble a third of the seasoning mixture over the eggplant. Cover with two more layers of eggplant slices, coating each one with the seasoning.

Ahead-of-Time Note: The dish may be assembled several hours in advance.

Baking and Serving: Cover the baking dish tightly with foil and bake for 20 minutes at 350° F, just until the eggplant is heated through and the flavors have time to mingle. Serve hot or at room temperature.

INGREDIENTS FOR 6 SERVINGS

For the eggplant
2½ pounds eggplants
6 to 8 tablespoons peanut
   or corn oil
Coarse salt
Freshly ground black pepper

For the seasoning
1 teaspoon cumin seeds
3 tablespoons fresh lemon juice
½ teaspoon salt
¼ teaspoon cayenne pepper
2 tablespoons sugar
1 tablespoon very finely minced
   fresh mint leaves

SPECIAL EQUIPMENT
SUGGESTED

1 or more flat baking sheets
A pastry brush
A small cast-iron skillet (for
   roasting the cumin)
A shallow baking dish, such as a
   lasagna dish, about 9 by 12
   inches
Aluminum foil

DANIEL BOULUD

Chef Daniel Boulud views his career as a work in progress. The original sketch began on his family's farm near Lyons, France, where he was surrounded by people who cared about food. "My grandmother made goat cheese. We raised all the animals you could name and made all our own charcuterie. We grew vegetables and herbs, and were doing the farmer's market twice a week." To avoid working in the fields, young Daniel hung around the kitchen and experienced the warmth and comfort of his grandmother's cooking. "She taught me a naturalness, but it was a far cry from the restaurant business."

At fourteen, Daniel apprenticed in a two-star Lyons restaurant that belonged to a family friend. "The picture got bigger," recalls Daniel, and it continued to grow when he left for La Mère Blanc, Georges Blanc's three-star restaurant north of Lyons. The kitchen was large and professional but still served what the local French call "la cuisine des mères," and Chef Daniel wanted to work on a larger canvas. He moved to the south of France and continued his work with Roger Vergé at Le Moulin de Mougins and Michel Guèrard in Eugénie Les Bains. "I was a very little boy in the corner of the kitchen, but all the young cooks were very high-caliber and all went on to be chefs."

In 1980 Daniel became chef at the EEC embassy in Washington, D.C., and from there moved to New York City. He was working at the Plaza-Athénée at Le Régence, then went to Le Cirque, where Sirio Maccioni asked him to be his chef. "It was a very big challenge for me but I knew I would learn a lot." Six years later Daniel opened his own restaurant, Daniel, where he is painting a masterful picture. Within one year, he has not only become a member of Relais & Châteaux but has earned the recognition of having the only North American restaurant on the *International Herald Tribune*'s World's Best Restaurants list (number nine in the world) and awarded four stars by *The New York Times.* Daniel demonstrated for us some of his restaurant's most popular dishes, such as his lovely and colorful fresh pea soup and his braised veal chops with sweetbreads—dishes that prove beyond a doubt what an amazing artist he has become.

CHILLED GREEN PEA SOUP WITH ROSEMARY

In the summertime, when all the peas are all around the town, Chef Daniel makes his glorious soup with five different varieties. Whatever peas you bring to the pot, this recipe will make you a beautiful pea-green soup. "Use what's available and fresh," he advises, "and if it has to be only one kind, use garden peas."

Nutritional Note: As to heavy cream—that deadly monster!—how dare he suggest it? He's put in half a cup of the heavy stuff! However, that makes only 1⅓ tablespoons of cream per person—hardly a fearsome amount. And how delicious it is, infused with rosemary and a touch of garlic. The little garnish of tiny croutons sautéed in olive oil and the dusting of pulverized crisp bacon add a needed touch of severity to the gentle green.

Manufacturing Note: As usual, being a recipe from an unusually talented chef, there are lots of bits and pieces here, but you can prepare all of them a day in advance—and it is such a remarkable soup that you will find the labor entirely worthwhile.

Technique: Directions for dealing with fava beans are in the box on page 96.

Preparing the Soup Base: Bring the stock to the boil and keep hot. In the large saucepan, over moderate heat, sauté the bacon until the fat is rendered and the meat is well browned. Discard the fat, retaining the bacon in the pan, and pour in the olive oil. Stir in the finely chopped vegetables and 1 rosemary sprig; sweat (cook very slowly) the vegetables for 10 to 15 minutes, adding more oil if necessary, until they are soft but not at all browned. Add the parsley leaves.

Cooking the Peas: Set aside about 1 cup of the mixed peas for garnish, and keep the favas in a separate bowl. Pour the remaining peas into the saucepan with the diced vegetables, season with salt and pepper, and sweat for 5 more minutes. Then add the favas and pour in the hot stock, adding enough to come just up to the level of the peas. Then bring quickly to the boil; cook slowly for 2 minutes or so, just until the peas are tender but still very green.

Cooling and Pureeing the Soup: Immediately remove the pan from heat and pour the soup into the large bowl set over ice and water. Discard the rosemary and bacon, and stir the soup slowly with a large spoon, reaching all over the sides of the pan to cool it down—quick chilling will set the bright

INGREDIENTS FOR 6 SERVINGS

For the soup base
*1½ to 2 quarts chicken stock
    (see page 87)*
*2-ounce slab of bacon, sliced ½
    inch thick, or 4 "thick-cut"
    slices in large dice*
*2 teaspoons olive oil, plus more as
    needed*
*The following vegetables finely
    chopped:*
*4 small leeks, washed, roots and
    tough green removed*
*4 small (2-inch) young white
    onions, or scallions, tender
    green left on, 1 cup chopped*
*6 tender stalks of celery
    (4 ounces = 1 cup chopped)*
*Four 6- to 10-inch sprigs of fresh
    rosemary (one for the soup,
    two for the rosemary cream,
    and one for the croutons)*

For the peas
*8 to 10 cups assorted fresh peas
    such as:*
1 pound shelled garden peas
*¾ pound sugar snap peas,
    washed, ends snapped and
    strings pulled*

(continued)

Chilled Green Pea Soup with Rosemary (continued)

green color. When the soup is cold, ladle it into the blender and puree in batches, blending each batch to a beautifully smooth pale green. Strain the soup, and taste carefully for seasoning. Keep refrigerated until serving.

Infusing the Rosemary Cream: Pour the cream into the small saucepan, bring to the boil, and add 2 sprigs of rosemary, the garlic, and salt and pepper. Boil gently for 5 minutes, then cover the pan and let infuse until cooled. Strain and refrigerate until serving.

Preparing the Garnish:

The Croutons. Cut the bread into neat ⅛-inch dice. Mince the leaves of one of the rosemary sprigs. Heat enough oil in the small frying pan just to coat the bottom, then fold in the bread and rosemary. Sauté, swirling the pan by its handle, until the croutons are lightly browned. Season with salt and pepper, and set aside.

The Bacon. Arrange the bacon strips in a jelly-roll pan and brown in a 375° F oven until fully cooked and crisp; drain well on paper towels, then pulverize either in the food processor or with a knife; pat dry again on clean paper towels.

The Peas. Blanch the peas reserved for garnish in salted boiling water for 2 minutes or so, until just tender, and immediately plunge into ice water to chill, thus setting the bright green color. Drain; cut the snow peas and sugar snap peas at an angle into ¼-inch slices.

Ahead-of-Time Note: You may complete all or parts of the recipe to this point a day in advance.

Presentation: At the moment of serving, pour the chilled soup into a tureen or individual soup plates. Drizzle the rosemary cream in dabs over the top, scatter a few of the blanched peas in the center, and sprinkle with the croutons and chopped bacon. Or, if you wish, the cream and all the garnishes may be served on the side in small bowls at the table, so that guests can help themselves.

¾ pound snow peas, washed, ends snapped and strings pulled

¾ pound shelled and peeled fava beans

¾ pound pea shoots (available in oriental groceries)

Salt

Freshly ground white pepper

½ cup (loosely packed) parsley leaves, washed and dried

For the rosemary cream

½ cup heavy cream

2 garlic cloves, crushed and peeled

Salt

Freshly ground white pepper

For the garnish

3 thin slices of homemade-type white bread, crusts removed

Olive oil

5 strips of thin-sliced bacon

SPECIAL EQUIPMENT
SUGGESTED

A 4- to 6-quart heavy-bottomed saucepan or soup pot

A 6-quart stainless steel bowl set over a larger bowl of ice and water

A ladle

An electric blender

A medium-meshed sieve (for sieving and draining)

Small saucepan

A 6-inch frying pan (for the croutons)

A jelly-roll pan (for the bacon garnish)

SWEET-AND-SOUR LEMON SLICES

Chef Boulud's preserved lemon slices add a pretty touch to any dish. He uses them here to decorate his braised veal chops, and their sweet-sour quality adds zest to both veal and sweetbreads. They will keep for weeks in the refrigerator, and it's nice to have something stylish on hand.

INGREDIENTS FOR 2 DOZEN OR MORE SLICES

3 lemons, cut in ⅛-inch slices and seeded
½ cup white wine vinegar
⅓ cup sugar
1 sprig of fresh rosemary, about 5 inches long

SPECIAL EQUIPMENT SUGGESTED

A 12-inch straight-sided stainless steel skillet or saucepan
A 4-cup saucepan

Arrange the lemon slices loosely in the skillet and pour in cold water to cover them by 2 inches. Bring to the simmer and let cook gently for 20 minutes. Lift out with care and drain. Pour the vinegar and sugar into the saucepan, and bring to the simmer, stirring, to dissolve the sugar completely. Return the lemon slices to the pan, lay in the rosemary, and simmer for another 20 minutes, until tender and cooked through. When cool, refrigerate in a wide-mouthed jar.

ROASTED VEAL CHOPS AND SWEETBREADS WITH LEMON AND ROSEMARY

For all lovers of veal, here is a masterpiece from Daniel Boulud. The meat is tender, subtly flavored by the aromatic vegetables that accompany it, and the meat juices and vegetable flavors combine to make one of those divine natural sauces that you long remember. The soft, almost melting contrast of sweetbreads and meat is a touch of genius that gives even more character to this really splendid dish.

Manufacturing Note: As in many of Chef Daniel's recipes, there is a lot going on here for the home cook alone in the kitchen. Method and general conception are important—his manner of preparation is what gives the dish its remarkably fine flavor. You may not want to use all of the vegetable garnish indicated, but certainly the onions, carrots, and some if not all of the garlic are needed for their aromatic flavor; the rest is up to you. Although in the television version, Chef Daniel started in on the meat, we suggest that you prepare the vegetables first, and then they'll be out of the way. Please note that special information on veal and veal sweetbreads appears in the accompanying box.

INGREDIENTS FOR 6 SERVINGS

The vegetables
12 ounces sweet onions (spring onions or Vidalia)
4 medium-size celery stalks
¾ pound carrots (about 12 small)
3 bulbs of fennel (about 1 pound)
6 ounces (or 2 bunches) French radishes or round radishes (about 20 pieces)

(continued)

Preparing the Vegetables:

The Spring Onions. Trim away the green stems and the root ends; cut in half and then into wedges 1 inch wide.

The Celery. Peel and cut into 2-inch pieces.

The Carrots. Peel, and trim the greens away, leaving ½ inch of stem (or use regular carrots and cut into thin slices).

The Fennel. Trim the feathery tops off and remove the two or three tough outer leaves; trim away the root ends and cut the bulbs into ½-inch wedges.

The Radishes. Leave whole but cut away the green leaves and the root ends.

The Turnips. Trim away the stems within ½ inch of the bulb and peel them with a paring knife; or trim all the ends from regular turnips, peel them, and cut into 1-inch wedges.

Ahead-of-Time Note: May be prepared several hours in advance; keep them separate, cover with plastic or a wet towel, and refrigerate.

Trimming and Tying the Meats:

The Sweetbreads. Poke a hole horizontally through the center of each sweetbread with a long skewer or a knife. Push a sprig of rosemary through the hole, leaving ½ inch of leaves protruding.

The Veal. Tie a piece of butcher's twine around the circumference of the chop to keep the meat securely in place. Cut 3 sprigs of rosemary into inch-long pieces and tuck them into the string surrounding the meat.

Preliminary Browning: (Preheat the oven to 475° F for the roasting, later.)

The Veal Chops and Sweetbreads. Season the chops and the sweetbreads with salt and pepper. Dust lightly with instant flour and pat off excess. Pour the

*6 ounces baby turnips (10 to 12)
    or regular small-size turnips*
*15 large garlic cloves, peeled
    and split*

The meat
*1¾ to 2 pounds sweetbreads,
    about 4 to 5 ounces each,
    trimmed and ready to cook,
    and kept in a bowl of ice and
    water (see box below)*
*6 sprigs of fresh rosemary, 10 to
    12 inches long (3 for meat and
    3 for decoration)*
*3 best-quality well-trimmed veal
    rib chops, about 1¼ inches
    thick, 8 to 10 ounces each*

For browning the meat
Salt
Freshly ground black pepper
*"Instant" flour (for dusting the
    veal)*
2 tablespoons vegetable oil
6 tablespoons unsalted butter

(continued)

NOTES FROM JULIA ABOUT VEAL AND SWEETBREADS

Veal is the meat of a young male calf, 3½ to 4 months old. For centuries veal calves were raised in barns, tied to their mothers, and consumed only mother's milk. Today, both in this country and abroad, top-quality professionally raised veal is nurtured on milk and milk by-products under carefully controlled conditions. When you are buying veal, look closely at the color—the meat of prime veal is pale pink, actually the shade of a raw chicken drumstick. Once a veal calf is off its special diet and roams green pastures, it is no longer veal—the flesh reddens and toughens, and finally the meat neither tastes nor cooks like veal.

Thus the term "free-range veal" is a misnomer—it is not veal at all; it is baby beef.

Veal sweetbreads are of two shapes: the long, narrow thymus gland and the smoother, rounder pancreas sweetbread. Although they are interchangeable, many prefer the pancreas because of its more pleasing shape. Some markets do carry sweetbreads, and frozen portion-size individually packaged ready-to-cook sweetbreads are now beginning to come in. Sweetbreads freeze well, fortunately, and those that I've had recently have been of excellent quality.

Roasted Veal Chops and Sweetbreads (continued)

VEAL *JUS*—JULIA'S OBSERVATIONS

Contemporary chefs have taken to making *jus* rather than stocks because they are lighter. We have several in this book and shall use Alfred Portale's duck broth (see page 132) as the model for all, but in each case we shall note any significant changes in technique or ingredients. You may always substitute your own stock in their place, or even use a canned chicken broth—it won't be the same, but it will do.

Chef Daniel uses 2 pounds of veal scraps and bones and browns them in oil on top of the stove for 20 minutes. He then stirs in and browns for 10 minutes more ½ cup each of chopped carrots, onions, fennel, celery, and 8 peeled and chopped garlic cloves. Finally, he simmers his ingredients in water to cover, adding ½ teaspoon of sugar and about ¼ teaspoon of fresh rosemary. He simmers it slowly until the liquid is reduced to 2 cups.

The seasoning

Salt and freshly ground black pepper

½ teaspoon sugar

The juice of 1 lemon

¼ cup dry white wine or dry white French vermouth

2 cups veal jus *(see box)*

For finishing the dish

6 sweet-and-sour lemon slices (see box, page 32), drained

½ teaspoon chopped rosemary

3 tablespoons finely chopped chives

3 tablespoons roughly chopped chervil leaves

SPECIAL EQUIPMENT SUGGESTED

Butcher's twine (unwaxed plain white cotton twine)

A heavy cast-aluminum roaster large enough to hold the chops, sweetbreads, and vegetables easily, or 1 or 2 large skillets for browning and a large roasting pan for the oven cooking

Tongs

oil into the large roasting pan and set over high heat. (Or use one or two skillets for this step, then transfer the contents to a roasting pan.) When very hot but not smoking, add the veal chops and the sweetbreads. Stir in 2 tablespoons of the butter and slowly brown the pieces on both sides.

The Vegetables. When the meats are nicely browned, push them to the sides of the pan, swish the remaining butter into the pan, and scatter the vegetables around the meat, sprinkling them with salt, pepper, and sugar. Stir gently over moderate heat for a few minutes, then drizzle the lemon juice over all, and pour in the wine.

Roasting: Set the hot pan in the middle level of the preheated 475° F oven and bake for 10 to 12 minutes, until the wine has reduced almost to a glaze, then add the veal *jus* or stock to the pan. Roast for another 15 to 20 minutes, basting occasionally with the pan juices until the veal is lightly springy when pressed, and cooked through.

Finishing the Dish: Remove the chops and sweetbreads from the pan; set them aside and keep warm. Return the roasting pan and vegetables to the oven for another 15 to 20 minutes, or until the vegetables are very tender and the cooking juices have reduced to 1 cup of liquid. Transfer the pan to the stove top over low heat, and stir in the chopped herbs, reserving a few tablespoons for the finished dish. Taste carefully for seasoning and keep warm.

Reheating the Lemon Garnish: Lay the lemon slices on a small baking sheet and warm in the oven for several minutes.

Presentation: Meanwhile, set the chops on a cutting board, discard the trussing strings, and work rapidly from now on. One at a time, leaving a serving of meat on each chop, neatly cut off three slanting ½-inch slices of meat, and arrange the slices in the center of your warm platter. Arrange the bone-and-meat servings around the slices. Remove and discard the sprigs of rosemary from the sweetbreads, and cut the sweetbreads into ½-inch slices. Lay them on the platter around the veal. Place the warm lemon slices over the meat. Spoon the vegetables and sauce over and around the veal, and decorate with the chopped herbs.

WARM CHOCOLATE UPSIDE-DOWN "SOUFFLÉ"

Everybody's favorite soufflé seems to be chocolate, and pastry chef François Payard from Daniel's Restaurant give us a recipe here where each may have his own soufflé, since the servings are baked in individual molds. This is a quite classic mixture, but the soufflés are more sturdy than usual since they are baked in a water bath, which somehow and fortunately renders them noncollapsible. Thus you don't have that breathless dash from oven to table; you may dally in a civilized way as you unmold them for serving.

Manufacturing Note: Chef Payard suggests using disposable aluminum cups for the soufflés since they are readily available in most supermarkets. If you have ceramic baking cups you may use those, and if you choose to you can serve the desserts directly from the dishes.

Technique: Directions for beating egg whites are in the appendix.

Preliminaries: Preheat the oven to 375° F. Carefully butter the inside surfaces of the cups, and roll enough sugar in them to coat the bottoms and sides completely with a light dusting. (If you have bare spots, the soufflés may stick and refuse to unmold!)

Preparing the Chocolate Base: Melt the butter in the small saucepan over moderate heat. Remove from heat and drop the chocolate pieces into the warm butter, stirring well with a whisk until the chocolate is melted and smooth; set aside. Start beating the egg yolks at moderate speed in the mixer, gradually adding the sugar until the mixture is thick and pale yellow, and a bit lifted on the beater falls back on the surface in a slowly dissolving ribbon—5 to 6 minutes. Pour the chocolate into the yolks and run the machine on low speed just until the ingredients are blended. Remove the bowl from the stand and fold the chocolate mixture briefly with the spatula to be sure all is blended.

Adding the Egg Whites: Pour the egg whites into the very clean, dry bowl of your mixer. When foaming, beat in the lemon juice and continue beating to soft peaks, beat in the tablespoon of sugar, and continue to stiff, shining peaks. Remove the bowl from the base and stir ¼ of them into the chocolate to lighten it, then gently fold in the rest. Spoon the mixture into the prepared cups.

INGREDIENTS FOR 8
INDIVIDUAL SOUFFLÉS

1¼ sticks (5 ounces) unsalted butter
6 ounces bitter (unsweetened) chocolate, cut into small pieces
4 "large" eggs, separated
⅓ cup sugar for the egg yolks, plus 1 tablespoon for the egg whites
2 teaspoons fresh lemon juice

For preparing the baking cups
Unsalted butter, at room temperature
Sugar

For serving
Lightly beaten whipped cream— sweetened or not, according to your taste

Baking: Set the filled cups in a baking pan. Place the pan in the oven and pour boiling water into the pan until it reaches about 1 inch up the sides of the cups. Bake 10 to 12 minutes, or until the top is firm to the touch and a knife inserted near the center comes out almost clean with only small amounts of chocolate visible.

Unmolding and Serving: Remove the pan from the oven and let the soufflés sit for 2 minutes. Turn the molds upside down on the dessert plates and poke a hole in the bottom of each mold with the sharp point of a small knife. Unmold them, giving a sharp little downward shake.

Serving: Top with an egg-shaped dollop or two of whipped cream, vanilla ice cream, or Charlie Trotter's yogurt sorbet (see page 68).

SPECIAL EQUIPMENT
SUGGESTED

A 6-cup saucepan (for melting the butter and chocolate)
An electric mixer with whip attachment—an extra bowl and set of beaters would be nice; otherwise transfer your chocolate to a mixing bowl and wash out the mixer bowl for beating the egg whites
A wide rubber spatula
8 disposable aluminum cups, 4-ounce size
A roasting pan large enough to hold the cups with a little space between
A kettle of boiling water
Warm dessert plates

cook's notes

JIM DODGE

Not many chefs trace their culinary heritage back two hundred years, but Jim Dodge does. His ancestors opened a hotel, Pendexter Mansion, near North Conway, New Hampshire, that long ago, and each generation has carried on the tradition. The family philosophy is that everyone must work in every aspect of the business—waiting tables, cleaning rooms, cooking. Discussions were always about taking care of people—and good food. "We were in a rural area and used a lot of local ingredients. We had our own sugar house, made our own maple syrup for the hotel, had vegetable gardens. It was a pretty special childhood."

Once in the kitchen, Jim knew that was where he wanted to specialize. With his father's encouragement, he trained with a Swiss pastry chef, Fritz Albicken, and then in his ten years at the Stanford Court Hotel in San Francisco, he himself became a star pastry chef. While there, Jim met cooking school owner Mary Risley, who encouraged him to teach. How fortunate for his students and for New England Culinary Institute, where he is now senior vice president! He is a confident, enthusiastic teacher—a result of his own constant interest in his subject. He teaches throughout the country as well as in Japan and Hong Kong, where he is part owner of the restaurant American Pie. "I wonder why some people have such a rigid outlook on food. It is important to understand and know your ingredients well. Then you understand their limitations as well as their capabilities. If you have a good knowledge of the fundamentals you can do a lot."

Jim's books, *The American Baker* and *Baking with Jim Dodge,* are fine examples of his unintimidating approach. With his glorious, all-American apple pie and lovely, layered, chocolaty chocolate cake, he shared with us his confidence-building techniques.

CHOCOLATE BUTTERMILK FUDGE CAKE

Here is one really great chocolate cake in all its aspects. It's high and mighty, it's the essence of choco-late, it's moist, and its fudge frosting is just right. And you can make it yourself in your own kitchen.

Techniques: Directions for melting chocolate are in the appendix, while methods for handling fragile cake layers are in the instructions on page 42.

Preliminaries: Set a pan on a piece of the parchment paper and trace a circle around the bottom; cut just inside the line to produce a circle that will fit comfortably inside the pan without wrinkling; make another for the second pan. Brush a light coating of melted butter all over the bottom and sides of the two pans, line them with the parchment, and butter the parchment. Sprinkle 1 tablespoon of flour into each pan, roll and shake it to cover the bottom and sides evenly, and knock out the excess. Preheat the oven to 325° F and set the rack on the lower level.

Preparing the Chocolate Base: Heat the buttermilk and butter pieces in a small saucepan over moderately low heat until the butter has melted and the temperature of the liquid is about 100° F. Meanwhile, stir the cocoa and ½ cup of the sugar together with the whisk in a large mixing bowl; when thoroughly mixed, blend in the baking soda and vanilla, and finally the warm buttermilk-butter mixture. Whisk gently until the sugar and cocoa are completely dissolved. Set aside while preparing the egg whites.

The Egg Whites: In the bowl of the electric mixer, whip the egg whites on high until foamy and then gradually add the remaining ½ cup of sugar, pouring it down the sides to avoid overwhelming and deflating the whites. Adding the sugar slowly will also ensure that it will dissolve. Continue whipping at high speed until peaks form. The result will be a meringue-type mixture that will hold its shape when folded into the chocolate base. Set the bowl of whites next to the chocolate mixture.

Finishing the Batter: Whisk the egg yolks into the preceding chocolate base, and then whisk in the flour until it is completely incorporated. Use the wide rubber spatula to transfer the egg whites onto the top of the chocolate and then to fold them in gently but thoroughly. Pour the batter into the pans, dividing it evenly between them. Rock the pans gently to spread the batter evenly. Proceed at once to the oven.

INGREDIENTS FOR A 4-LAYER 8- BY 3½-INCH CAKE

For the cake pans
2 tablespoons unsalted butter, melted
2 tablespoons flour

For the cake
½ cup buttermilk
1 stick (4 ounces) unsalted butter, cut into 8 pieces
⅓ cup cocoa powder, preferably Dutch process
1 cup sugar
1 teaspoon baking soda
1 teaspoon pure vanilla extract
5 "large" eggs, separated
1 cup (scooped and leveled) bleached cake flour (see box, page 43)

For assembling the cake
Chocolate Fudge Frosting (see page 41)
Optional decorating suggestions:
Crystallized rose petals (see box, page 92)
Fresh raspberries

(continued)

All-Purpose Flaky Pie Crust Dough (continued)

Finishing the Dough: Sprinkle your work surface with flour and turn the dough out onto it. Roll it out, lifting the sides with the scraper and folding them back on top of the dough to make a bulky package. Don't worry if it is not perfectly smooth at this point. If you are concerned that there is not enough water, pick up a small piece of dough and squeeze it in your palm; it should hold together. Roll the dough into a 9- by 14-inch rectangle, then fold the rectangle into thirds. Roll it out again to an 8- by 9-inch rectangle. Use the scraper to fold it in half again. The dough will be loose and crumbly, not smooth. Carefully lift it onto a sheet of plastic and wrap it. Press the dough together by gently rolling the pin back and forth over the package; chill at least 10 to 15 minutes, and it is ready to use.

Ahead-of-Time Note: The dough will keep 2 to 3 days under refrigeration. Chef Jim lets chilled dough become malleable by massaging the package with the palms of his hands—he never beats it, since that could fuse the butter pieces with the dough itself, causing it to lose its flakiness.

SPECIAL EQUIPMENT
SUGGESTED

An 8-quart mixing bowl
*A good professional rolling pin
    (see introduction to recipe,
    page 43)*
A pastry scraper
*A rubber spatula with extra-wide
    blade, about 2½ inches across*

HARVEST APPLE PIE

Chef Jim's beautiful old-fashioned, everybody's favorite-American-national-hero pie is our example of how to make and bake any beautiful pie, from cherry, rhubarb, or apple to steak and kidney. It's the real technique from a master baker.

Preheat the oven to 425° F and set the rack on the lowest level.

Preparing the Apples: Peel the apples and cut them in half. Use the melon baller to remove the cores. Cut each half into three wedges and then cut across the wedges, slicing each into thirds. Thoroughly blend the sugar, spices, and tapioca or arrowroot in the mixing bowl, and toss with the apples, coating them evenly. Press a piece of plastic wrap onto the apples to make an airtight covering, and set aside.

Lining the Pie Pan: Remove the dough from the refrigerator and massage through the plastic for several minutes, just until it is pliable enough to roll out. Divide it in half, and chill one half. Sprinkle your work surface and the top of the dough lightly with flour, and start rolling it into a circle that is to be 10 inches across and about ⅛ inch thick. Chef Jim says it is quite all right for you to roll the pin back and forth, as long as you do not roll over the

INGREDIENTS FOR ONE 9-INCH
2-CRUST PIE

For the apple filling
*6 large firm early-crop apples
    (for notes on the right apple to
    use, see page 47)*
½ cup sugar
¼ teaspoon ground allspice
1 teaspoon ground cinnamon
*1 tablespoon tapioca flour or
    arrowroot*

(continued)

Harvest Apple Pie (continued)

edges. As you roll, lift and swish the dough on the counter to keep the bottom well-floured. Fold the circle in half and pick it up; brush off excess flour, and lay the dough in the pie pan with the fold at the center. Open the dough out to fill the pan, then lift the edges to coax it down into the pan, pressing it so that it lines the pan tightly.

In Go the Apples: Empty the apples into the crust using the rubber spatula to be sure that all the juices and seasonings go with them. Push them around so they are nicely arranged with a slight dome at the center. Brush the edges of the dough, where it rests on the edge of the pan, with the egg white. Roll the second piece of dough as the first; fold it and drape it over the apples; unfold and press the edges together to seal them, actually lifting the two pieces gently in your fingers to press them together, and at the same time folding them under to make a 1-inch lip all around. Then push the edges up to make an upstanding rim that does not overhang the sides; otherwise the crust will droop during baking. Crimp or flute the edges by pressing the index finger of one hand against the inside rim of the dough while pressing the dough lightly around that finger from the outside rim, using the thumb and index finger of your other hand. Continue around the dough at intervals of about 1 inch. Brush the center of the dough—but not the crimped edge—with more egg white, and sprinkle on the sugar. Note that the edge cooks first and fastest, and the egg white and sugar would cause too much browning.

Manufacturing Note: Chef Jim prefers egg white to water for sealing the crusts together since water could produce steam which would pry the edges apart.

Baking the Pie—about 1 hour in all, starting at 450° F: With a sharp knife poke four neat holes for steam release in the top of the crust—not on the downward slopes where the juices could seep out. Bake in the lower level of the preheated oven for 10 minutes, then rotate the pie a half turn and reduce the heat to 375° F. Continue baking 45 to 50 minutes more, until the top is golden brown.

When Is It Done? The apples should be tender when poked with a cake tester or small sharp knife through the steam holes in the crust. Any juices that bubble out should be slightly thickened and clear.

Remove the pie to a wire rack and let cool for an hour before cutting and serving.

1 recipe Jim Dodge's flaky pie dough (made with 2½ cups flour; see page 43), chilled and ready to go

For glazing the top
1 "large" egg white, beaten in a small bowl just until smoothly broken up
1 teaspoon sugar

SPECIAL EQUIPMENT SUGGESTED

A vegetable peeler
A melon baller
A 3-quart mixing bowl
A rolling pin
A pastry scraper
A rubber spatula with extra-wide blade, 2½ inches across
A 9-inch metal pie pan with sloping sides
A pastry brush

JULIA'S ADVICE ON AVOIDING THE WRONG APPLES

It is not always easy to find the right apple for cooking since many markets have only a limited selection—which is because we, the public, do not express ourselves. Apple choices depend, of course, on the time of year and also on the area where you live. If you are fortunate enough to be in a region growing apples for pie makers and apple-slice canners, you will have much the best choice. What we are concerned with now is apples that will hold their shape for baking and for pie and tart making. Here they are:

Golden Delicious, York Imperial, Greenings, Newtons, Monroes, Northern Spy. (Others reputed to be good but which I have not personally tried are: Stayman, Winesap, Baldwin, Grimes Golden.) Cortlands have worked for me when new, fresh, and firm. I have had disasters with the Gravensteins and the McIntosh. When you must

absolutely have baked apples or apple slices that will hold during cooking, however, the firm and fresh Golden Delicious is the old reliable.

Chef Jim used Empire apples for his Harvest Apple Pie but advises that one should always choose early-crop apples, since late-in-the-season examples can be soft and mushy, or can even burst out of shape, like late-harvest Granny Smiths.

How many apples do I need?

3 medium apples = 1 pound, or about 2⅔ cups, sliced apples

12 medium apples = 4 pounds, or about 3 quarts, sliced apples

ORANGE WALNUT BISCOTTI

The Italians traditionally dip these crisp almond cookie-breads into their sweet wines. The Americans eat them with everything from coffee to ice cream, and they have indeed become one of the most popular cookies in this country today. So popular are they that all cooks seem to have their own secret recipe for the very best. "Oh, this biscotti is great," they say, munching away on a rival batch. "But wait'll you taste mine—they're the greatest!" Here is Jim Dodge's greatest.

Preliminaries: Preheat the oven to 350° F. Line the jelly-roll pan with a piece of parchment paper cut to fit the inside bottom of the pan exactly.

Preparing the Dough: Blend the flour, walnuts, baking powder, and baking soda in a large bowl until the nuts are evenly mixed in. Set it aside nearby. Break 2 of the eggs into a 2- to 3-quart mixing bowl, separate the third egg, and drop the yolk into the bowl but reserve the white in a small bowl. Whisk the eggs, adding the sugar, the zests, and the orange oil. Gradually whisk in the melted butter, and when all is well blended, pour it into the bowl of flour and other dry ingredients. Fold and push all ingredients together until the liquid is absorbed and the dry ingredients have been completely incorporated. Empty it out onto your lightly floured work surface, and knead and squeeze it into a quite stiff, doughy mass.

INGREDIENTS FOR 6 DOZEN COOKIES

3⅔ cups (scooped and leveled) all-purpose flour

2 cups (8 ounces) walnut pieces

1 teaspoon double-action baking powder

¼ teaspoon baking soda

3 "large" eggs

1⅓ cups sugar

2 tablespoons zest (colored part of peel only) from 1 large fresh lemon

(continued)

Orange Walnut Biscotti (continued)

Forming the Dough into Logs: Divide the dough in half and roll and press each half into a log 14 inches long; press the ends in as you roll to keep them neat. Lift each log as shaped onto the parchment-lined pan, and press the top to flatten slightly—the logs will be oval in shape. Beat the reserved egg white with a fork until smooth and brush it lightly over the tops of the logs.

2 tablespoons zest from large shiny orange

1 teaspoon pure orange oil (available in specialty stores)

1 stick (4 ounces) unsalted butter, melted

SPECIAL EQUIPMENT SUGGESTED

A jelly-roll pan, approximately 9 by 15 inches
Parchment paper
A wire whisk
A rubber spatula
Wire cooling racks
An airtight storage container

The First Baking: Bake until the logs are light brown but still give slightly when the tops are pressed, about 30 minutes. Remove the pan from the oven and reduce the temperature to 325° F. Let the logs cool on the pan for 15 minutes.

The Second Baking: One at a time, remove the logs to a board and cut them on a diagonal into ½-inch slices—the characteristic biscotti shape. Lay the slices on their sides and return the sheet to the oven. Bake until the cookies are light brown, about 15 minutes. Set them on wire racks, and when the biscotti are thoroughly cold, store them in the airtight container, where they will keep for weeks.

cook's notes

ZARELA MARTÍNEZ

I t's a long way from her roots on El Rancho in northern Mexico to her restaurant on Second Avenue in New York, but in many ways Zarela Martínez has managed to weave a tight, multifaceted bond between the two. She is a thoroughly modern American chef and entrepreneur, who, although educated as a social worker, began her own catering company, frozen food business, and restaurant. And yet, her food and her writings are undeniably steeped in the culture and tradition of an old Mexico.

It hasn't always been that way. Zarela admits that she got a bit off-track in the beginning of her culinary career. When she married a widower with three kids and became pregnant with twins, her sister suggested that she cater in order to supplement their income. She took classes at the Culinary Institute of America, learned the business end from a California caterer, and set up business in El Paso. "I was fearless. I tried everything—everything except Mexican food. I didn't think it was special enough." Zarela says that she created some pretty weird combinations—well done but weird. And then, in 1981, she took classes with Paul Prudhomme, who diplomatically and thankfully suggested that she concentrate on Mexican food. Two weeks later she found herself at the Tavern on the Green preparing a Chaîne des Rôtisseurs dinner for seven hundred. "I brought my mother with me. She's like a John Deere tractor; she believes that you just do it! She did the cooking and I got the press."

The press led Zarela and her mother to catering parties for such celebrated people as Warner LeRoy and Lauren Bacall and for the Reagan White House, where they needed authentic Mexican recipes for the visiting Queen Elizabeth. The attention was abundant and it proved enticing. Craig Claiborne suggested that she come to his kitchen to cook a meal, offering to do an article about the event. She spent all her money to get there, but the article brought so much publicity that she decided to move with her children to New York. She had some false starts, but in 1987 opened the immediately successful Zarela. Her charming book, *Food from My Heart,* was published in 1992 and offers not only authentic dishes from her native Mexico but also her remembrances. She shared both with us in my kitchen.

SALSA DE CHILE COLORADO
RED CHILE SAUCE

This is Zarela's mother's recipe for a rich chile sauce that is delicious on cooked pork or chicken, on enchiladas and with various hearty Mexican soups like menudo *(tripe soup) and* pozole *(hominy soup). Zarela uses it here to sauce the pork for her tamales. You will note it is not a difficult sauce: dried chiles are soaked to soften, then are pureed, and finally are simmered in a lard and flour roux, giving it its very special taste and depth of flavor.*

Reconstituting and Pureeing the Chiles: Soak the chiles in warm water to cover until softened, 15 to 20 minutes, then drain. Remove the stems and seeds from the chiles and puree in the blender with the stock, using enough to make a thick paste that will hold its shape on a spoon. Strain through the sieve and set aside.

Making the Roux and Sauce: Melt the lard in a heavy saucepan. Add the garlic and push it around the pan with the spatula to release its flavor. Remove the garlic when it is lightly browned and quickly stir the flour into the fat to prevent lumps. Cook the roux until golden but not brown. Add the strained puree and simmer, stirring frequently, for 10 minutes.

Ahead-of-Time Note: The sauce will keep a week or so in the refrigerator. Zarela does not freeze hers; she feels the sauce separates and loses quality when frozen and thawed.

INGREDIENTS FOR ABOUT
1½ CUPS

For the chiles
*10 large dried medium-hot
 red chiles (New Mexico, ancho,
 guajillo, or Anaheim)*
*1½ cups or more pork or chicken
 stock*

For the sauce
¼ cup lard
3 smashed and peeled garlic cloves
2 tablespoons all-purpose flour

SPECIAL EQUIPMENT
SUGGESTED

A blender
A fine-meshed sieve or strainer
A heavy 1½-quart saucepan

MEXICAN EQUIPMENT TALK

Zarela says that a food processor just does not produce the texture that is needed for Mexican cooking. In Mexico, as soon as someone earns enough money, he or she buys an electric blender. The old way of doing it was by hand or with a stone tool similar to a mortar and pestle.

If you plan to do a lot of Mexican cooking, you should invest in a good heavy cast-iron griddle. The Mexicans use a terra-cotta griddle called a *comal* for grilling and charring vegetables before they are peeled—a technique which gives that special "Mexican" flavor to recipes.

RENDERING PORK FAT FOR LARD

Chicken fat, goose fat, beef fat

To render fat means to heat raw pieces of fat to extract the fat itself from the fatty tissue in which it is embedded, leaving just the liquid fat—such as lard—which congeals when cool. You can then refrigerate it in a covered container for weeks, or freeze for months. Lard is much used in Mexican cooking, as in Zarela's tamales. Chicken fat is used in Jewish cookery, and goose fat is particularly effective for sautés, especially potatoes. Beef kidney fat (or suet) is prominent in classical English cookery. Whatever the fat, the rendering is the same. I shall take pork fat as the example—look for fresh pork fat in ethnic markets, or order it from a butcher.

Nutritional Note: Ever since fear of fat entered the scene, lard has been looked upon with horror. According to our sources, store-bought lard is lower in cholesterol than butter, but higher in saturated fat because it has been hydrogenated. It is neither bad nor good, just like butter. However, home-rendered lard is not hydrogenated and is therefore not saturated fat. It ranks with olive oil on the nutritional scale.

INGREDIENTS FOR ABOUT 3 CUPS
2 pounds fresh unsalted pork fatback
1 cup water

SPECIAL EQUIPMENT SUGGESTED
A heavy 3-quart saucepan with cover
A fine-meshed sieve
1 or 2 sturdy screw-top jars

Remove the rind if any covers the meat—you might package and freeze a sizable piece, and use it sometime to tie around a piece of meat that is to braise—it works as an automatic baster.

Cut the fat into ½-inch dice and bring to the boil with the water. Cover the pan and simmer slowly for 20 minutes to draw the fat out of the tissues. Then uncover the pan and boil slowly to evaporate all moisture—you will hear sputtering noises as the evaporation proceeds. As soon as the sputtering stops, remove at once from heat—the fat has rendered. The liquid will be clear and yellowish, and the tissue particles—the cracklings—will have browned slightly. Let cool a few minutes, then strain through the sieve into the jar or jars.

The Cracklings. Knock the cracklings out of the sieve onto paper towels. Chop them into bits if necessary, and toss with a little salt, pepper, and allspice. Sprinkle over a salad, poached eggs, broiled fish or meat, and so forth. Deliciously crunchy little bits they are.

CORN RELISH

Zarela tucks this Mexican corn relish inside her tamales and it is delicious. It would be right at home on a summer picnic table alongside hamburgers or grilled steaks.

Preliminaries: With a sharp knife, remove the kernels and juices from the corncobs, preserving the juices—you should have about 2 cups. (See also Dean Fearing's ingenious kernel removal using the large holes of a grater, page 183.) Heat the griddle or skillet over moderately high heat until a drop of water sizzles on contact. Arrange the peppers on the hot surface, turning often to cook evenly until the skins are blackened and the flesh is somewhat softened. Remove the peppers and wrap them in a kitchen towel, letting

INGREDIENTS FOR ABOUT 2½ CUPS

2 large ears of fresh corn
2 fresh poblano chiles
2 tablespoons vegetable oil
1 medium onion, minced
2 medium garlic cloves, peeled and minced

(continued)

them steam for several minutes to loosen the skin. Then peel, discard the seeds and veins, and coarsely chop them.

Making the Relish: Heat the oil in the frying pan, stir in the onion and garlic, and sauté for several minutes, stirring frequently, until they are softened but not browned. Blend in the peppers and sauté one minute, then stir in the corn and continue sautéing for 4 to 5 minutes, just until tender. Stir in the cilantro, and salt lightly to taste.

cook's notes

About 3 tablespoons chopped cilantro
Salt to taste

SPECIAL EQUIPMENT SUGGESTED

A corncob stripper or 4-sided grater
A cast-iron griddle (or use a heavy cast-iron or cast-aluminum frying pan)
Tongs (for turning the peppers)
A 10-inch frying pan, preferably no-stick

MEXICAN INGREDIENTS

Tomatillos: These golf-ball-size green tomatoes, cloaked in their papery husks, are native to Mexico, where they are known as *tomate verde,* literally "green tomatoes." In American markets they are called tomatillos, or "little tomatoes." Oddly enough, they are not tomatoes at all but a relative of the Cape gooseberry. The tomatoes have a glutinous quality that naturally thickens sauces. To use, simply peel away the husk and wash them well. When she has the time, Zarela lets them sit in a bowl of cold water for about an hour. They will peel easily and be well washed.

Fresh Poblano Chiles: Poblano chiles are long—4 to 6 inches—shiny, dark green chiles with a distinctive flavor that varies from mild to hot. Available in many large markets, poblanos are used often for stuffing and also as a flavoring once they are charred and peeled. You can substitute Anaheim or New Mexico long green chiles in their place.

Epazote: This is stinkweed. It has a pungent flavor and many people think of it as the most Mexican of culinary herbs. The plant is characterized by pointed, serrated pale green leaves with tiny green balls for flowers. It is not easy to find in its fresh state but is available in specialty markets dried. Many people substitute the more readily available cilantro and it is fine to do so, although the flavor will be entirely different. (Some people insist that a little fresh epazote cooked with dried beans minimizes their gaseous effects.)

Hoja Santa: The delicate anise-like hoja santa, which can be found in Mexican markets in large U.S. cities, can be replaced if necessary with an anise infusion. In that case, boil 1 cup water with 1 teaspoon anise seed (or 8 star anise pods) in a small saucepan until reduced by half; strain the liquid and add to the blender instead of the ½ cup of water.

Pure Ceylon Cinnamon: Pure Ceylon cinnamon, which comes in sticks, has a softer bark and a subtler flavor than the more common cinnamon. It's one of those flavorings that defines Mexican food.

MOLE VERDE
GREEN MOLE SAUCE

Mole means "ground," and a mole sauce is a puree in which a number of flavorings are blended. The most typical mole sauce is red and has chocolate in it, but this mole verde sauce with its green tomatillos is characteristic of the ancient Oaxaca region of Mexico. Zarela points out that its slightly tart character goes especially well with white beans and pork dishes. She serves it with pork-flavored tamales (see page 58).

Pan-roasting the Tomatillos and Peppers: Set the griddle or skillet over moderately high heat until a drop of water sizzles on contact. Spread the tomatillos and the poblano on the hot surface. Turn frequently until blackened and somewhat softened, about 10 minutes. Transfer the tomatillos to the blender. Wrap the chile in a kitchen towel and leave for several minutes to steam so that the skin loosens, then peel, halve, and remove seeds and veins. Transfer the chile to the blender.

INGREDIENTS FOR 4 CUPS

The tomatillos and the chile
1 pound fresh tomatillos, husked and washed (about 12 large tomatillos)
1 fresh poblano chile

Other ingredients
3 large garlic cloves, peeled
1 medium onion, peeled and coarsely chopped
¼ cup coarsely chopped fresh parsley sprigs
Either 3 large hoja santa leaves (fresh or dried) and 4 sprigs fresh epazote leaves or 1 tablespoon dried (see box, page 53)
Or a medium handful of fresh cilantro
½ cup water
1 tablespoon masa harina (see box), mixed to a paste with 1 tablespoon water
Salt to taste
Sugar to taste

MASA

The word *masa* means "dough," and in Mexican cookery it refers to corn dough, a staple of the Mexican diet—the basis of all corn tortillas and an integral part of most tamales. Fresh masa is made by soaking dried corn kernels in a lime solution (calcium oxide) until the skins flake off—a process similar, but not identical, to that of making hominy. The kernels are then pounded to a moist paste. This is fresh masa, which has its own unique flavor; you can buy it at tortilla factories. If there is a factory near you, you will want the coarse grind for masa dough; the finer grind is for tortillas. Since fresh masa keeps only a few days before going sour, buy 10 pounds or so and store it in 1-pound bags in your freezer, where it will keep nicely for several months.

Lacking fresh masa, you can still do well with the dried version, masa harina, sold in 5-pound bags in many supermarkets. (Zarela recommends Quaker Oats and Maseca as two good brands.) Here is how to reconstitute it:

To Make Masa from Masa Harina— for 3 pounds

4½ cups masa harina
4 or more cups warm chicken stock
Place the masa harina in a large bowl and beat in enough of the chicken stock with a wooden spoon to make a firm but pliable dough—the consistency of a fairly stiff bread dough. The dough is now ready to use in the tamale filling on page 58—you may freeze what you don't use.

(continued)

Pureeing: Add to the blender the garlic, onion, parsley, and the hoja santa and epazote or cilantro. Puree briefly, then pour in the water and the masa harina paste. Puree until smooth, about 3 minutes. Taste carefully; season with salt and, if you think it too tart, a little sugar.

Simmering the Sauce: Set the saucepan over high heat, add the lard, and when almost smoking, stir in the puree and bring to the boil. Reduce heat to low and simmer uncovered for 10 minutes, stirring occasionally. Taste for seasoning, adding more salt and, if still too tart, a little more sugar.

Ahead-of-Time Note: Mole sauce will keep covered in the refrigerator for about 5 days.

For simmering the sauce
2 tablespoons lard

SPECIAL EQUIPMENT
SUGGESTED

*A griddle or heavy cast-iron
   skillet*
Tongs
An electric blender
*A 2- to 2½-quart heavy-
   bottomed saucepan*

POBLANOS RELLENOS
STUFFED POBLANO CHILES

Preparing the Stuffing: Set the frying pan over moderate heat, add the butter, and when bubbling, stir in the garlic and onions. As soon as the onions are tender and translucent, in 3 to 4 minutes, stir in the dried fruits and olives; continue cooking another 3 minutes. Blend in the spices and pork, mixing well, and let cook for 5 to 7 minutes to combine flavors. Taste carefully for seasoning, remembering when you add salt that the olives are salty.

Ahead-of-Time Note: May be prepared a day or two in advance; cover and refrigerate.

Frying the Chiles: Make a slit 1 to 1½ inches long in each chile, and dry in a kitchen towel. Pour ½ inch of oil into the saucepan and set over high heat until the oil is almost smoking. Being sure the chiles are completely dry (to prevent the oil from spattering), fry them two at a time, turning once or twice, until they puff up and take on an olive-beige color. This goes very fast. Remove them from the pan as they are done and continue with the rest. Carefully peel the chiles under cold running water and very gently pull out the seeds through the slit in each, being sure not to tear the flesh. Set aside.

Ahead-of-Time Note: You may stuff them a day in advance; cover and refrigerate.

Stuffing and Baking the Chiles: Preheat the oven to 500° F. Being careful not to tear them, stuff the chiles through their slits. Arrange on the oiled

INGREDIENTS FOR 8 SERVINGS

For the stuffing
4 ounces (1 stick) unsalted butter
*2 large garlic cloves, peeled and
   minced*
*1 medium onion, chopped (about
   1 cup)*
½ cup each, coarsely chopped:
Pitted prunes
Dried apricots
Dried peaches
*½ cup pimento-stuffed green
   olives, sliced*
1½ teaspoons each:
Ground cumin
Ground cloves
*Ground imported Ceylon
   cinnamon (if available) or ½
   teaspoon regular ground
   cinnamon*

(continued)

Poblanos Rellenos (continued)

baking sheet and roast for 7 to 8 minutes in the middle level of the preheated oven. They should just heat through.

Serving: Spoon the tomato sauce onto individual plates or onto a large serving platter and arrange the warm chiles on top.

2 cups shredded pork (see page 58)

Salt to taste

For the chiles

8 large fresh poblano chiles (see box, page 53)

Vegetable oil (for frying)

For serving

Salsa de Tomate Asado (Roasted Tomato Sauce; see page 61)

SPECIAL EQUIPMENT
SUGGESTED

A heavy 12-inch frying pan

A deep saucepan, about 10 inches across and 8 inches deep (for frying the chiles)

An oiled baking sheet

THE PERFECT MARGARITA

If tequila is the Mexican national drink, certainly a margarita, which is made with tequila, has become the Mexican national cocktail. Tequila is produced only in Mexico, and is distilled from the juices of the maguey, or agave plant. The best tequila is made from the blue agave plant, which grows only in four of the Mexican states, one of which surrounds the town of Tequila. Zarela makes a mean margarita, and insists on the best ingredients in equal proportions—the finest white tequila, the best-quality orange liqueur, and the very freshest and fattest limes. Drink it straight up over ice, or whiz it in a blender with ice cubes—which our serious tasting team preferred. One cocktail is perfect; two, plenty; three—watch out!

Preliminaries: To make the traditional ring of salt around the rims of the glasses, pour a little tequila into one of the saucers, and the salt into the other. Turn the glasses upside down; one by one, dip the rim first into the tequila, shaking off excess liquid, then into the salt; and set the glass upright.

Making the Cocktail: Measure the fresh lime juice, tequila, and orange liqueur into the container of the blender, pour in the ice, and puree, pulsing the machine on and off for a few seconds. If you want a uniform frozen effect, puree until you hear no ice crackling; otherwise leave in a few bits of ice—a matter of taste. Serve at once, pouring into the middle of each glass so as not to disturb the ring of salt.

cook's notes

INGREDIENTS FOR A QUARTET
OF DRINKS

For decorating the glasses
About 1 tablespoon tequila
About 1 tablespoon table salt

The formula
  2 ounces (¼ cup) each:
Fresh lime juice
White tequila
Triple Sec or Cointreau
8 ice cubes, 1¼-inch size
  (making about 1 cup in a
  quart measure)

SPECIAL EQUIPMENT
SUGGESTED

2 saucers (for dipping the glasses
  into)
4 coupes (shallow wide-mouthed
  wineglasses), about ¾-cup
  capacity
An electric blender

PUERCO COCIDO
SIMMERED PORK BUTT

Simmered, shredded pork is an important ingredient in many Mexican recipes, such as the Colorado red sauce filling for tamales on page 51 and the stuffing for poblano chiles on page 55. It's easy to do and nice to have on hand.

Cooking the Pork: Set the pork in the pan and pour in enough cold water to cover the meat by 2 inches. Add the garlic, peppercorns, bay leaves, and salt, and bring to the boil. Reduce heat to the simmer, cover partially, and occasionally skim off scum which will accumulate on the surface. Simmer for 1½ to 2 hours, or until a fork will pierce the meat easily and can be removed readily. The pork must be cooked enough to be shredded when cool, but it should not be dried out. When cool, cover and store overnight in the refrigerator; the pork will remain moist and absorb the flavors of the stock.

Shredding the Pork: Use two forks to pull the meat apart into thin shreds, or cut into shreds with a large knife. Pull or cut along the grain. This is not a quick process because the meat must be very thin shreds.

A 2½- to 3-pound boneless well-trimmed pork butt
1 whole head of garlic, unpeeled, halved crosswise
10 whole peppercorns
4 large bay leaves
1 teaspoon salt

SPECIAL EQUIPMENT SUGGESTED

A saucepan or pot just large enough to hold the meat comfortably

TAMALES

A tamale is food that is folded or wrapped in a leaf of some sort, usually corn husks. A recipe for the traditional tamale follows. The corn husk is spread with prepared masa dough into which a flavoring or garnish is tucked; the husk is then folded around it, and the tamale is steamed.

Soaking the Corn Husks: Place the corn husks in a large bowl, cover with boiling water, and let soak while you're preparing the rest of the ingredients—at least ½ hour.

Making the Masa Filling: Beat the masa in the bowl of the mixer while gradually adding large spoonfuls of lard. Continue beating 3 to 4 minutes (longer if you do not have a heavy-duty mixer), until the mixture is very light, fluffy, and fully aerated. Beat in tablespoons of warm chicken stock if the masa appears stiff—it should be almost the texture of whipped cream. Beat in the

INGREDIENTS FOR ABOUT 30 TAMALES

30 untreated corn husks

For the prepared masa dough filling
1½ pounds fresh masa or prepared masa harina (page 54)

(continued)

salt, then test the masa by dropping a small dollop on top of a cup of chicken stock or warm water—if it floats it's ready.

Manufacturing Note: If you are using commercial lard instead of your own rendered lard, reverse this process: first whip the lard, then add the masa bit by bit.

Forming and Filling the Tamales: Remove the corn husks from the water and gently squeeze out excess, then pat dry with a kitchen towel. Lay the husks on the counter with the rough, outside edge down and the narrow, pointed end away from you. Spread about ½ cup of the masa over ⅔ of the husk, leaving the pointed end uncovered. Spoon a few tablespoons of one of the flavorings into the center of the masa. To enclose the filling, fold the sides of the husks together, overlapping them, then fold the pointed top down. The bottom remains open.

Ahead-of-Time Note: The tamales may be prepared a day ahead to this point and refrigerated or frozen.

Steaming the Tamales: Arrange the tamales in the steamer with their open ends facing up. (You may wish to place a ball of foil in the center of the steamer as a prop.) Pour 1 inch of boiling water into the steamer pan and lay a clean, damp towel over the tamales—this helps hold in the steam. Cover tightly and bring to the full boil; reduce heat to maintain a gentle bubbling, and steam for 45 minutes to 1 hour, replenishing with boiling water as necessary.

When Is It Done? The tamales are ready when the filling is firm to the touch. Remove from the steamer and let stand 10 minutes before serving.

Serving: Either serve the tamales in their husks or unwrap them and place on individual plates with the sauce and corn relish on the side.

(continued)

½ pound best-quality lard, preferably home-rendered (see box, page 52)
1¼ tablespoons salt
Several tablespoons tepid chicken stock (if needed)

For flavoring the tamales
Either *Corn Relish (see page 52)*
Or *Pork with Red Chile Sauce (see pages 51 and 58)*

For serving
1 to 1½ cups Green Mole Sauce (see page 54)
About one cup Corn Relish (see page 52) or cooked corn

SPECIAL EQUIPMENT
SUGGESTED

A heavy-duty electric mixer with paddle attachment, ideally; otherwise a large bowl, a wooden spoon, and elbow grease
A steamer with a basket or steaming insert

Tamales (continued)

Manufacturing Note:

Frozen Tamales. Either steam frozen tamales in their frozen state, allowing a little extra time, or microwave on high for 10 minutes.

Reheating Steamed Tamales. Either steam until warmed through or reheat in the microwave.

SALSA DE TOMATE ASADO
ROASTED TOMATO SAUCE

Pan-roasting vegetables brings out their natural sugar and produces a slightly smoky taste, which, when combined with cream, gives some complexity to this essentially simple, earthy sauce. Don't be too fanatical about peeling the tomatoes and onions—leave in a few blackened bits—if you want an authentic Mexican flavor.

Pour the cream into the saucepan and simmer over moderate heat until reduced by half.

Meanwhile, set the griddle over high heat until a drop of water sizzles on contact. Spread the onion and garlic on the hot surface and brown on all sides, turning frequently until the garlic is softened and the onion is partly blackened and fragrant. Set them aside. Then pan-roast the tomatoes, turning several times until blistered all over. Set aside.

Peel the onion, scraping away any extremely charred bits. Cut out and discard the root and then cut the onion into chunks and drop into the blender. Squeeze the garlic cloves out of their skins into the blender. Peel the tomatoes directly over the blender (leaving on a little of the charred skin) and drop them in, seeds and all. Puree on medium speed until smooth.

Finishing the Sauce: Stir the puree into the reduced cream. Season with salt and simmer for about 5 minutes, or until the sauce loses its raw taste.

Ahead-of-Time Note: The sauce can be made a day or two ahead, covered, and refrigerated.

INGREDIENTS FOR ABOUT
4 CUPS

1½ cups heavy cream
1 medium onion, unpeeled, halved crosswise
8 large garlic cloves, unpeeled
3 to 4 large ripe tomatoes (about 2¾ pounds), unpeeled
Salt

SPECIAL EQUIPMENT
SUGGESTED

A 2- to 2½-quart heavy-bottomed stainless steel saucepan
A heavy cast-iron griddle or skillet
An electric blender

CHARLIE TROTTER

When Charlie Trotter was working toward his political science degree at the University of Wisconsin, he and his roommate had cooking contests to see who could outdo the other. He must have won more than his fair share because after graduating, Charlie decided to forget the political science degree and try his hand at a professional food career. Finding it difficult without a culinary degree, he looked for anyone who would hire him to do anything. He pounded on a lot of doors and finally hit the jackpot with Norman Van Aiken in Chicago. Once he began to apprentice, he knew that all that pounding was worth the effort. "It was love at first sight!" recalls Charlie. Charlie continued his journeyman apprenticeships with such noted chefs as Gordon Sinclair and Bradley Ogden in Chicago and San Francisco, and spent time in Europe. "I read every cookbook I could get my hands on and ate out incessantly." The menus from leading international restaurants that adorn his walls attest to the feeding frenzy.

As he traveled, Charlie began mentally to formulate his dream restaurant, and in 1987 it became a reality. He spent eighteen months working closely with architects and construction crews to ensure that every detail fulfilled his ideal. A ceiling-high wine rack in the entrance bar of the renovated brownstone that houses Charlie Trotter's is bold testimony to Chef Charlie's sensitivity to the total dining experience. "Wine is as important as food in the eating-out scenario," he says. In addition to the wine, critics and diners alike have great praise for the chef's ability to marry what he calls the "earth, sea, and sky in a vegetable- and fruit-driven cuisine." He demonstrated his talents for us with his innovative use of carrot broth, curry butter, and deeply flavored sorbets.

SMOKED SALMON NAPOLEON

A beautiful dish of many parts is typical Charlie Trotter, a cook's cook. He is full of invention, and his recipes are definitely for those who love the pure act of cooking. Nothing is difficult here— there are just a lot of steps, some of which you may ready hours or even a day in advance. The original Napoleon is a pastry—thin, buttery, crunchy layers of puff pastry filled with custard. Chef Charlie's Napoleon replaces pastry with thin slices of smoked salmon sandwiched between crushed avocado and slices of pickled papaya. Crisp potato wafers give the crunch, and a beautiful green herbal sauce binds the flavors to make a handsome as well as toothsome first course.

Manufacturing Note: Remember this is a chef's recipe, and chefs in restaurants, unlike home cooks, have all sorts of delicious edibles right on hand, such as exotic mushrooms, cunning sauces, chopped fresh herbs, and the like. If you don't happen to have, for instance, a teaspoon of fresh tomato pulp or half a papaya, either improvise or omit. That's what Charlie Trotter himself would do, and what he would encourage you to do.

Preparing the Herb Sauce: You may make this by hand, but the blender is fast and easy, as follows: Drop the 2 egg yolks into the blender with 1 teaspoon of vinegar and another of lemon juice. Puree for several seconds, until the egg yolks are a thick pale yellow; then slowly, by dribbles, begin pouring in the herbal oil, and continue until the mixture forms a thick mayonnaise. Finally, pulse in enough of the herbal juice (about ⅓ cup) to thin the mayonnaise to a sauce-like consistency. Season with salt, pepper, and lemon juice as needed. Pulse in the habanero pepper or hot pepper sauce, and set aside.

Ahead-of-Time Note: The herb sauce may be made a day in advance. Store in the refrigerator, and if it separates, whisk or blend it back to its original consistency.

Preparing the Pickled Papaya: Pour the water, vinegar, sake, sugar, and all the seasonings into a saucepan and bring to the boil; reduce the heat and simmer for 10 minutes. Taste the syrup and adjust the seasoning or cook a little longer so it has a good spicy flavor. Slice the papaya as thin as possible and place it in a bowl. Strain enough of the hot liquid over the sliced papaya just to cover. Let stand for 5 minutes, then drain and season with salt and pepper.

INGREDIENTS FOR 4 SERVINGS

For the herb sauce
2 egg yolks
1 teaspoon rice wine vinegar or white wine vinegar
1 teaspoon fresh lemon juice, plus more as needed
½ cup Herbal Oil (see box, page 73)
About ⅓ cup Herbal Juice (see box, page 73)
Salt
Freshly ground black pepper
1 teaspoon finely minced habanero pepper or a few drops of hot pepper sauce

For the pickled papaya
¾ cup water
¾ cup rice wine vinegar or white wine vinegar
2 tablespoons sake (Japanese rice wine)
2 tablespoons sugar
6 to 8 whole cloves

(continued)

Smoked Salmon Napoleon (continued)

Preparing the Pulped Avocado: Mash the avocado with a wooden spoon until roughly broken up into ¼-inch pieces. Fold in the tomato and the chives. Stir in the lemon juice and seasonings to taste.

Preparing the Lemon Vinaigrette: Pour the oil into a small bowl and whisk in the lemon juice. Taste, carefully adding more lemon juice if needed. Season with salt and pepper and stir in the chives.

Assembling the Dish—just before serving: Spread about 1 tablespoon of the avocado in the center of each of 4 luncheon-size plates. Cover the avocado with 2 squares of the salmon, and arrange 2 or 3 slices of papaya over the salmon and cover with a potato wafer. Continue building the Napoleon with layers of avocado, salmon, papaya, and a potato wafer; repeat, ending with a wafer. Drizzle the herb sauce on the plate around the Napoleon and spoon the lemon vinaigrette on top. Serve at once.

1 tablespoon mustard seeds
1 cinnamon stick
4 Turkish bay leaves
1 tablespoon whole allspice
½ papaya, peeled and seeded
Salt
Freshly ground black pepper

For the avocado
½ ripe unblemished avocado,
  pitted and peeled
2 teaspoons ripe, peeled and
  seeded chopped tomato
1 teaspoon minced chives
Drops of juice from ½ lemon
Salt
Freshly ground black pepper

For the lemon vinaigrette
¼ cup excellent olive oil
Drops of juice from the other
  ½ lemon
Salt
Freshly ground black pepper
1 tablespoon chopped chives

The rest of the dish
¾ to 1 pound smoked salmon,
  very thinly sliced, cut into
  16 two-inch squares
12 crisp Potato-Thyme Wafers
  (see page 118, but make them
  about 2 inches long)

SPECIAL EQUIPMENT
SUGGESTED

An electric blender

CURRY BUTTER

What do you do to transform a very white fillet of poached fish into something exciting to see and to eat? You follow Charlie Trotter's lead and create some flavored butters; then, with a small assortment in your freezer, you have the power to turn a plain broiled chicken breast into an Indian curry, or to transform plain spaghetti or simple boiled rice into a dream of Tuscany. These "compound" butters, as they are often called, provide instant flavoring. Chef Charlie Trotter's special butter has a lovely light curried quality, and he whisks it into an otherwise mild but healthy vegetable broth to give it character and texture. First he makes a strong curry paste, then he whips it into unsalted butter and rolls it into logs, which will keep for weeks in his freezer.

Manufacturing Note: For a quick method of producing a small amount of curry butter, see the box on page 68.

Preparing the Curry Paste: Roughly cut the stick of butter into chunks and melt in a 6-cup pan, adding the onion and garlic. Sweat (cook very slowly) until they are just softened but not colored. Add the apple pieces and cook 3 minutes more, then stir in the curry powder, turmeric, paprika, salt, and pepper; continue cooking slowly for 15 minutes, stirring occasionally. Transfer the contents to a food processor and puree 30 seconds, then push through a strainer and let cool to room temperature.

Preparing the Curry Butter: Whip the butter until light and fluffy, add the cool curry paste, and continue whipping until well incorporated.

Ahead-of-Time Note: The curry butter will keep several days in the refrigerator; or, when cool, roll it into 3 or 4 log shapes, wrap in foil, and freeze. Slice off pieces of the frozen butter to melt on top of cooked foods or to whisk into sauces.

INGREDIENTS FOR ABOUT
2 CUPS

1 stick (4 ounces) unsalted butter

1 small white onion, finely chopped (¼ cup)

2 large garlic cloves, peeled and coarsely chopped

½ Granny Smith apple, peeled, cored, and diced

2 tablespoons fragrant curry powder

1 teaspoon turmeric

½ teaspoon paprika

Salt

Freshly ground white pepper

1 pound unsalted butter, at room temperature

SPECIAL EQUIPMENT
SUGGESTED

An electric blender

A strainer

An electric mixer with paddle attachment, or a bowl and wooden spoon

SEARED SCALLOPS WITH CURRIED CARROT BROTH

Chef Charlie Trotter's handsome scallop dish makes a splendid first course, with its succulent sea creature sitting atop a richly flavored bed of earthy vegetables and napped with a delicately curried carrot broth. Chef Charlie likes to serve an Alsatian Gewürztraminer wine with his scallops, and he uses "diver" scallops if he can find them. These usually giant examples, also known as "dry-packed" or "day boat" scallops, are hand-harvested, sold in their natural state—no processing, no preservatives—and therefore must be exceedingly fresh. If you cannot find them, use large, very fresh sea scallops.

Preparing the Carrot Broth: Bring the carrot juice to the boil in a heavy saucepan, spooning off and discarding the foaming solids as they collect on the surface. When the juice is clear, pour it through the strainer. Return the broth to the pan and bring it back to the boil; turn down the heat and simmer until the juice is reduced to 1 cup. Set aside; bring just to the simmer at serving time, at which point you will add the curry butter.

The following steps take place immediately before serving. Have everything at the ready—food, implements, warm plates, and so forth—and, after the bacon has browned, plan to cook everything at once—as though you were a restaurant.

Cooking the Bacon: Sauté the bacon in one of the frying pans with 1 tablespoon of butter, cooking over low heat until the fat is rendered and the bacon is nicely browned but not too crisp. Remove from the pan with a slotted spoon and set aside on a plate.

Sautéing the Chard or Spinach: Sauté the strips of chard or spinach briefly in the bacon drippings and salt lightly; when just wilted, remove it to the plate with the bacon. Add the remaining tablespoon of butter and the mushrooms to the pan; salt lightly and sauté for 2 to 3 minutes, until the mushrooms have wilted. Toss the *haricots verts* into the mushrooms to heat through, and squeeze on a little lemon juice; taste very carefully, adding more seasonings as necessary.

Cooking the Scallops: Meanwhile, season the scallops with salt and pepper. Set the second frying pan over moderately high heat and add the butter; when its foam has almost subsided, lay in the scallops. Sear and brown them approximately 2 minutes on each side, until just cooked through—they will

INGREDIENTS FOR 4 SERVINGS

For the carrot broth
2 cups carrot juice (either homemade in a vegetable juicer or bought from a health food store)

For the garnish of bacon and vegetables
2 to 3 ounces slab of bacon, rind removed, or thick-sliced bacon (3 or 4 slices), diced
2 tablespoons unsalted butter
½ pound Swiss chard or spinach, washed, stems removed, leaves cut into long thin strips
Salt
Mushrooms:
Either ½ cup each:
Black trumpet mushrooms, wiped clean
Shiitake mushrooms, stems removed, wiped clean and sliced
Oyster mushrooms, wiped clean and sliced

(continued)

feel springy when touched, neither squashy nor stiff. Remove the pan from heat and season the scallops again with salt and pepper.

Serving: Divide the chard or spinach among the four warm soup dishes. Scatter some of the mushrooms and *haricots verts* around the chard and strew the bacon pieces on top. Place the scallops over that; whisk the curry butter into the warm carrot broth, taste for seasoning and add salt and pepper, and ladle the broth around the edges of the plate. Serve at once.

Or *1½ cups other wild mushrooms, wiped clean and sliced*
2 ounces (a handful) haricots verts *(small thin young green beans), trimmed and blanched (boiled) for 1 minute*
1 fresh lemon

For the scallops
4 large "diver" scallops or 12 ounces large sea scallops
Salt
Freshly ground black pepper
2 tablespoons unsalted butter

For finishing the broth
4 tablespoons Curry Butter (see page 65, or see box on page 68 for a simpler version)
Salt
Freshly ground white pepper

SPECIAL EQUIPMENT SUGGESTED

A strainer lined with washed cheesecloth set on top of a bowl
2 no-stick frying pans, 10-inch size
4 large soup plates with rims, warmed

JULIA'S SUGGESTIONS FOR QUICK CURRY BUTTER AND OTHER FLAVORED BUTTERS

Simple flavored butters can be fast and easy to make, and give instant new flavor to grilled fish, broiled chicken, boiled or steamed vegetables, and so forth. You can squeeze it out of a pastry tube to decorate appetizers, or you can chill it and cut it into fancy shapes for seasoning hot foods or to accompany bread. Here are a handful of suggestions to get you started.

Quick Curry Butter: Puree a small garlic clove and mash it in a bowl with ½ teaspoon or so of fragrant curry powder and ½ stick (2 ounces) of softened unsalted butter; season with salt and pepper. Use as is, or chill.

Variations: Using the same general system, and ½ stick of softened unsalted butter, here are some more combinations:

Maître d'Hôtel Butter: Mix ½ tablespoon very finely chopped shallots and 1 to 2 tablespoons finely chopped fresh parsley into the butter along with drops of lemon juice.

Mustard Butter: Blend in 1 to 2 tablespoons prepared Dijon-type mustard, along with 1 tablespoon finely chopped parsley or other herbs.

Anchovy Butter: Blend in 1 tablespoon mashed anchovies, drops of lemon juice, and pepper.

Garlic Butter: Blanch 2 or 3 peeled garlic cloves in boiling water, and puree the cloves, then mash with the butter and add minced herbs and lemon juice.

A TRIO OF SORBETS

Homemade sorbets are easy indeed with one of the modern ice cream makers. Store-bought sorbets, unfortunately, are rarely made with fresh ingredients and too often are super sweet. If it has to be store-bought, I'd personally rather skip the sorbets and sherbets and settle for vanilla ice cream.

Manufacturing Note: Sorbets are sweetened with a sugar and water solution known as "simple syrup." Once made, the syrup will keep almost indefinitely in the refrigerator and is useful to have on hand as a general sweetener not only for sorbets but for fruits, iced drinks, and so forth—you may wish to double the recipe here. The fruit purees may be made a day in advance, but the sorbets themselves should be churned only the day they are to be served or they will become too icy and rigid.

Making the Simple Syrup: Stir the sugar and water into a 6-cup saucepan, bring to the simmer over moderate heat, swirling the pan by its handle frequently, until the sugar is completely dissolved and the liquid is perfectly clear. Set it aside.

Preparing the Blackberry Puree: Puree the berries and simple syrup in the blender. Strain, and taste for a balance of flavors; the berry flavor should be strong but not too tart. Add more simple syrup if necessary; the juices should be decidedly sweet. Add a few drops of lemon juice to spark the flavor. Chill until ready to freeze.

INGREDIENTS FOR ABOUT
10 CUPS

For the simple syrup
2 cups sugar
2 cups water

For the blackberry sorbet
2 cups blackberries
½ cup of the simple syrup, plus
    more if needed
Fresh lemon juice, as needed

For the yogurt sorbet
2 cups plain yogurt
½ cup of the simple syrup
The juice of 1 lime

(continued)

Preparing the Yogurt Mixture: Whisk the yogurt in a bowl to smooth it out. Stir in the simple syrup and the lime juice. Chill the mixture until ready to freeze.

Preparing the Watermelon Puree: Our team found that the watermelon was so watery it could use a little denser sugar syrup, so begin by taking the standard syrup from above and heating it with the additional ¼ cup sugar until the sugar is dissolved; set aside. Puree the 3 cups of watermelon in the blender or processor until it is liquidized. Strain the juice into a bowl; you should have 2 cups. Stir in the simple syrup, taste carefully, adding more syrup if necessary to make a sweet taste. Add a few drops of lemon juice to balance the flavors and then chill the puree. Chill the diced watermelon separately, until ready to freeze.

Freezing the Sorbets: Freeze the sorbets one at a time in the ice cream freezer according to the manufacturer's directions. When the watermelon sorbet has solidified, add the reserved watermelon and run the machine until the pieces are completely incorporated and pureed. Spread the sorbets in freezer containers; cover and freeze. Before serving time, remove the sorbets and let them sit at room temperature just until they are soft enough to spoon easily.

For the watermelon sorbet
½ cup of the simple syrup, plus more if needed
¼ cup sugar
3 cups seeded, chopped watermelon
Fresh lemon juice (if needed)
1 cup finely diced watermelon (for finishing the sorbet)

SPECIAL EQUIPMENT SUGGESTED

A blender or a food processor
A fine-meshed strainer
An ice cream freezer

WARM PEACH SOUP WITH A TRIO OF SORBETS

A delightful summer soup—diced ripe peaches and watermelon bathed in a sweet puree of cooked peach, surrounded by homemade sorbets and decorated with homemade fruit chips. As is usual with Charlie Trotter's dishes, this is one for those who love to cook and to try out new techniques. If you don't choose to do all the steps, you could just make the fruit and the soup, topping them with vanilla ice cream and mint leaves. But the parts do make a great whole!

Preparing the Peaches: To peel the peaches, drop them into the pan of boiling water, leave them for exactly 30 seconds, and remove them with the slotted spoon to the bowl of ice water. Leave to cool for a moment, then remove the peel with a sharp paring knife—it will come off easily. Cut the peaches in half and discard the pits. Quarter two of the peaches and set aside. Cut the remaining peach into ⅜-inch dice, squeeze a few drops of lemon juice over them, and set aside with the diced watermelon.

INGREDIENTS FOR 4 SERVINGS

For the peaches
3 large ripe peaches (about 1½ pounds total)
Drops of fresh lemon juice
2 cups water
¼ cup sugar

(continued)

Warm Peach Soup (continued)

Ahead-of-Time Note: When preparing in advance, leave 1 blanched peach unpeeled, and dice it shortly before serving.

Poaching the Peaches: Simmer the sugar and water in a 6-cup saucepan, stirring and swirling the pan by its handle until the sugar has dissolved completely. Carefully lift in the peach quarters, and add the ginger, cinnamon, and pepper. Bring the liquid just back to the simmer, cover the pan and remove it from heat; let the peaches steep for at least 30 minutes while they absorb flavor.

Pureeing the Peach Soup: When the peaches have steeped, discard the ginger and cinnamon, and transfer the peaches to the blender with a slotted spoon. Pour 1½ cups of the peach-cooking syrup into the blender and puree. It should look like a thin cream soup—pulse in additional droplets of syrup if necessary, then pour the soup into a stainless steel saucepan and set aside until serving time.

Ahead-of-Time Note: May be prepared several hours in advance.

Assembling the Dessert: When ready to serve, heat the soup to warm. Mix the diced peaches with the watermelon and divide among the soup bowls or plates, spreading them in the bottom of each. Either form egg-shaped scoops of each sorbet with the soup spoons, or form small balls with an ice cream scoop, setting one of each over the diced fruits. Tuck a fruit chip into each sorbet. Rapidly pour a ladleful of the warm peach soup into each bowl or plate, and scatter on the mint chiffonade. Serve immediately.

Serving Alternative: To save yourself a mad dash to the table to avoid melting the sorbets with the warm soup, bring each guest a bowl with the sorbets and diced fruit scattered with the mint. Then circle the table, pouring on the soup from a pitcher—as they do in the restaurant.

2-inch piece of fresh ginger root, peeled and quartered
1 cinnamon stick
¼ teaspoon freshly ground white pepper

For serving
1 cup diced watermelon on a plate (⅜-inch pieces, cut from the melon used for the following sorbet)
Yogurt, blackberry, and watermelon sorbets

For the garnish
Oven-Dried Fruit Chips (see page 72)
6 large fresh mint leaves, cut into chiffonade (very narrow strips)

SPECIAL EQUIPMENT SUGGESTED

A slotted spoon
A pan of boiling water (for blanching the whole peaches)
A bowl of ice and water (for cooling the peaches)
An electric blender
A strainer
2 soup spoons or a small ice cream scoop (for serving the sorbets)
4 wide soup bowls or soup plates

OVEN-DRIED FRUIT CHIPS

Master chefs have many trade tricks for making simple foods appear elegant, as well as making elegant dishes even more so. The dried fruit chip trick is one of these—tuck a chip of apple and another of strawberry into a serving of store-bought vanilla ice cream, scatter a chiffonade of mint leaves around, and you have created "A Dessert." Three examples are described here, but many other fruits may be used, including kiwis, of which Charlie Trotter is fond.

Preheat the oven to 250° F and place the rack in the middle of the oven.

Cut the fruit into very thin slices, about as thick as your thumbnail. Lay them out in one layer on the baking pan and set in the oven for 25 to 30 minutes, or until the pieces are thoroughly dry and crisp. If some of the thinner pieces are dry first, remove them.

Ahead-of-Time Note: The fruits will stay crisp for several hours stored in a tightly sealed plastic bag.

1 banana, peeled

1 cup strawberries, quickly rinsed and hulled

1 Granny Smith apple, peeled, cored, and quartered

SPECIAL EQUIPMENT SUGGESTED

A no-stick baking sheet

cook's notes

HERBAL JUICE AND HERBAL OIL

Herb-flavored oils are treasures to have on hand either for making mayonnaise-based sauces or for seasoning cooked chicken or fish or vegetables or eggs or anything that would enjoy an herbal lift, since they give an explosion of flavor more intense than that of plain chopped herbs. Charlie Trotter blanches his fresh herbs briefly in boiling water and then "shocks" them in ice water to stop the cooking and to set their vibrant green color. He purees them in ice water for herbal juice to use in sauces and soups, or in oil for mayonnaise and salad dressings.

Manufacturing Note: The proportions here make a restaurant-size quantity, which may be too much for your needs. Feel free to cut everything down to a more reasonable size, and feel free also to use what herbs you personally like—it is the method that counts. However, it is very important that you use only best-quality fresh unflavored oil, such as grape-seed, sweet almond, or canola, which will not mask the flavors of your herbs. The following combination is one that Chef Charlie favors.

HERBAL JUICE

2 bunches (4 cups, loosely packed) fresh flat-leaf Italian parsley sprigs
1 cup watercress leaves
1¼ cups tarragon leaves
⅓ cup ice water
¼ cup fresh flavorless oil
Salt
Freshly ground white pepper

HERBAL OIL

The reserved half-portion of pureed green herbs
2 cups fresh flavorless oil
Salt
Freshly ground white pepper

SPECIAL EQUIPMENT SUGGESTED

A large saucepan of boiling water
A Chinese wire-mesh dipper-outer (useful but not essential)
A large bowl of ice and water
An electric blender
A fine-meshed sieve or chinois (conical-shaped strainer)

Preparing the Herbal Juice: Drop the parsley into the saucepan of rapidly boiling water and lift out immediately with the wire-mesh strainer; plunge at once into ice water to stop the cooking. Drain and scatter on a perfectly dry kitchen towel; roll up the towel and squeeze tightly to extract as much water as possible. Repeat with the watercress and tarragon. Chop the herbs roughly, then puree in the blender with the ice water, oil, salt, and pepper. Divide the puree in half and reserve one half for the herbal oil. Pour the rest through the strainer into a bowl, pressing on the solids to extract the beautiful green liquid—this is the herbal juice; set aside. Do not wash out the blender, since you will use it again for the herbal oil.

Preparing the Herbal Oil: Transfer the reserved half of the pureed herb mixture to the blender and pour in ½ cup of the oil. Turn on the machine and start to drizzle in the remainder of the oil through the top. Puree on medium-high speed until the mixture is bright green, 1½ minutes or so. Strain, pressing on the herbs left behind in the strainer to extract as much of the oil as possible. Discard the herbs, pour the liquid into a glass pitcher, and refrigerate for at least 6 hours, or overnight. By then, sediment will have sunk to the bottom of the oil; carefully pour the clear green oil from the top into a clean screw-top jar.

Ahead-of-Time Note: The herbal juice will keep in the refrigerator for several days; the oil, at least a week.

GEORGE GERMON
AND JOHANNE KILLEEN

When George Germon and Johanne Killeen—or, as friends of the couple call them, "Mr. and Mrs. Al Forno"—opened their first, twelve-seat Providence restaurant in 1980, they did it so they could support artistic careers. The chefs, both art graduates of Rhode Island School of Design, needed a source of steady income. "But," says George, "we fell in love with the restaurant within the first three days and decided to give up everything else." The art community's loss was definitely the food world's gain.

When Johanne and George moved and enlarged Al Forno in 1989, the steady beat of customers and worldwide accolades continued undiminished. "We have a friend whose theory is, whatever you want to do in life, don't study for it; what you decide to go into you'll go into with such a passion that you'll devour everything in sight." That's just about what the couple does, traveling and tasting every minute they can. They have been known to eat as many as five meals a day in as many different restaurants in order to expand their knowledge.

The restaurant's overwhelming popularity and astounding reputation (*The International Herald Tribune* named it the number one restaurant in the world for casual dining in 1994) was built not only on the incredible Italian-inspired flavors of its dishes but also on its dedication to cooking everything to order. Desserts such as the meltingly warm, tangy-sweet citrus tart on page 81 don't go into the oven until customers order them; pasta is never precooked; and the uniquely flavored, ash-cooked "Dirty Steak" recipe that they shared with us isn't even on the menu because if too many are ordered at once, the steaks smother the fire; diners know about it only through word of mouth.

GEORGE GERMON'S HOT FANNY SAUCE

"Why the name, George? Hot Fanny Sauce?" No explanation. He just likes the sound of it, and he likes to serve it with his Dirty Steak (see page 76), and with broiled chicken, and with barbecued ribs; it goes nicely indeed with egg dishes, too. He makes an intensely brown caramel for this very special sauce, and lets the onions cook in it until they are browned and themselves caramelized. There's no sweetness here, since when sugar caramelizes, the sweet has gone out of it, leaving only a unique flavor that gives this sauce its unusual character.

INGREDIENTS FOR ABOUT 1 QUART

For the sauce base
1 cup sugar
2 pounds onions, minced (7 to 8 cups)
1 jalapeño pepper, seeded and finely minced
4 cups chicken stock
1½ teaspoons kosher salt
⅛ cup medium-dry sherry

For finishing the sauce
½ cup red wine vinegar
1 green bell pepper, roasted, peeled, and seeded

SPECIAL EQUIPMENT SUGGESTED

A heavy 2-quart saucepan
An electric blender

Preparing the Sauce Base: Measure the sugar into the saucepan and cook over medium heat, stirring often and watching carefully until the sugar caramelizes, turning a rich mahogany-brown—6 to 8 minutes. Stir in the onions and jalapeño pepper; as they release their juices they will blend with the caramel. Let them cook over moderately high heat, stirring occasionally, until very soft and brown—8 to 10 minutes.

Reducing the Sauce: Add the stock and the salt, and bring to a boil over moderately high heat. Reduce by a third—to about 1½ cups—10 to 15 minutes. Stir in the sherry, cook another minute, and remove from heat.

Pureeing and Finishing the Sauce: Transfer the sauce to the blender and, holding the top down firmly to prevent accidental burns and splatters, turn the machine on to moderately slow. With the machine running, add the vinegar and the green pepper through the hole in the top. Close the top and puree at high speed for a moment. Pour back into the saucepan, and reheat when needed.

Ahead-of-Time Note: Cover and refrigerate when cool; the sauce will keep for several days. Or freeze it for several weeks.

A BARBECUE TIP FROM GEORGE GERMON OF AL FORNO

Build the fire in a pyramid shape and when you are ready to cook spread the coals out so they are evenly distributed over the bottom of the grill. If you need to add more coals, pour them around the rim and they will catch quickly without disturbing the glowing center coals. You'll know that they are ready for cooking when you can barely hold your hand 4 inches above them for 1 second.

GEORGE'S SILKY PEPPERS

Rather than having to roast, bag, and peel your peppers, try Chef George's simple marinated red peppers to serve with meats, fish, poultry, salads, fried eggs, and so forth. They're awfully good, and so easy to do.

Preliminaries: Wash the peppers and dry them thoroughly with paper towels. Halve them lengthwise, seed them, cut each half into thirds, and remove the inner ribs.

Cooking the Peppers: Toss the pepper slices in a 12-inch skillet with the vinegar, brown sugar, and salt. Cook at the barest simmer until they have softened but still retain their shape—10 to 12 minutes. Remove with a slotted spoon to a serving dish, leaving the cooking juices in the pan.

Marinating the Peppers: Increase the heat under the skillet and let the juices reduce almost to a syrup for several minutes, scraping up any bits adhering to the pan. Stir in the olive oil, thyme leaves, and parsley, heating just to warm the oil. Pour over the peppers; while they are cooling and marinating, a half hour or more, they will soften and absorb flavor. Serve at room temperature. Refrigerate leftovers in a screw-top jar, where they will keep nicely for several days.

INGREDIENTS FOR 6 TO 8 SERVINGS

For simmering the peppers
6 to 8 red bell peppers
½ cup balsamic vinegar
1 tablespoon (firmly packed) brown sugar
1 teaspoon kosher salt

For the marinade
¼ cup virgin olive oil
1 tablespoon fresh thyme leaves
2 tablespoons chopped flat-leaf Italian parsley

DIRTY STEAK

One very busy evening at his restaurant, Chef George was looking desperately for one of the four fine fat rib-eye steaks that he had put on the grill. He knew there were four, but where was that fourth steak? There it was! It had fallen upon the hot coals. He picked it up. It looked pretty good, so he turned it over and let it finish cooking directly upon the coals. It continued to look very good and he sliced off a piece. Delicious! And so was born his new technique, which he shared with a friend who enthusiastically tried it. Unfortunately, his friend used charcoal briquettes instead of pure hardwood. The briquettes stuck to the meat and when he plopped it down in front of his wife, with the lumpy bits still attached, she responded indignantly, "I'm not going to eat that dirty old steak!" Hence the name, and it is a favorite at the Al Forno restaurant.

(continued)

Manufacturing Note: You'll probably have to special-order this beautiful cut of meat. Although you could use a loin strip, the rib eye is George's choice. He also warns that you should be sure to get yourself pure unadulterated natural wood charcoal, since he feels that treated woods or briquettes will impart a chemical or petroleum taste to the meat.

Preliminaries: Build the fire in a pyramid shape, and when you are ready to cook, spread the coals out so they are evenly distributed over the bottom of the grill. If you need to add more coals, pour them around the rim and they will catch quickly without disturbing the glowing center coals. You'll know that they are ready for cooking when you can barely hold your hand 4 inches above the coals for 1 second.

Cooking the Steaks: Just before cooking the meat so it will remain fresh, cut it crosswise into 3 steaks about 1¼ inches thick. Dry them with paper towels and keep them separate—not piled upon each other where they could ooze juice. Pat each dry again as you lay them one by one on the hot coals. Let them cook for 4 minutes, turn on the other side with tongs, and let cook an additional 4 minutes. They will be very rare at this point. Transfer them with your tongs to the rack, and cover loosely with foil. Let them rest for 8 to 10 minutes and the juices will be reabsorbed into the meat as the intense residual heat from the fire finishes the cooking.

Ahead-of-Time Note: If he has a longer wait, Chef George sets them uncovered on their rack in a 160° F oven, where they hold nicely for an hour or two. (Our team has tried this, and it works very well indeed—I would have thought they would overcook at this temperature, which is nutritionally correct for bacteria-free meat, but it works.)

Serving: Carve the steaks across the grain into slanting slices ¼ inch thick and arrange on warm plates or a platter. At Al Forno they spoon a ribbon of Hot Fanny Sauce over the slices, and accompany them with their special mashed potatoes and silky red peppers.

INGREDIENTS FOR 8 SERVINGS

A fine well-aged, well-marbled 3-pound beef rib-eye roast (the trimmed prime roast beef area, minus the ribs and back bones)

FOR SERVING

Hot Fanny Sauce (see page 75)
George's Silky Peppers (opposite)
Gremolada Mashed Potatoes (see page 78)

SPECIAL EQUIPMENT SUGGESTED

A wood-burning kettle-shaped grill
Natural hardwood charcoal
Tongs
A rack set over a shallow baking pan

JOHANNE'S GREMOLADA MASHED POTATOES

Chef George likes to serve his beautiful steaks with his wife's equally beautiful mashed potatoes. She leaves the skins on for extra flavor, and always mashes them with one of those old-fashioned (but still obtainable) hand mashers with big holes or the kind known as an S-type masher. These are great non-diet potatoes, with plenty of butter and cream and taste.

Cooking the Potatoes: Wash, scrub, and quarter the potatoes—leave the skins on. Set in a saucepan with cold water to cover by 1 inch. Add the kosher salt and bring to the boil. Lower the heat and cook at a fast simmer for about 15 minutes, or until the potatoes are tender when pierced with a small sharp knife. Cut into and taste a potato to be sure it is tender throughout—but not mushy.

INGREDIENTS FOR 6 SERVINGS

For cooking the potatoes
2 pounds small red potatoes
1½ teaspoons kosher salt per quart of water

(continued)

Finishing the Potatoes: Drain the potatoes at once, return them to the saucepan, and set them over very low heat. Coarsely mash them, gradually adding the cream and butter and tasting to correct seasoning as you go. Then fold in all but ½ tablespoon of the gremolada. Transfer to a pretty bowl, sprinkle with the remaining gremolada, and serve piping hot.

Ahead-of-Time Note: If done somewhat in advance, omit the gremolada until just before serving, and set the pan in a larger pan of almost simmering water. Place a wooden spoon in the pan, and top with a cover—you must allow some air circulation. Stir up now and then, and the potatoes will keep their fresh taste.

For mashing the potatoes

½ cup heavy cream

8 tablespoons unsalted butter, softened

Kosher salt to taste

For the gremolada

2 tablespoons finely chopped fresh Italian parsley

The zest of 1 lemon (colored part of peel only)

1 teaspoon peeled and finely minced garlic

SPECIAL EQUIPMENT SUGGESTED

A hand-held potato masher

LIME CURD

A curd is a custard—and vice versa, by the way—and there's nothing wrong with having either or both on hand. In addition to using lime curd on her Triple Citrus Meringue Tart, Johanne spreads it on cakes for a quick filling, adds it to strawberry shortcake, and finds it wonderful as a base for fresh fruit tartlets. George likes to spread it on buttered toast, but Johanne claims that he usually stands at the refrigerator and eats it with a spoon.

INGREDIENTS FOR 2 CUPS

2 "large" eggs
2 egg yolks
½ cup sugar
¾ cup fresh lime juice (6 to 8 small limes)
½ cup heavy cream

SPECIAL EQUIPMENT SUGGESTED

A 6- to 8-cup heavy-bottomed stainless steel or flameproof glass saucepan
A wire whisk
A large bowl with ice and water (for cooling the custard)

Break the whole eggs directly into the saucepan. Using a whisk and being careful not to beat too vigorously and cause air bubbles, blend in the yolks, sugar, lime juice, and cream. Set over moderately low heat and, stirring rather slowly but constantly to reach all over the bottom and sides of the pan, bring the custard to the boil; it will thicken into a mayonnaise-like cream. If by any chance it is not smooth and free of little lumps, pass it through a fine-meshed sieve. Then set the saucepan into the ice water and stir occasionally, until the curd is cool. Cover and store in the refrigerator.

Ahead-of-Time Note: Lime curd will keep in the refrigerator for a week.

Variations:

Lime Butter Cream: You can turn lime curd into a buttercream filling or frosting simply by beating into the cool finished curd 6 to 8 tablespoons of softened unsalted butter, a tablespoon at a time. Very nice for special-occasion cakes and petits fours.

Orange and Lemon Curds and Butter Creams: Follow the exact same system substituting oranges or lemons for the lime.

JOHANNE'S SWEET TART DOUGH

This Al Forno recipe not only produces a crisp, light crust that is a delight to eat but also employs an excellent and efficient food-processor technique that will work every time. Chef Johanne uses this method herself every day in her restaurant, and this is the recipe she teaches to her chefs. I have made pie dough a number of different ways and was impressed with this technique. I stood right there when she demonstrated it for our television series—and I ate it, and loved it.

Preliminaries:

The Butter. It is essential that the butter be very cold when making this tart dough. Cut it into ½-inch cubes and return the cubes to the refrigerator for at least 10 minutes while you set up the food processor and gather the dry ingredients.

The Liquid. Remove the zest (colored part of the peel) from the orange and chop very fine; you should have about 2 teaspoons. Squeeze 2 tablespoons of the orange juice into a 1-cup measure and add ice water to the ¼-cup mark. Stir in the orange zest and refrigerate until needed. Return the ice water to the refrigerator in case it is needed.

Mixing the Dough: Place the chilled butter and liquid at your side. Measure the flour, sugar, and salt into a plastic bag and toss together. Add the well-chilled butter, tossing and turning the bag quickly to coat each cube with flour (this is to prevent the butter cubes from sticking together). Transfer the mixture to the bowl of the food processor. Pulse on and off about fifteen times, until the butter particles are the size of small peas. Then immediately, with the motor running, pour in the cold liquid all at once. Process for 10 seconds, then stop the machine and test the dough—it should just hold together when squeezed between your fingers. If too dry, briefly process in an additional teaspoon of ice water and test again. It is better for the dough to be a little too moist than a little too dry. Turn it out onto a sheet of aluminum foil, pressing any loose particles into the mass of dough. Handling the dough as little as possible to prevent it from toughening, form it into a rough 7-inch disk. Cover completely with aluminum foil and refrigerate for an hour or more.

Ahead-of-Time Note: The dough will keep for 2 days under refrigeration. Chef Johanne is not enthusiastic about freezing it.

INGREDIENTS FOR 18 TO 20 OUNCES OF DOUGH (ENOUGH FOR 1 LARGE TART, TWO 9-INCH TARTS, OR 4 LITTLE TARTS FOR TWO)

8 ounces (2 sticks) cold unsalted butter

1 cold orange

A 2-cup measure with ice and water

2 cups (scooped and leveled) unbleached all-purpose flour

¼ cup superfine sugar

½ teaspoon kosher salt

SPECIAL EQUIPMENT SUGGESTED

A zester
A 2-quart plastic bag
A food processor with steel blade
Aluminum foil

TRIPLE CITRUS MERINGUE TART

One of George's favorite desserts is his "auntie's" lemon meringue pie. He wanted Johanne, who develops all the desserts for the restaurant, to use it on the menu. Johanne said that she would make a lemon meringue pie but it couldn't be anything so humdrum and unimaginative as the standard auntie-type American pie, and that she would develop her own unique recipe. What she did was to take all the elements—the crust, the lemon custard, and the tender meringue—and put them together in a new way. She even went a step further for us, turning the basic lemon meringue affair into an absolutely stunning triple citrus tart. You will have a divine mouthful of warm, sweet meringue with its tart base of lime and be greeted by a warm, buttery crust—an experience to dream about.

Preheat the oven to 450° F in time for baking.

Preparing the Crust: Beat and roll the dough (it will be somewhat recalcitrant!) into an 11-inch circle, sprinkling a little flour as needed onto both the dough and the rolling surface—the circle need not be perfect. Roll it up on your pin and unroll it onto the baking sheet. Sprinkle on 1 tablespoon of the sugar.

Preparing the Lemon Filling: With the mandoline or very sharp knife, make paper-thin crosswise slices of lemon and carefully poke out the seeds from each. Leaving a 1½-inch border all around, cover the dough with the lemon slices starting in the center and working your way toward the outside in concentric circles. Sprinkle 2 tablespoons of sugar over the lemon slices. Raise the plain dough border to enclose the sides of the tart, letting it drape gently over the fruit. Gently pinch the soft pleats that form from the draping. (The center of the tart will remain uncovered.) Press the dough down onto the baking sheet, snugly securing the sides and the bottom of the pastry.

Ahead-of-Time Note: The tart may be prepared to this point about an hour or so before baking. Cover loosely and refrigerate.

The First Baking—The Shell: Bake the tart for 15 to 20 minutes, until the dough is golden and the lemon slices have begun to caramelize. Transfer the baking sheet, with the tart shell on it, to the rack.

Preparing the Meringue: Whip the egg whites in a clean, dry bowl until frothy (complete directions for beating egg whites are in the appendix). Sprinkle in the remaining superfine sugar, one tablespoon at a time, while

INGREDIENTS FOR ONE 9-INCH TART, SERVING 6

½ recipe Johanne's Sweet Tart Dough (opposite)

About ½ cup unbleached all-purpose flour (for dusting the dough and counter)

⅔ cup superfine sugar (3 tablespoons for the tart crust; the remainder for the meringue)

1 large organic lemon or 1 large regular lemon, dropped into boiling water for 30 seconds

For the meringue

½ cup egg whites (4 "large")

For baking and serving the tart

2 to 3 tablespoons lime curd (see box, page 79)

Confectioners' sugar (for dusting)

(continued)

Triple Citrus Meringue Tart (continued)

whipping. After all the sugar is incorporated, continue to whip until the egg whites form stiff peaks.

The Second Baking—Finishing the Tart: Spread the lime curd over the lemon slices, then cover the entire surface of the tart with the meringue, mounding it as high as possible. Pull at the meringue to form irregular peaks, as shown in the finished tart. Return the tart to the oven for 4 to 5 minutes, until the meringue is golden brown. Dust with confectioners' sugar and serve at once.

SPECIAL EQUIPMENT
SUGGESTED

A rolling pin
A lightly buttered baking sheet
A mandoline or a very sharp smallish knife (for making very thin lemon slices)
A cake rack (for cooling the tart)
A freestanding electric mixer (for the egg whites)
A rubber spatula

cook's notes

JEAN-GEORGES VONGERICHTEN

Jean-Georges Vongerichten grew up in a rural area of Alsace, where his grandfather had a coal business. The employees would stay for lunch every day and his grandmother cooked traditional French food for all of them. "The kitchen was starting at six o'clock in the morning; ten people for dinner and forty for lunch—every single day. It was like a restaurant." It was an atmosphere Jean-Georges found quite appealing, and when he was a teenager he told his parents that he wanted to cook for the crew also. Fortunately for the food world, they told him that if he wanted to cook he would have to go to professional cooking school.

After a traditional French culinary work-study program and still in his early twenties, Jean-Georges won a position at the posh Oriental Hotel in Bangkok, where he discovered the wonders of Asian ingredients, which have since become an integral part of his food. "The flavor of lemongrass, cilantro, ginger, curries, and coconut milk exploded like a bomb in my life," he recalls. From 1980 to 1985 he opened hotel-based restaurants for Swisshotel in Singapore and Hong Kong. There his love of the newfound flavors grew, and they have found full expression in the dishes he created for his restaurant Jo-Jo, which opened in New York in 1991, and Vong, which opened two years later. His passion is deliciously expressed in his delicate Crab Spring Rolls and his Thai-Marinated Beef with Rice Noodles with its many layers of flavor.

One might expect that Chef Jean-Georges's combinations of French and Asian foods would seem contrived, and yet what is amazing is how natural they are. His background from the coal days taught him that food is basically about feeding people. "People in New York go to restaurants five nights a week. They want simple and very direct food. That is what we provide them." Sounds much like his grandmother's place.

RED CHILE PUREE

This is an aggressive raw chile puree. Chef Jean-Georges chops the peppers up, seeds and all, which gives the puree its extra fire. He uses it atop his Thai-Marinated Beef (see page 86) to add color and heat to the dish. Anytime your recipe calls for a puree of red chiles, this is certainly it! But keep in mind that a little dab goes a long way, so use it with caution.

Note: You can find both ready-made raw and cooked chile purees in some specialty food stores.

Place all the ingredients in a blender or food processor and puree to a paste. Refrigerate in a covered jar, where it will keep for several weeks.

INGREDIENTS FOR ¾ CUP

8 fresh Thai finger chile peppers
1 large garlic clove
1 tablespoon sugar
1 tablespoon white wine vinegar
    or rice vinegar

JUS-RÔTI
LIGHT ROASTED CHICKEN-WING BROTH

Many of our contemporary chefs are making this light broth out of chicken wings, or duck wings, or meat scraps, and so forth. Chef Jean-Georges favors it particularly for his Asian-style dishes and uses it with much of his food since he feels it is lighter than a formal brown chicken stock.

Manufacturing Note: Jean-Georges's broth calls for flavoring his wings not only with onions and a whole head of garlic but also with a touch of the Far East—lemongrass and ginger. Other chefs will use other flavorings instead, like carrots, celery, and leeks. Whatever the flavor items, the general procedure is the same. Home cooks should note that recipes for simple chicken stock and brown chicken stock are in the box on page 87.

Place the rack in the upper middle position and preheat the oven to 500° F.

Pat the chicken wings dry in paper towels, film the pan with the oil, and set over moderately high heat. Sauté the wings, tossing and turning, until lightly browned—6 to 8 minutes. Set the pan in the preheated oven and roast for 30 minutes, tossing and turning several times to brown evenly. Stir in the onion, garlic, lemongrass, and ginger; roast another 15 minutes. At this point, pour the contents of the pan into a colander to drain off the fat.

**INGREDIENTS FOR 2 CUPS,
REDUCED TO ½ CUP**

*3 pounds chicken wings, chopped
    into 1-inch pieces*
2 tablespoons olive oil
*1 large onion, peeled and cut in
    eighths*
*1 whole head of garlic, unpeeled,
    cut horizontally in half*
1 stalk of lemongrass
1 slice of unpeeled ginger root
About 3 cups water

(continued)

Jus-Rôti (continued)

Return the ingredients to the pan and add just enough water to cover them—3 cups or so. Return to the stove and simmer for 30 minutes, skimming any fat off the surface. Strain into a clean saucepan, skim thoroughly, and reduce (boil down) to ½ cup.

Ahead-of-Time Note: The stock will keep for a few days under refrigeration, or may be frozen.

SPECIAL EQUIPMENT
SUGGESTED

*A cleaver (for chopping up
the wings)*
*A large ovenproof sauté pan or
frying pan (for browning and
for roasting in the oven)*

THAI-MARINATED BEEF WITH RICE NOODLES

This dish is quite typical Vongerichten, with a goodly number of little garnishings and maneuverings—definitely one for the dedicated and adventurous cook. Those with a more sober approach may, of course, include only those elements that fit their culinary mood. Jean-Georges's Thai-Marinated Beef is a splendid introduction to the increasing number of Asian ingredients available in our markets. The special marinade both flavors the meat and acts as a tenderizer. Because the loin is already tender, the role here is more for flavor than texture, but when you have to settle for the tougher cuts, like flank, chuck blade, and rump, it is a marinade to keep in mind.

A Note on Ingredients: If you cannot find some of the items in your market or in the Asian markets in your area, either omit or substitute—for the mushrooms, as an example, use whatever fresh mushrooms are available and seem suitable.

Preliminaries—the day before:

Marinating the Meat. Trim away all fat from the outside of the steaks. Puree the marinade ingredients in the blender or food processor and process until very smooth. Spread the mixture over all sides of the steaks and place them in one layer on a plate or in a glass or enameled baking dish. Cover tightly with plastic wrap and refrigerate—4 to 6 hours at least but 12 hours are preferable.

Preliminaries—2 hours before:

Soaking the Noodles. Cover the noodles with warm water and let them soak for 2 hours.

INGREDIENTS FOR 4 SERVINGS

The meat
*4 well-aged and well-marbled
7- to 8-ounce top-sirloin
steaks, ¾ inch thick*
*About 2 tablespoons canola oil
(for the final cooking)*

For the marinade (½ cup)
*1 stalk of lemongrass, ends
trimmed, stalk chopped*
*8 lime leaves, roughly chopped, or
2 tablespoons fresh lime juice*
2 small shallots, peeled and diced
1 teaspoon sugar

(continued)

CRAB SPRING ROLLS

Chef Jean-Georges's spring rolls reflect his years in the Far East, where he learned how to combine that culture's special genius with his classical French background to create a delectable contrast of textures, temperatures, and flavors. When you bite through the fresh, crisp wrapper here, you are met by tender crab filling as well as the cool salad and herb exterior, juxtaposed against a burst of sweet and sour in the dipping sauce. Sheer rapture! The rolls are surprisingly easy to make, but in order for them to be perfection, be sure to afford yourself the luxury of fresh new oil for the frying.

Manufacturing Note: We have tried substituting shrimp and lobster for crab, but for this formula neither is nearly as fine and delicate as crab.

Preparing the Crab Meat: Pick over the crab meat very carefully to remove any pieces of shell. Gently fold in the mayonnaise, tamarind paste, chile, and salt; taste carefully for seasoning.

Filling the Wrappers: One by one, lay a wrapper down on the counter diamond-shaped, its corners pointing north, south, east, and west. Place a heaping tablespoon of filling in the center, shaping it into a horizontal log 4 inches long—you will want 1 inch of space between the end of the log and the east and west points. Fold the west and east corners over the filling so that their points just touch each other over the filling. Pick up the southern corner and drape it forward over the filling, giving the filling a firm push to remove any air pockets. Using the pastry brush, generously paint the beaten egg yolk over the northern or top half of the wrapper, beginning at the northern point. Then roll up snugly toward the north to enclose the filling completely. Set aside, and continue rapidly with the rest.

Ahead-of-Time Note: May be prepared to this point, covered with plastic, and refrigerated 6 hours before cooking—but no longer or they will get soggy; bring to room temperature before frying. The crab mixture itself may be made a day in advance, covered, and refrigerated.

Preparing the Dipping Sauce: Puree all the ingredients, except the oil, in the blender, liquidizing them completely. Very slowly at first, with the machine running, pour the oil through the top in a steady stream of droplets so that the mixture forms an emulsion. Taste very carefully, pulsing in more sugar if the sauce is too tart or more tamarind paste for acidity and thickness. The

INGREDIENTS FOR 10 ROLLS

For the crab filling
1 pound top-quality crab meat
1 tablespoon mayonnaise
1 tablespoon tamarind paste
*   (a recipe for making your own*
*   is on page 22)*
1 Thai bird chile, finely minced
Salt

For the rolls
10 spring roll wrappers, about
*   7 inches square (get the thin*
*   "dumpling" wrapper made*
*   with egg yolk)*
1 "large" egg yolk, lightly beaten
A fresh quart bottle of canola or
*   vegetable oil (for deep-frying)*

For the dipping sauce
¼ cup rice vinegar or white wine
*   vinegar*
2 tablespoons nam pla or nuc
*   man (fermented fish sauce)*
*   or 1 teaspoon soy sauce*
1 garlic clove

(continued)

Carta Musica (continued)

so thin you could almost read a sheet of music through it. Either using the floured peel or your hands, transfer the disk onto the hot baking surface and cook about 1 minute on each side, or until golden and crisp. Remove to a rack and continue with the rest.

Ahead-of-Time Note: Baked *carta musica* disks may be stored for at least a week in an airtight container. If they get soggy, recrisp in a hot oven.

NOTES FROM JULIA ON FAVA BEANS

Fava beans (*Vicia faba*) are known in England as broad beans, and in Germany as *dicke Bohnen,* or "thick beans."

Fava beans have quite recently made their almost all-year appearance in our chic restaurants and specialty groceries. Jane Grigson, the wonderful British cook and writer, speaks of home gardeners who pick baby favas, 2 to 3 inches long, in the English springtime, when they are so tender you simply boil them whole and serve them with just a little butter. Unless you grow them yourself, the ones you buy will most probably be mature fat green bean-shaped objects the circumference of your thumb, and ranging in length from 4 to 6 inches. The thick, bright green, shiny outer pod of a fine fresh mature fava is lined with what looks like close-cropped white fur, and nestled upon it are 4 to 6 large lima-bean-shaped pale green beans. Inside this rather thick and somewhat bitter enveloping pale green sheath lies the pretty green bean-kernel itself. This is the part you eat, and when young enough, it has the pleasant taste of fresh green peas. (Stale and overmature beans, by the way, will have little flavor, a dry texture in the mouth, and you will wonder why anyone bothers with them at all.)

Getting at the green kernels of a mess of fava beans is definitely labor-intensive, which is obviously why restaurants serve you just a small handful as a garnish. To accomplish the task, first remove the green outer shell by grasping the tip and pulling down on it to split the shell open, then collect the beans. Now you must remove the outer skin, and there are two ways to do so.

Boiling—for Salads: When you want the beans cooked through and plan to use them cold, drop them into a pan of salted boiling water and boil slowly for 5 minutes. Drain, drop them into cold water for a moment, then peel off the enveloping skin—when you open one of the short ends, you can usually squeeze the other end and pop out the bean, which more often than not separates horizontally into matching kidney-shaped halves. The beans are now cooked and ready to use.

Blanching—for Serving as a Hot Vegetable: In this case, I like to blanch the shelled beans first, by boiling them for 1 minute, then peeling off the skin as described. Then I simmer them for 4 to 5 minutes in a covered saucepan with a little salt, ¼ inch of water (adding spoonfuls more if needed), and a bit of butter—½ tablespoon per cup. You could add a little finely minced shallot as you cook them, or toss in a sprinkling of freshly minced chives at the end. When the beans are tender and just cooked through, the water should have evaporated, and the beans will be glistening in their modest coating of butter.

Weights and Measures: I recently purchased 12 assorted fava beans weighing 1¼ pounds. They produced 75 beans which, skins on, measured 1½ cups, and skins off, 1⅛ cups. They took me almost half an hour to prepare, and served only three people with an adequate but small sampling—however, they make good eating.

The Stuffing (continued)

3 ounces provolone cheese, cut
    into ¼-inch dice

2 teaspoons salt, or to taste

10 or more grinds of fresh black
    pepper

½ cup fresh peas, boiled until
    tender, or frozen peas, thawed

STUFFED BRAISED BREAST OF VEAL

Here's a magnificent dish that will serve a crowd, and presents a happy challenge to those who love to cook. The whole bone-in breast from a side of veal—from the collarbone down to the thirteenth rib—is stuffed with a savory mixture of ground veal and pork, diced mortadella, cheese, fresh herbs, pistachios, and fresh green peas. It is then slowly braised in wine and aromatic vegetables, and this is a true braise in the classic sense, where the meat absorbs delicious flavors from the surrounding liquid, and the liquid acquires depth and flavor from the veal and its stuffing. You will want to cook it a day or two in advance so that the meat and stuffing will firm into shape. Then you either cut it into chop-size portions and reheat in the oven, or broil or grill it. Grilling increases the complexity of flavors, but if a grill isn't available, it will still be delicious. One of Chef Jody's signature dishes at Michela's restaurant, this recipe was inspired by her continuing research into Italian regional dishes.

(continued)

Manufacturing Note: You will undoubtedly have to order the veal from a specialty butcher, who can prepare the pocket for you, although if you like working with meat, it is a simple matter to do so yourself. Be sure you have the right-size pan and that it will fit into your oven—you can always remove several rib portions if you can't squeeze the breast into the pan.

Preparing the Breast: If the breast is too long for your pan, cut off one or more rib sections and braise the piece, unstuffed, along with the main section. Trim away excess, flabby fat from the top of the veal, leaving a thin layer attached, and trim off any loose miscellaneous bits on the underside. Working from the top of the ribs and being careful not to pierce through the surface of the meat, make a pocket by cutting close to the rib bones, to separate meat from bone to within 1 inch of where the ribs are attached at the sides, and at the bottom of the opening. Trim off any excess fat from the inside of the pocket. Season inside with salt and pepper.

Stuffing the Breast: Spoon the stuffing into the pocket and tap it down into the bottom of the pocket; the pocket should be filled to within 2 inches of its opening at the top. Lay the meat on its side and massage the outside to move the stuffing around so it will be as evenly distributed as possible. So that it will keep its shape while cooking, make a firm tie around the meat between each rib with butcher's twine.

Ahead-of-Time Note: The veal may be prepared a day ahead up to this point. Preheat oven to 450° F.

Preliminary Browning of the Veal: Pour the vegetable oil into the roasting pan, scatter in the carrots, celery, onions, and garlic halves, toss well and sauté over low heat until the vegetables are lightly browned, then push them to the edges of the pan. Season both sides of the veal with salt and pepper and set, rib part down, in the middle of the pan. Roast for 30 minutes, or until the meat browns nicely, then remove the pan from the oven and set over a burner on the stove. Reduce oven heat to 300° F.

Braising the Veal: Pour the Marsala around the veal; follow with the tomatoes, and enough chicken stock to come a third of the way up the sides of the meat. Turn the heat to high and bring the liquid to the boil. Remove from heat, tuck the herb bundle into the liquid, cover the pan tightly with aluminum foil, pressing it down so it touches the meat and rests just over the stock, then cover with the second pan and/or a second layer of foil—the

The meat

1 large fine top-quality breast of veal (7 to 7½ pounds, untrimmed)

Salt and freshly ground black pepper

About 6 cups stuffing (see page 99)

The flavorings

¼ cup vegetable oil, plus more if needed

3 carrots, peeled and cut diagonally into 1-inch pieces

3 cups peeled and coarsely chunked celery (2 large stalks)

3 cups coarsely chunked onions (2 medium)

2 garlic heads, washed and cut in half across the cloves

3 cups dry Marsala wine

2 cups fresh Italian plum tomatoes, washed and cut into sixths, or 1 cup drained canned plum tomatoes

6 cups rich brown chicken stock (see page 87)

The herbs, tied together in a neat bundle

4 bay leaves

6 sprigs of fresh thyme

8 to 10 sage leaves

2 to 3 sprigs of marjoram

For serving

Polenta or mashed potatoes, such as those on page 78

Fresh peas or green beans

(continued)

Stuffed Braised Breast of Veal (continued)

pan must be well sealed because the veal cooks a long time with only a small amount of liquid, and you want to be sure that those beautiful juices do not evaporate and burn before the breast is done. Return it to the oven.

When Is It Done? It should be done in 3½ to 4 hours, when the meat is very tender. Test by inserting a long fork or metal skewer half its length into the meat: it should slip easily in and out. Set aside to cool, then cover and refrigerate for several hours or overnight.

Preparing the Sauce: Pour the pan juices and vegetables into a strainer set over a saucepan; pick out the garlic halves and set aside. Push on the vegetables with the back of a ladle or wooden spoon to draw all the juices into the saucepan, then discard the vegetables and the herb bundle. Thoroughly degrease the juices, and boil down slowly until thickened enough to coat the back of a spoon lightly. While boiling, squeeze the garlic out of its skin and into the liquid, whisking to blend (discard the skins). Taste, and correct seasoning. This will be a deliciously rich brew, and fat-free!—if you did your degreasing job well.

Ahead-of-Time Note: When cool, cover and refrigerate (it will keep for several days), or freeze.

Carving the Breast: When the veal is cold and firm, remove the strings and cut the meat into portions between the ribs—bearing down hard when you hit an occasional cartilage. The portions will not all be the same size, and you will probably want to cut a few in half—this is a rustic dish! Tie the bones to the meat in two spots to form a secure package.

Grilling the Veal (optional, see introduction to recipe): Prepare a fire in the grill, and when the heat is at a moderate temperature, brush the ribs with vegetable oil and grill on all sides until slightly charred and heated through, 15 minutes or so.

Alternately, preheat an oven to 400° F. Put the ribs in a roasting pan and spoon the juices over the top. Roast for 20 minutes, or until heated through.

Serving: Remove the string from the ribs and put each rib on a very large plate, spooning some sauce on top and around. If desired, make a bed of polenta or potatoes on the plate first, set the rib on top, and scatter the peas or beans and sauce over all. Decorate with sprigs of fresh herbs.

SPECIAL EQUIPMENT
SUGGESTED

A very sharp boning knife
*Butcher's twine (unwaxed plain
    white cotton twine)*
*A 20- by 16-inch roasting pan,
    3 to 4 inches deep, and a pan
    to cover it (or the largest pan
    that your oven will hold); or a
    large turkey roaster*
Heavy-duty aluminum foil
*A very sharp heavy knife
    (for carving the breast)*

PICKLED RED PEPPERS

Bring the ingredients for the pickling liquid to a boil in the saucepan and simmer for 10 minutes. Meanwhile, cut the peppers into quarters and remove the seeds, ribs, and stems. Turn them into the pickling liquid, cover the pan, and cook for 2 minutes, stirring occasionally to make sure all the peppers spend some time submerged in the liquid. Remove from heat and let the peppers cool in the liquid. One by one, remove them from the liquid, and peel them—the skins will come off quite easily. Slice them into neat ⅛-inch julienne, and drop into the glass jar. Pour on the cooking liquid, cover, and store in the refrigerator.

Ahead-of-Time Note: The peppers will keep for several months.

INGREDIENTS FOR 1½ CUPS

The pickling liquid
½ cup white wine vinegar
2 tablespoons sugar
½ teaspoon pickling spices
2 large garlic cloves, peeled and
    coarsely chopped
1 cup water

The peppers
2 large red bell peppers

**SPECIAL EQUIPMENT
SUGGESTED**

A 6- to 8-cup stainless steel
    saucepan
A 2-cup screw-top jar

SFOGLII SAOR
SWEET-AND-SOUR SOLE, VENETIAN STYLE

Always interested in Italian regional dishes, Jody Adams has adapted this spicy fish recipe from the Venetian repertoire. The finished dish, which can be served hot or at room temperature, is based on an old Italian method of keeping fish from spoiling in a hot climate—it was the large amount of vinegar that did the work. Jody has tamed and sweetened it for modern tastes. It is a fascinating combination of flavors, with its spicy peppers, garlic, raisins, pine nuts, and orange juice.

Preparing the Sole: Season the sole fillets with salt and pepper and dredge in the flour, shaking off the excess. Heat the frying pan with ⅛ inch of olive oil. When very hot but not smoking, sauté the sole until golden brown on each side and just cooked through, about 5 minutes per side. Transfer to a platter.

Preparing the Sauce: In the same frying pan, over moderate heat, add the shallots and sauté a minute or two, just until tender. Add the garlic and cook

INGREDIENTS FOR 4 SERVINGS

For the sole
8 fresh skinless and boneless sole
    fillets (imported channel sole
    or gray sole), 4 to 5 ounces
    each and ⅜ inch thick
Salt

(continued)

an additional minute. Stir in the red pepper flakes, the raisins with their Marsala or sherry, and the pine nuts; reduce to a glaze—a minute or so. Swirl in the orange juice and boil down by a third. Then whisk in the olive oil to thicken the sauce; stir in the vinegar, and season with salt and pepper. Spoon the sauce over the fish, and garnish with the red pepper strips.

Serving Suggestions: Chef Jody suggests you accompany the dish with garlic mashed potatoes (see page 78) and fresh spinach.

cook's notes

Freshly ground
1 cup all-purpos
   dredging the f
Excellent olive oil

For the sauce
4 large shallots, peeled and thinly
   sliced (⅓ cup)
1 large garlic clove, peeled and
   minced
¼ teaspoon hot red pepper flakes
1½ tablespoons raisins, soaked in
   2 tablespoons Marsala wine or
   sherry
1½ tablespoons pine nuts, toasted
½ cup fresh orange juice
4 tablespoons excellent olive oil
1 to 2 teaspoons champagne
   vinegar or white wine vinegar
Salt and freshly ground pepper

For the garnish
16 pieces pickled red peppers,
   either homemade (see opposite)
   or store-bought

SPECIAL EQUIPMENT SUGGESTED

A 12-inch no-stick frying pan

MICHAEL LOMONACO

When Michael Lomonaco became executive chef at The '21' Club in 1989, he revitalized the menu of this New York landmark, which was once a speakeasy, in such a way as to attract the attention of critics and new customers while continuing to please the palates of the long-standing clientele. No easy task! But then, Chef Michael has talent, passion—and fate on his side. In 1982, he was driving a New York City taxi to subsidize a promising but financially unsteady acting career. He happened to pick up Master Chef Patrick Clark, who extolled the benefits of the culinary profession. Michael had grown up in a home where food was abundant and good, but until the chance meeting he had not considered cooking as a career. After the fateful encounter, he enrolled in the culinary program at Patrick's alma mater, New York City Technical College, where he found that his old and new professions had similarities. "The theater is a lot like the restaurant business in terms of the front of the house, the back of the house and waiting for the curtain to go up."

Chef Michael refined his skills in New York with Swiss and French chefs; he especially credits Alain Sailhac and Daniel Boulud, with whom he worked at Le Cirque. With them he discovered that the culinary profession has a shared history and tradition. "Just as in music and theater, a classical food background helps you find your own freedom." Michael found his stride in his fresh interpretation of the American cuisine upon which The '21' Club had staked its reputation for decades, such as adding vibrant berry relishes to a traditional mixed grill of carefully chosen game.

What does Michael think now about his second career? He doesn't hesitate. "It's a wonderful life!"

BERRY RELISH

This tangy berry relish is one that Michael Lomonaco likes to serve with the mixed game grill dinner that follows. But why save it for a grilling day? It is equally delicious with roasted or grilled chicken, with grilled sausage, or, unusual as it may seem, with spicy grilled shrimp. Think of it as a chutney.

Ahead-of-Time Note: The relish is best made a day or so in advance so that the natural pectins have a chance to lend some body.

Bring the berries, sugar, port, citrus zests and juices, cayenne, and ginger to the boil in a heavy-bottomed saucepan. Reduce to a simmer for several minutes, until the berries begin to burst; then remove the pan from heat; taste for seasoning. When cool, turn into a screw-top jar and refrigerate. Will keep for several weeks, at least, under refrigeration.

INGREDIENTS FOR ABOUT
2 CUPS

*1 pound huckleberries or black
    or red currants (jarred or
    frozen if fresh berries are not
    available)*
⅓ cup light brown sugar
⅓ cup port wine
*2 teaspoons orange zest
    (colored part of peel only)*
The juice of 1 orange, strained
*2 teaspoons lemon zest
    (colored part of peel only)*
The juice of 1 lemon, strained
2 teaspoons cayenne pepper
*2 teaspoons peeled and grated
    fresh ginger root*

MIXED GAME GRILL

Cook a barbecue of mixed game either indoors or out, but when it grills over an open fire, it is at its best. And when you throw in a handful of wood chips for additional flavor, it has the rustic, woodsy character of the great outdoors. This recipe calls for a mild smoking to give the food a special aroma and taste without overpowering its natural flavors. Chef Michael proposes an intriguing choice for his grill: a rack of venison, bacon-wrapped duck livers, boneless quail, and homemade rabbit sausage.

MICHAEL'S BARBECUE TECHNIQUE

Michael says he has the best results when he builds his coals at opposite sides of his barbecue bowl, leaving the center third of the bowl free. He can then brown his meats over the hot coals at the sides, and finish by indirect heat

(continued)

Mixed Game Grill (continued)

with the meat at the center. Before he starts cooking, he lets his coals burn to a white ash, then adds his water-soaked wood chips. He covers his grill briefly during the final cooking, allowing some of the smoky flavor to penetrate. Thus he achieves the desired effect without blackening the meat, since charring and burning toughen the surface of the meat and leave a bitter taste.

THE MEAT CHOICES
Try specialty markets for some of these:

Venison usually comes fresh from New Zealand in Cryovac packages. Substitute lamb for venison if you wish.

Quail are readily available in specialty markets—either fully boneless quail or boneless except for the breastbone. Substitute half a Cornish game hen for one quail if you wish, and allow a little extra cooking time on the grill.

Rabbit. Rabbit legs or the saddle go well on a grill. (However, you'll want boneless rabbit meat to make Michael's sausages.) Chicken may stand in for rabbit.

Duck livers or chicken livers. Use either one here, but duck livers have more flavor.

Wild boar bacon cured in "natural" smoke is Chef Michael's choice for wrapping around his livers, but he will accept regular bacon on occasion.

Pork fat. You can often find this in ethnic markets. Or you may order it from your butcher.

Preparations for Grilling:

The Venison. This is to be a "frenched" rack, meaning that just the "eye" of the meat is attached to the top portion of the rib bones, and the rib ends are scraped clean—making a neat package. If a butcher can't manage this for you, it is not at all a difficult job to do yourself. First remove the chine bone (backbone) and the outside (or top) flap of meat, leaving just the "eye" of the rib meat. Now "french" the rib ends, meaning cut in between the bones, then scrape them clean. (Save the scraps for stock, as described on page 87.)

Mix the chile paste and garlic together, season with salt and pepper, and rub over the meat. Refrigerate in a covered container and let marinate for at least 3 hours, or overnight.

The Quail (or Game Hens). Stir the olive oil, soy sauce, and maple syrup

INGREDIENTS FOR 6 SERVINGS

For the venison
*3 pounds venison rib rack
(or enough to provide 12 ribs)*
*2 tablespoons chile paste
(see page 113)*
*1 garlic clove, peeled and finely
chopped*
*Salt and freshly ground black
pepper to taste*

For the quail
2 tablespoons olive oil
*2 tablespoons soy sauce
(Chef Michael prefers
low-sodium soy)*
¼ cup maple syrup
1 orange
1 lemon
*1 tablespoon juniper berries,
crushed (with a rolling pin in
a plastic sandwich bag)*
2 bay leaves
*1 tablespoon black peppercorns,
crushed*
6 boneless quail

(continued)

together in a deep glass or stainless steel dish. Halve the orange and lemon crosswise, squeeze the juice from each into the dish, and drop in the squeezed pieces. Add the crushed juniper berries, bay leaves, and peppercorns. Mix well and add the quail, basting them with the marinade—plan to baste and turn the quail several times during their marinade of several hours, or overnight.

The Sausage. Grind the rabbit and pork fatback together, letting the meat drop into a mixing bowl—do not grind it too fine; it should have some texture. Using a wooden spoon, beat in the cumin, cilantro, cayenne, port, salt, and pepper. When thoroughly mixed, sauté a spoonful to check the seasoning. Either fill the sausage casing, or form sausage patties.

Ahead-of-Time Note: If made in advance, refrigerate in a covered container; the sausages or sausage meat will keep for several days.

The Liver and Bacon. Inspect the livers to clean them of any fat traces or green or black bile marks. Wrap each liver piece in a slice of bacon, folding it around twice if necessary. Thread 3 or 4 on each skewer, and keep refrigerated until you are ready to grill. Season with salt and pepper just before grilling.

Grilling the Meat and Finishing the Dish:

When the coals are ready, brush the grill rack with oil to ready it for the meats. Lay the venison and quail on the hottest areas of the coals and brown nicely on both sides for several minutes, then move them to the center to the indirect heat area. Brown the liver skewers briefly in the same manner, and move to join the venison. Prick the sausages in several places with the sharp end of a skewer (to prevent them from bursting over the coals), and

For sixteen 5-inch rabbit sausages
2 pounds boneless rabbit meat (one 3-pound rabbit)
¼ pound fresh pork fatback
1 tablespoon ground cumin
2 tablespoons finely chopped cilantro
2 teaspoons cayenne pepper
¼ cup port wine
1 teaspoon salt
1 teaspoon freshly ground black pepper

For the liver and bacon
12 duck or chicken livers (about ½ pound)
12 strips of boar bacon or thick-sliced regular pork bacon
Salt and freshly ground black pepper to taste

For serving
Berry Relish (see page 107)
French-style grainy mustard

(continued)

Mixed Game Grill (continued)

set them also in the indirect heat area. Strew the soaked wood chips over the hot coals and set the cover over the grill (with the cover vent open, if applicable); let cook covered for 5 minutes, to give the meats a light and pleasant smoky flavor, then remove the cover. Keep turning and moving the meats as they cook, setting them a little closer to the hot coals during the last few minutes, to give them a rich, dark, burnished look.

Timing. The rack will take approximately 20 minutes in all for medium rare; the sausage, 20 minutes for fully cooked. The quail will probably grill in under 15 minutes, and the liver and bacon skewers about 12 minutes.

Serving. Chef Michael likes to serve mustard and berry relish with his game, and to accompany it with home fries (see page 112) and a fresh green vegetable, like asparagus. He also suggests a Rhône-type red wine and sourdough country-style bread.

SPECIAL EQUIPMENT
SUGGESTED

For the sausages
A meat grinder
If you have sausage-stuffing equipment, follow the directions, using about ½ pound of natural lamb sausage casing for nice thin sausages about 5 inches long. Otherwise, form the sausage meat into 2-inch patties ½ inch thick, which you might then wrap in pork caul fat— a spiderweb-like membrane laced with streaks of fat often available in Italian markets. (See also box on page 52.)
4 or 5 skewers, 6 to 8 inches long
An outdoor grill with cover and natural wood charcoal
2 handfuls (2 cups) oak chips, soaked for 1 hour in a pan of water
Vegetable oil and a pastry brush (for greasing the grill rack)
Tongs

HOME FRIES

Home fries!—and you are remembering Grandmother's cozy kitchen the way it was (or the way it ought to have been), with her wonderful gutsy food, and especially her skillet-fried potatoes. They are (or ought to be) everybody's favorite potato dish—but they don't always come out like Grandma's. Perhaps because they weren't cooked like Michael's, who certainly seems to have blessed us with grandmotherly secrets in the following recipe. The potatoes are peeled and boiled until almost tender, then they are cut into wedges and sautéed before being combined with cooked onions and seasonings.

Bring the potatoes to the boil in a saucepan of cold water, and boil slowly for 12 to 15 minutes, just until a knife pierces them with no resistance—they should be very slightly undercooked, still slightly firm. When they have cooled to tepid, quarter them into wedges.

Heat 1 tablespoon of the oil in a 10-inch no-stick frying pan and add the onions. Cook over moderately low heat for several minutes, until they are soft and translucent, then raise heat to medium high, tossing them occasionally until the onions are golden brown and actually begin to caramelize—10 to 15 minutes. Turn the onions into a side dish and reserve. Heat the remaining olive oil and butter in the same pan until the butter foams and is beginning to brown. Immediately, add the potato wedges, and cook, turning frequently, until they begin to brown and crisp. Fold in the onions, the paprika, the salt and pepper, and toss over moderately high heat for 2 to 3 minutes.

If you are not serving shortly, keep them warm, partially covered, in a 150° F oven, but the sooner you serve them the more delicious they will be. Toss in the fresh thyme just before bringing them to the table.

INGREDIENTS FOR 6 SERVINGS

2 pounds yellow finn, Yukon gold, or red bliss potatoes, 2 inches or less in diameter, washed and peeled

3 tablespoons olive oil

2 Vidalia or Spanish onions, diced (about 4 cups)

2 tablespoons unsalted butter

1 tablespoon paprika

2 tablespoons fresh thyme

Salt and freshly ground black pepper

CHILE PASTE

You'll find ready-made chile paste in many ethnic markets, but Michael likes to make his own because then he knows exactly what's in it, and it reflects his own tastes. He uses a combination of chiles which gives the paste a complex and concentrated flavor, as well as bringing out the real personality of the peppers. He keeps jars of his homemade paste in the refrigerator, and uses it whenever chile powder or red pepper flakes are called for, such as in chile mayonnaise, chile con carne, spicy salad dressings, and so forth.

PROPORTIONS FOR ABOUT ⅓ CUP

2 ounces dried peppers, any combination of serrano, chipolte, and ancho

Proportions to Use: Michael's chile paste is strong and vigorous! A little bit of it goes a long way. Substitute ½ teaspoon of it for every tablespoon of chile powder called for in a recipe.

Cover the peppers with hot water and soak until softened—15 to 20 minutes. Drain, seed, and stem. (Careful of the volatile oils! Michael washes his fingers in milk to counteract the heat.) Either puree the peppers in a food processor, then sieve the puree to get rid of the skins, or puree through a food mill, in which case sieving is not necessary.

Storing. Refrigerate in a screw-top jar, where the paste will keep almost indefinitely.

cook's notes

CHRISTOPHER GROSS

When he was twelve years old, Christopher Gross's passion led him to the restaurant business—a passion for bikes, not for food. Christopher wanted a dirt bike and his mother said he would have to buy it himself. So he worked in a steak house and earned the money. He's now *on* his twelfth bike and *in* his twelfth restaurant. The bike infatuation has been constant, but his love affair with food was not. "As a kid, I ate such a small selection of food that my mother asked the doctor if I was going to be all right. I didn't even try pizza until I was sixteen."

His eyes opened at seventeen, when the steak-house chef transferred to the Adams Hotel and took Christopher with him. It was a professional kitchen with European chefs, one of whom became intent on teaching him something new every day. Christopher's culinary passion took hold. Heeding his chef's advice, he headed for Los Angeles and the Hyatt Hotel. His chef had advised him to call first to see if they were hiring—Christopher called from the lobby. The chef could not ignore someone so insistent and he told him about a position at the Marina City Club. Christopher then worked at the Century Plaza under Walter Roth, and by that time knew that he wanted to study in Europe. His chef gave him a lead—in London—and again, he called from the lobby and got that position, and then one at the Parisian restaurant Chez Albert.

Chef Christopher's varied apprenticeships have found an exciting expression at his two Arizona restaurants, Christopher's and Christopher's Bristo. Perhaps there is a hint of his original steak-house influence in his Alder-Smoked Loin of Beef, but the lovely rich shallot sauce is classic French. His Potato-Thyme Wafers and Chocolate Towers display the same superb combination of American ingenuity and traditional French techniques.

ALDER-SMOKED LOIN OF BEEF WITH RED WINE AND SHALLOT SAUCE

To home-smoke a cut of beef takes only 15 minutes, and is far easier than you might think. All you need is a package of hardwood sawdust, which you can get in a hardware store, a wok, a rack, and a stove top. When you serve the beef in a sophisticated red wine sauce and garnish it with braised shallots, people will think you have a chef in the kitchen—perhaps one named Christopher! He marinates the meat in flavored oil, either truffle oil or a mixture of olive oil and fresh herbs. He then very lightly smokes it before he browns and roasts it. Chef Christopher is partial to beef with shallots since it reminds him of his Paris days, and here he garnishes his roast with sautéed chopped shallots, accompanies it with braised whole shallots, and serves it with a red wine and shallot sauce.

Marinating the Beef: At least a day (preferably 3 days) before you are serving, dry the meat thoroughly in paper towels, then rub all over with the truffle oil, or with olive oil, thyme, and pepper. Refrigerate it in a tightly closed plastic bag—overnight is good, but 3 days has a pronounced tenderizing effect.

Smoking: When you are ready to smoke the beef, mound the hardwood sawdust in the bottom of the wok, insert the rack, and set the wok or pan over moderately low heat. If necessary, cut the meat in half lengthwise to make it fit into the smoking contraption. In a few minutes, when the sawdust is smoking, arrange the meat on the rack and put the cover on. Stuff aluminum foil between the wok or pan top and cover if necessary, to prevent smoke from escaping. The beef is to smoke for 15 minutes, but it is not to cook—in other words, keep the heat low throughout the smoking process: it should feel only tepid to the touch. When the 15 minutes are up, remove the meat to a side dish.

Timing Note: You may accomplish the following steps an hour or so in advance of the final cooking and serving. Preheat the oven to 375° F 20 minutes before you plan to roast the beef. Then, while the beef is resting after roasting, reheat the various elements, and you are ready to carve and serve. A little help in the kitchen at this point will not be amiss!

INGREDIENTS FOR 6 SERVINGS

The loin of beef

A 2½- to 3-pound well-aged and nicely marbled top-quality loin strip of beef, neatly trimmed of all covering fat and ready for roasting

2 to 3 tablespoons truffle oil (see page 116), or extra virgin olive oil with several sprigs of fresh thyme, plus several grinds of black pepper

2 cups alder wood sawdust (or, if unavailable, use apple wood or hickory—and change the name!)

A little more olive oil (for browning the meat before roasting)

Salt

(continued)

Alder-Smoked Loin of Beef (continued)

Preliminaries to the Finale:

Browning the Beef. Film the bottom of a heavy frying pan with oil, and brown the meat nicely on all sides. Remove it to a baking pan. Carefully spoon the browning fat out of the frying pan, leaving in any meat juices. Set the pan aside, unwashed.

The Red Wine Sauce. Set the meat-browning fry pan over medium heat and add the chopped shallots. Stir for several minutes to soften, but do not brown. Then blend in the thyme, pepper, and red wine. Boil down by half, and add the stock. Let boil slowly until reduced to ½ cup. Transfer to a saucepan and set aside.

The Braised Whole Shallots. Place the 12 whole shallots in a small covered saucepan and simmer very slowly for 20 minutes or so in the chicken stock—they should remain whole but be thoroughly tender when pierced with a small knife. Remove them to a side dish and boil down the cooking stock almost to a syrup, add the cream, let boil for a moment, correct seasoning, and return the shallots to the pan.

The Shallot Garnish. Slowly sauté the freshly minced shallots in a spoonful of olive oil, until tender and translucent—6 to 8 minutes. Season lightly with salt and pepper, and set aside. Reheat just before serving and blend in the minced chives.

Roasting the Meat. Place the roasting pan with the browned beef loin in the middle level of the preheated 375° F oven and roast to rare or medium rare—120° to 130° F on an instant meat thermometer—it will rise almost 10 degrees out of the oven. *Timing:* If the meat is still warm, 10 to 15 minutes should suffice; count on 20 to 25 minutes if the meat has cooled.

TRUFFLE OIL

Truffle oil adds a special touch to Chef Christopher's Alder-Smoked Loin of Beef, but it may not be easy to find. Many specialty stores and mail-order catalogs do offer it, but the chef has some suggestions if you cannot find it. You can make your own by letting truffle peelings steep in a light olive oil. Keep the oil covered in the refrigerator and use it for a special taste on salads or drizzle some over pasta. Or you could make an herb oil by bringing 2 cups of light olive oil to a simmer, then adding herbs such as ¼ cup basil or the leaves from several sprigs of thyme, and so forth. Puree the mixture in a blender and refrigerate overnight; strain the next day. For a greener color, add some parsley to the mixture before pureeing. Also see the notes on herb oil in Chef Charlie Trotter's chapter, page 73.

The red wine and shallot sauce

3 tablespoons peeled and chopped shallots (3 large shallots)

1 sprig of fresh thyme

4 grinds of black pepper

3 cups healthy young red wine, such as a Merlot or Zinfandel

3 cups strong veal or chicken stock

Salt and freshly ground black pepper to taste

2 or more tablespoons unsalted butter

The braised whole shallots

12 fairly large fine fresh unblemished shallots, neatly peeled

3 cups or more chicken stock

2 or more tablespoons heavy cream

Salt and freshly ground black pepper

1 tablespoon unsalted butter

The shallot garnish

1 tablespoon olive oil

⅓ cup peeled and finely minced freshly cut shallots (about 5 large)

2 tablespoons chopped fresh chives

Salt and freshly ground black pepper

(continued)

The Finale: When the meat is done, remove it to a cutting board and let it rest a few minutes while you deglaze the roasting pan by pouring in 1 cup of red wine and scraping up any roasting juices. Transfer this winy pan juice to the wine and shallot sauce; boil rapidly to reduce down to 1 cup or so; correct seasoning, and, off heat, swirl in a tablespoon or so of butter. Heat up the braised shallots and swirl in another spoonful of butter. Reheat the sautéed chopped shallots and whatever other elements you may have, such as vegetable garnishes, sauces, etc.

Serving: Rapidly cut the beef into neat thin slices and arrange on either a hot platter or hot dinner plate, ringing the meat with the sauce and garnishing with the chopped shallots. Position the braised shallots attractively, napping them with their sauce. Chef Christopher completes each serving with egg-shaped ovals of that exotic grain, fareki, in which he stands a couple of his crisp potato wafers—an inviting dish indeed.

For serving

Fareki (see page 119) or rice or
cous-cous
Potato-Thyme Wafers
(see page 118)

SPECIAL EQUIPMENT
SUGGESTED

A wok or other deep pan which
can hold a rack or steamer
basket for the meat, and a
tight-fitting cover (for smoking
the beef)
Aluminum foil

POTATO-THYME WAFERS

One evening when Chef Christopher was dining with Michel Richard, chef-owner of Citrus in Los Angeles, he was so intrigued with Chef Michel's description of some remarkable potato chips, made out of mashed potatoes, that Christopher set off on an experimental spree. It ended with this perfect recipe for crisp delicious chips actually made out of mashed potatoes. His chips go beautifully with the smoked beef loin, or with any roast meat. They are irresistible tidbits, too, as appetizers for special occasions— a welcome addition to anyone's repertoire, especially since there's no deep-fat frying involved.

Manufacturing Note: You'll have to experiment a bit on your first try here, such as how wide to make your template, your technique on the baking sheets, etc. You'll find it well worth your while since these potato wafers could well be one of your famous house specialties—one of your "signature" dishes.

Boiling and Mashing the Potatoes: Peel and quarter the potatoes, boil until tender in lightly salted water, and puree into a bowl. Beat in the butter, then whisk in the egg whites. Season nicely to taste with salt and pepper and let rest 30 minutes.

Ahead-of-Time Note: May be prepared to this point several hours in advance.

Forming and Baking: Preheat the oven to 350° F. Either paint a light film of clarified butter over the baking sheets, or coat with cooking spray (we preferred the spray—less greasy!). Place the template on the baking sheet and spread a small amount of the potatoes very thinly into the teardrop area. Lift off the template and position it on the baking sheet for the next wafer. Continue to make shapes on the pan, spacing them about 1 inch apart. Sprinkle the thyme over the

INGREDIENTS FOR 5 TO 6 DOZEN WAFERS

2 large baking potatoes (1 pound)
4 ounces (1 stick) unsalted butter, at room temperature
½ cup egg whites (4 "large")
Salt
Freshly ground white pepper to taste
About ½ cup clarified butter (see appendix) or no-stick cooking spray (which our team preferred)
3 tablespoons minced fresh thyme leaves

SPECIAL EQUIPMENT SUGGESTED

A potato ricer or a vegetable mill
A template for shaping the potatoes—a swelling teardrop shape 4 inches long and 3 inches at its widest point, cut out of something like a shirt cardboard from the laundry or a paper plate (we preferred the paper plate)

(continued)

potatoes and bake for 8 to 10 minutes, or until golden brown. Lift them off the sheet and cool on a rack.

Ahead-of-Time Note: The chips may be made a day ahead. Store uncovered so they will stay crisp.

2 or 3 no-stick flat (edge on one side only) baking sheets

An offset spatula—a special pastry spatula with a bent blade—desirable but not essential

A cake rack (for cooling the wafers)

FAREKI

Fareki is a Middle Eastern grain, and, according to our Mediterranean specialist, Paula Wolfert, it is immature wheat, eaten in those regions where food must be provided when the new grains have not yet been harvested. To make immature wheat palatable, it is toasted, which gives it its special, slightly smoky flavor. You'll find fareki in stores carrying Middle Eastern foods, and, according to our source, it provides not only an especially interesting grain food but is unusually nutritious. All is not nutritional heaven, however, since before cooking, fareki must be picked over bit by bit to remove stems and other debris. To make up for that labor, Chef Christopher spikes his fareki with his excellent homemade red pepper and chile harissa (see page 120).

Cleaning the Fareki: Turn the fareki out onto a large tray, and, using something like a credit card, separate it into small portions as you pick it over, discarding stems, stones, and other debris. Then turn the fareki into a large sieve set over a bowl of cold water, swish it about, drain well, and it is ready for cooking.

Cooking the Fareki: Set a heavy-bottomed 8-inch pan about 2 inches deep over moderately high heat, add the oil, stir in the fareki, and sauté for several minutes so that it is well heated or "toasted" but not burned. Stir in the garlic, shallots, and warm stock; bring to a boil, reduce the heat to a slow simmer, and cover the pan. Let cook 35 to 40 minutes, checking now and then, and adding a little more stock (or water) if the fareki seems too dry. When the grain is tender, the liquid should be almost completely absorbed. Season to taste with salt and pepper, and stir in the harissa. Just before serving, stir in the chives.

Ahead-of-Time Note: The fareki may be prepared a day in advance. When cool, cover and refrigerate; reheat before serving.

INGREDIENTS FOR 6 SERVINGS

For the grain
¾ pound fareki (about 2 cups)
1 tablespoon olive oil
2 tablespoons peeled and minced garlic
About 5 tablespoons peeled and minced shallots
3 cups warm chicken stock
Salt and freshly ground black pepper
2 to 3 tablespoons harissa (see page 120)
3 tablespoons chopped fresh chives

HARISSA
SPICY RED PEPPER AND CHILE PUREE

Chef Christopher Gross likes a few tablespoons of red pepper puree stirred into his Middle Eastern grain dish, fareki. He makes a lot of this puree because he also serves it with cold fish and chicken, as well as hard-boiled egg dishes. He loves it as a topping for garlic toast, and as an accompaniment to cold cuts. In fact, he serves his harissa with anything that goes with the fresh taste of pureed sweet red peppers. You may wish to halve or quarter the proportions here, although it's useful to have a number of small jars of harissa on hand in the freezer.

Manufacturing Note: If you've seen the television show, you will note that I've changed his order of battle slightly so that the garlic will be really pureed and therefore won't stick in your teeth. (A blender purees garlic more efficiently than a food processor.)

Roast, peel, halve, and seed the red peppers. Place 2 pepper halves in the container of the blender along with the garlic, onion, and chile powder or chiles. Blend to a fine puree. Then add the remaining peppers, ¼ teaspoon salt, and several grinds of pepper; blend in several spurts, just enough to break up the red peppers—you want to leave some texture in the final puree.

Ahead-of-Time Note: Refrigerate in a screw-top jar; it will keep several days. For longer storage, pack into small jars and freeze.

INGREDIENTS FOR ABOUT
3 CUPS

5 fine medium-size unblemished red bell peppers (about 1 pound)

3 large garlic cloves, smashed and peeled

1 small onion, roughly chopped (about ½ cup)

¼ teaspoon dried red chile powder or 4 dried serrano chiles

Salt
Freshly ground white pepper to taste

SPECIAL EQUIPMENT
SUGGESTED

An electric blender

SAUCE THICKENER

Chefs are so used to working "on the line" in bustling kitchens that they become quite adept at last-minute corrections or adaptations when a dish needs pampering. Chef Christopher has a nifty trick for a light brown or white sauce that tastes fine but is texturally a bit too thin. His quick emergency solution is to plop on top of it a dollop of whipped cream the moment before serving, and gently fold it in. The air bubbles in the cream puff up the sauce and give it temporary body.

PARNASSIENNE AU CHOCOLAT
CHOCOLATE TOWERS

Christopher named his handsome dessert, this latticework tower, in honor of the tower of Montparnasse in Paris. When he was working at the Parisian restaurant Chez Albert, he noted that the chef named a favorite scallop recipe Parnassienne de Coquilles Saint-Jacques and he liked the idea. It's a lovely dessert, and far easier to execute than the length of this recipe would suggest— you should see it first on the TV!

Manufacturing Note: The towers are chocolate mousse that is formed and frozen in paper cylinders; the paper is peeled off when the dessert is decorated, then thawed and served. So that you may plan your time, note that you will want two sets of cool melted chocolate: one for the mousse in the first step, and the other for the chocolate lattice decoration.

Techniques: Complete details on beating egg whites, and melting chocolate can be found in the appendix.

Forming the Towers: As a test, cut a piece of the parchment paper into a rectangle 3½ inches wide and 5 inches long. Using either a dowel or thin rolling pin, or just your hands, form it into a cylinder 5 inches tall and 1½ inches in diameter. Close the side with a piece of sticky tape; be sure you have made it so it stands up straight or it will tip over when filled. Measure the opening. It should be 1½ inches across in order to hold the right amount of mousse. If it is not, cut your parchment, say, 5½ inches long. When you are satisfied, make the 8 cylinders and set them aside upright.

Making the Mousse:

Melting the Chocolate. Pour 2 inches of water into the saucepan and bring to the slow simmer. Set a stainless steel bowl on top of the pan, and add the chocolate and butter. Stir occasionally as the chocolate melts; when smooth and lump-free, in about 5 minutes, remove and let the chocolate cool to room temperature.

Whipping the Cream. Pour the cream into the stainless steel bowl set over ice and water. Beat by hand or portable beater, whipping in as much air as possible, until you form quite stiff peaks.

INGREDIENTS FOR 8 TOWERS

For the chocolate mousse
5½ ounces semisweet chocolate (preferably "couverture"), broken into pieces
3 tablespoons unsalted butter (sliced for easy melting)
¼ cup heavy cream
1¼ cups egg whites (about 10 "large")
4 tablespoons superfine sugar

For the lattice and final decorations
3 ounces semisweet chocolate (preferably "couverture"), cut into pieces
6 ounces white chocolate, cut into pieces

For the garnish
Espresso Sauce (see page 124)
Fresh berries and mint leaves

(continued)

Chocolate Towers (continued)

Beating the Egg Whites. Beat the egg whites to soft peaks, whip in 2 table-spoons of sugar, and continue beating to stiff peaks, sprinkling in the rest of the sugar as you do so.

Combining the Ingredients. Whisk a quarter of the egg whites into the cool melted chocolate, then gently fold in the rest. Now fold in the cream rapidly and deftly, deflating as little as possible.

Filling the Towers: Fill the pastry bag with the mousse and pipe it into the tubes, leaving ½ inch of space at the top. Keep them standing up on the tray, drape a sheet of plastic over them, and set in the freezer for about 1 hour, until they are frozen solid. (Freeze any remaining mousse and use as a quick and elegant dessert.)

Melting the Chocolates for Decoration: Melt the dark chocolate as previously described, and let cool to room temperature. Melt the white chocolate the same way, but it will need occasional supervision since it hardens quickly—let cool, but keep over the hot water when you are not using it.

Preparing the Dark Chocolate Lattice Decoration: For decorating the towers, cut eight 5-inch squares out of the parchment paper. Fill a paper decorating cone with some of the dark chocolate, and drizzle free-form diagonal lines no more than ¼ inch apart in a lattice pattern across each of the parchment squares. As each square is done, lay it flat on one of the baking sheets, and when all are finished, put the sheets in the freezer until the chocolate is set, 5 minutes or so. Reserve the remaining melted chocolate.

Adding the White Chocolate and Finishing the Towers: Remove one dark chocolate lattice square from the freezer. With the offset spatula, spread 2 to 3 tablespoons of the white chocolate in a very thin layer on top of the lattice, leaving a 1-inch strip uncoated at one side—scrape off any excess white chocolate. Unwrap one frozen mousse tower and lay it on top of the white chocolate, parallel to and opposite the uncoated strip. Quickly wrap the parchment around the mousse, handling it as little as possible and being careful to leave the uncoated flap of the paper overlapping; you will grasp this to unwrap the tower later. Return each finished tower to the freezer and continue with the rest. (The papers can be peeled off after about five minutes, and the chocolate lattice will remain intact around the mousse.)

(continued)

SPECIAL EQUIPMENT
SUGGESTED

Two 8-inch stainless steel bowls set on top of 2 saucepans (for melting chocolates)

A 10-inch stainless steel bowl set over a larger bowl of ice and water (for whipping cream)

A very clean bowl and beater (for whipping egg whites)

Parchment paper (a full box, just to have enough)

6 homemade paper decorating cones

2 large baking sheets (for decorating work)

Sticky tape

A pastry bag fitted with a ½-inch star tube

An offset spatula—a special pastry spatula with a bent blade—desirable but not essential

A hand-held mixer

Chilled dessert plates

Chocoate Towers (continued)

Ahead-of-Time Note: The towers may be completed to this point and will keep, well covered, for several weeks in the freezer.

Presenting the Towers: Remember to allow about 30 minutes in all for the towers to defrost before serving. One at a time, unwrap the frozen mousse towers, and stand each upright in the center of a dessert plate. Now decorate the dessert plates: fill one paper decorating cone with espresso sauce; pour ½ cup of espresso sauce into a cup, blend with the remaining chocolate, and insert it into the second paper cone. Pipe alternating ½-inch dots of each sauce around the towers. Tuck fresh berries into the depression at the top and garnish each with a sprig of fresh mint. Combine the sauces in a serving bowl and pass separately.

ESPRESSO SAUCE

A rich coffee-flavored custard sauce goes beautifully with Chef Christopher's handsome dessert. He decorates the plates with dots of it, and passes the rest separately. Leave out the coffee beans and you have a rich custard sauce. Substitute milk for cream and you have the classic French sauce, crème anglaise, *without which many desserts and ice creams would not exist. It is therefore most definitely part of any good cook's culinary baggage, and a note on it is appended here, at the end of Christopher's recipe.*

Heat the half-and-half cream with the vanilla bean, and when almost at the simmer, remove from heat and cover the pan—or heat the cream with the vanilla extract. Meanwhile, start beating the egg yolks with the hand-held mixer or whisk in the 8-cup pan until thick and lemon-colored. Gradually beat in the sugar; then, by driblets, blend in ¼ cup of the hot cream to warm the yolks slowly—note that you are to blend rather than beat, to minimize air bubbles. Finally, remove the vanilla bean from the remaining cream, and blend the cream into the yolk mixture. Pour in the espresso beans and set over low heat, stirring slowly and constantly until the mixture is thick enough to coat the back of a spoon—be careful of the heat here; the sauce must warm enough to thicken, but if it comes to the simmer, the egg yolks will lump. Strain through the fine-meshed sieve into a bowl and let cool. Serve warm, tepid, or chilled.

INGREDIENTS FOR ABOUT
2 CUPS

*1½ cups half-and-half
    (light cream)*
*½ fragrant vanilla bean or
    1 teaspoon pure vanilla extract*
6 egg yolks
⅔ cup sugar
*1 cup (2 ounces) espresso
    coffee beans*

(continued)

Ahead-of-Time Note: When cool, cover and store in the refrigerator, where the sauce will keep for several days.

SPECIAL EQUIPMENT
SUGGESTED

A 6-cup saucepan (for heating the cream)
An 8-cup stainless steel pan (for making the sauce)
A hand-held mixer or a whisk
A wooden spatula or spoon
A fine-meshed sieve

FROM JULIA: CRÈME ANGLAISE— CUSTARD SAUCE AND OTHER SAUCES INCLUDING LIQUEURS AND/OR CHOCOLATE

Substitute 1½ cups of milk for the cream and you have the classic French custard sauce. You may use either low-fat milk or whole milk. You may enrich it by whisking into the finished sauce 2 to 3 tablespoons of unsalted butter, and/or you may flavor it at the same time with 2 tablespoons of rum, Cognac, or other liqueur, or with 2 to 3 ounces of semisweet chocolate. A more complete recipe is in the box on page 207, including the fast restaurant technique.

cook's notes

ALFRED PORTALE

Design and craftsmanship have always meant a lot to Executive Chef Alfred Portale, who once trained to be a jewelry designer. Before that career took off, however, Portale became enamored of the culinary arts, an obsession that began innocently when a friend showed him some classic French cookbooks, such as *Larousse Gastronomique.* Portale was drawn into the festive world displayed in the book's depictions of banquets of the past.

"It was love at first sight. I was taken by those pictures of *chaud-froids* and all those elaborate cold buffets, and began considering a career shortly thereafter."

Portale enrolled in the renowned Culinary Institute of America, where he graduated first in his class. He went on to work with Michele Guérard, who was opening an upscale shop for his gourmet food products in New York. When Guérard returned to France, Portale joined him in the kitchen of his restaurant and spa. "He helped shape my ideas about cooking," recalls Portale, who continued to travel and work in the great kitchens of France, spending time with the Troisgros brothers and Jacques Maximin.

Returning to the United States, Portale was eager to combine the techniques he had absorbed overseas with his innate designer's instincts: "I had the idea that it would be nice to apply everything I learned in France—an appreciation of the beauty and possibilities of food, the sophisticated flavors and combinations—but serve them in a manner and a setting removed from all pretension." He found a home for this notion nine years ago at the Gotham Bar and Grill, a festive, approachably elegant restaurant in Greenwich Village. There, Portale became one of the pioneers of New American Cuisine, combining classic training with a revolutionary playfulness and abandon. Diners and critics of the day responded rapturously to this inventive cuisine, and have been coming back faithfully ever since.

FOIE GRAS RAVIOLI

Ravioli are surprisingly easy to make, especially now that you can buy thin dough wrappers ready-made. Alfred Portale's ravioli filling is a well-seasoned puree of white beans topped with a small chunk of foie gras. They are light and delicate, and as the ravioli cook, the bean puree absorbs the melting juices flowing from the foie gras so none of the flavor is lost—they may be made several hours in advance of serving, and they cook in 10 seconds or so. Chef Portale serves them as a little touch of luxury on top of the turnips and mushrooms and fresh duck meat in his beautiful soup on page 129. If not in a soup, you might serve them alone in a warm soup plate, moistened by a big spoonful of richly flavored broth—an elegant first course.

Filling the Ravioli: Work with no more than 5 wonton skin wrappers at a time so they won't dry out, keeping the rest under plastic wrap. Lay the wrappers down on a clean work surface. Place 1 teaspoon of the bean or potato puree in the center of each wrapper, and set a piece of the foie gras on top. Using the pastry brush, paint egg wash on the wrapper, being sure to cover the entire surface around the filling. Immediately lay a second wrapper on top and press all around the filling with the balls of your fingers, to be sure the two wrappers are securely glued together. Don't worry if there are pleats and folds as long as the two wrappers are solidly glued together.

Cutting the Ravioli: Position the cutter directly over the filling and press through the two layers, making a round ravioli. Press a ½-inch decorative edging around the circumference with the tines of a table fork, to secure the two layers. As the ravioli are finished, arrange them in one layer on the tray—previously sprinkled with cornmeal to prevent the ravioli from sticking to the pan. Cover tightly with plastic wrap until ready to cook.

Ahead-of-Time Note: The ravioli may be refrigerated 4 to 6 hours before cooking. They will become soggy if they wait any longer.

Serving: Bring 4 quarts of lightly salted water to the boil. The moment before serving, drop in the ravioli and boil gently for 10 seconds; carefully remove them with the wire-mesh strainer and serve immediately, either in hot broth or as your recipe directs.

INGREDIENTS FOR 18 TO 20 RAVIOLI

40 wonton skin wrappers (available in Asian markets)

½ cup (4 ounces) mashed cooked white beans seasoned with salt, freshly ground white pepper, and a very small garlic clove, pureed, or very well-seasoned mashed potatoes

8 ounces foie gras (either block, terrine, or mousse), cut into 20 even chunks

Egg wash: 1 "large" egg beaten with 1 teaspoon water

SPECIAL EQUIPMENT SUGGESTED

A 1¼-inch round ravioli cutter, cookie cutter, or glass

A small pastry brush

A tray or baking sheet sprinkled with cornmeal

A wire-mesh strainer

DUCK VARIETIES

Peking or Long Island Duck: This is the most common species, found in all supermarkets. It is a good all-purpose bird that will serve in any of the recipes here and most of those elsewhere in this book. It is smaller than the other varieties, and an average boneless half breast weighs about 6 ounces.

Muscovy Ducks: The Muscovy has a greater proportion of meat to bone than the Peking, and in addition the Muscovy has a more pronounced duck flavor. It is a versatile breed, well suited to roasting, sautéing, and braising. These ducks are not readily available; you'll have to order them from your market. One side of the boneless breast, skin on, weighs around 14 ounces.

Moulard: The moulard duck, a cross between the Peking and the Muscovy, is considerably larger than other breeds. It is raised primarily for its liver—foie gras—and for its large breast—known in French as the *magret,* which has a rich beefy taste. Again, as for the Muscovy, it must usually be special-ordered. One side of the boneless breast, skin on, will weigh 14 ounces to 1 pound.

Mallard: The mallard is a wild duck with dark flesh. It is a lean bird with a somewhat tough texture; many cooks prefer to braise rather than roast it.

See illustration below on varieties of duck: top left is the familiar Peking duck; to the right of it a Muscovy duck; then the moulard; in the foreground, a mallard.

DUCK SOUP WITH FOIE GRAS RAVIOLIS

Alfred Portale's splendid duck soup is a hearty combination of duck meat, turnips, mushrooms, a handful of white beans, and generous homemade ravioli stuffed with duck foie gras. It makes a wonderful main course for a winter luncheon dish or a Sunday supper. Each of the ingredients in this soup maintains its own distinct flavor because it is cooked separately rather than being simmered together with everything else. The duck meat, freshly cooked on the bone especially for the soup, is from the thigh, a particularly succulent and juicy part of the bird. This is truly a great soup!

Manufacturing Note: As in many of our chef recipes, there is a lot going on at the end, the moment before serving. A friendly and knowing hand is always helpful in the kitchen, but you can swing it yourself if you get everything prepped, as the chefs say, and ready to go. Arrange the garnitures in each warm soup bowl and bring to the dining room, then go around the table ladling the hot broth into the bowls.

Cooking the Duck: Season the duck liberally with salt and pepper. Pour the oil into the frying pan, set over moderately high heat, and when it is very hot but not smoking, add the duck, skin side down. Sauté for 6 to 8 minutes, occasionally moving the pieces around with your tongs, until the skin is decidedly crisp and brown. Turn and continue on the other side for another 6 to 8 minutes, until cooked to medium—the juices, when the meat is pricked deeply with the sharp prongs of a fork, will run almost clear yellow and the meat, when pressed, will be fairly soft—not squashy like raw meat, not springy like rare meat, and not hard like overdone meat! Let the duck rest for 10 minutes, then remove the bones and cut the meat into thin slices; keep warm. Wash out the frying pan.

Preparing the Turnips: Add 1½ teaspoons of salt per quart to the saucepan of boiling water. Meanwhile, slice the tops off the baby turnips if you are using them, leaving about 1 inch of stem still attached. Set the tops aside. Drop the turnips (baby or regular) into the boiling water and let boil for 5 to 6 minutes or so, until just tender; remove to a large bowl of cold water with a slotted spoon. One by one, dry the turnips with a kitchen towel, rubbing gently to remove the skins, which will come loose easily. Slice the turnips into ¼-inch rounds. Wash the tops (or the chard), spin dry, and remove the stems from the leaves. Roughly cut the leaves into strips about 1½ inches wide, and set aside for later cooking.

INGREDIENTS FOR 6 SERVINGS

For the duck
*4 bone-in duck thighs
    (about 4½ ounces each)
Coarse salt and freshly ground
    black pepper
About 2 teaspoons excellent
    olive oil*

For the vegetables
Either *18 baby turnips, with tops*
Or *2 to 3 fine fresh white turnips,
    peeled and cut into ½-inch
    dice (making about 1 cup),
    and ¼ pound stemmed Swiss
    chard leaves*

(continued)

Duck Soup with Fois Gras Raviolis (continued)

Sautéing the Mushrooms: Trim the ends off the mushrooms and wipe the caps clean with a slightly dampened towel. If the stems are very dirty, scrape them with a small paring knife. Then cut the mushrooms into slices ¼ inch wide. Pour the oil into the duck frying pan, and when it is very hot but not smoking, toss in the mushrooms. Salt and pepper them, and sauté over moderately high heat, tossing occasionally for about 3 minutes, until lightly browned. Transfer to a small bowl and set aside.

Finishing the Soup: Bring 4 quarts of water to the boil for the ravioli in the second saucepan. At the same time, bring the duck broth to the simmer in the first saucepan; and keep hot over a low heat. Taste the broth and season carefully with salt and pepper. Shave the truffle into the broth, or slice into very thin pieces and add to the broth. Empty the mushrooms and the juices that collected in the bowl into the broth. Stir in the turnips and the white beans. Drop in the turnip tops, which will wilt quickly—chard will take a little longer. Turn up the heat, add the duck pieces, and simmer just until all the ingredients are very hot. Use a slotted spoon to divide the duck and vegetables among the soup dishes, and then ladle the broth around them. Add salt to the boiling water and drop in the ravioli; boil for 10 seconds and then retrieve them with the strainer; float 3 on top of each soup. Scatter on the chives and garnish with sprigs of chervil. Serve immediately. (See also the home-serving suggestions at the beginning of the recipe.)

cook's notes

10 ounces chanterelles or porcini, cremini, or button mushrooms or a combination of fresh and reconstituted dry mushrooms
2 teaspoons excellent olive oil
Coarse salt
Freshly ground white pepper

For the soup
1 quart duck broth (see page 132)
Salt
Freshly ground black pepper
1 or 2 fresh black truffles, walnut-size (optional but desirable)

For the garnish
⅓ cup cooked white beans, at room temperature
18 to 20 foie gras or mushroom ravioli (see page 127)
4 tablespoons finely chopped chives
¼ cup (lightly packed) sprigs of fresh chervil

SPECIAL EQUIPMENT SUGGESTED

A 10-inch heavy-bottomed frying pan (first for the duck, then for the mushrooms)
Tongs
A 4-quart saucepan of boiling water (first for the turnips, then for the soup itself)
A wire-mesh strainer
A second 4-quart saucepan of boiling water (for the ravioli)
Heated soup plates or wide bowls

DUCK BROTH

This fine strong, classically made duck broth is the model we use in this book whenever a "rich stock or broth" is called for. The ingredients may vary, but the method should be the same. Chef Alfred Portale uses this particular formula for his duck soup on page 129, and to make the sauce for his duck breasts on page 135. Chef Alfred, by the way, considers this a broth and not a stock because it has a higher proportion of meat to bone than a stock, which often has more bone than meat. By whatever name you wish to call it, this is one very superior concoction.

Manufacturing Note: You will note that no salt is included, since that is up to you. It is a good idea to go very light on salt—a little bit will help you judge the flavor of the broth, but since you may be reducing it considerably later on, a normal amount of salt at the beginning could make far too much in your final dish. For a different type of broth, popular with many chefs today, see the *jus-rôti* on page 85, and the simple white and brown stocks in the box on page 87.

Cooking the Duck: With the heavy knife or cleaver, cut and chop the duck and bones into 2-inch pieces—small pieces will brown evenly and release their flavor more quickly. Film the larger pan with oil, set over moderately high heat, and when it is very hot but not smoking, add the duck—it should sizzle as it goes in—stir and toss frequently for even browning. (If the pan is too small for all the pieces to fit in comfortably, brown in two batches.) When nicely browned, in 8 to 10 minutes, drain off the fat. Pour in the wine and turn up the heat, using a wooden spoon to deglaze the pan by scraping up the browned bits clinging to the bottom. Transfer the duck and pan juices to the stockpot.

Cooking the Vegetables: Meanwhile, film the second pan with oil, set over moderately high heat, and sauté the vegetables until they are nicely browned—slightly caramelized, as the chef says. Stir in a cupful of the water to deglaze the pan, and scrape the contents into the stockpot.

Simmering the Broth: Pour the water into the pot, bring slowly to the boil, then reduce to the simmer. Skim off any fat and scum that comes to the surface for 15 minutes or so, then add the seasonings. Simmer, partially covered, for 2½ hours, adding a little boiling water if too much liquid evaporates—you should end up with about 2 quarts of finished broth.

INGREDIENTS FOR ABOUT 2 QUARTS

The duck

4 pounds fresh uncooked duck pieces (neck, wings, legs, bones, and gizzards)

About 2 tablespoons vegetable oil

1¼ cups hearty, healthy, dry red wine

1½ quarts water, plus more as needed

For the vegetable flavoring

2 tablespoons vegetable oil

The following vegetables, roughly sliced into ¼-inch pieces:

6 large shallots, unpeeled

1 medium celery stalk, halved

1 leek, washed and halved lengthwise

1 whole head garlic, unpeeled, cut in half horizontally

(continued)

Finishing the Broth: Ladle the broth through the strainer into the clean saucepan, pressing hard on the solids to extract as much liquid as possible. Simmer, skimming fat off the surface, and taste carefully for strength and flavor—you may wish to continue simmering to reduce the volume and concentrate flavor.

Ahead-of-Time Note: When cool, pour into a covered container and refrigerate for several days, or freeze for several weeks.

For the seasonings
½ teaspoon whole black
   peppercorns
5 sprigs of fresh thyme, about
   4 inches long
¼ teaspoon fennel
¼ teaspoon caraway seeds
2 small Turkish bay leaves
2 star anise

**SPECIAL EQUIPMENT
SUGGESTED**

A heavy knife or cleaver
A 10- to 12-inch heavy-bottomed
   straight-sided sauté pan or a
   frying pan (for the duck)
A 10- to 12-inch frying pan
   (for the vegetables)
A 6-quart heavy-bottomed
   stockpot or saucepan
   (for simmering the broth)
A cover for the pot
A clean 4-quart saucepan
   (for the finished broth)
A sturdy fine-meshed sieve or
   a chinois

JULIA'S INSTRUCTIONS ON CUTTING UP A DUCK

Only a very young duck, the kind we supermarket shoppers never see, can be roasted whole with success. Our usual 4½- to 5-pound "roaster ducklings" are still young, but if we roast them in the ordinary way and want rosy breast meat, we do get rosy breast meat, but we also get tough legs and thighs. If we want tender legs, we get gray breasts, and if we want crisp skin, we get shredded meat. The way around this dilemma, according to Chef Alfred Portale, is to cut up the duck and cook the parts separately. It's good training for the cook, too, since when you know where all the parts are located, you'll be a better bird-carver, while on the practical side you'll have the carcass and scraps for a super stock, plus all that duck fat, which is yours for rendering and for crunchy cracklings.

Removing and Separating the Leg-Thighs: With the duck sitting on its back, grab one of the legs by the knee and, bending it slightly toward your work surface, cut the skin between the knee and the vent, then from the knee down to the small of the back. Bend the knee all the way down to your work surface, which will pop the thigh bone out of its socket at the backbone. Remove the thigh along with the two "oysters" of meat, one lying forward of the ball joint at the small of the back; the other, along the side of the tail. Turn the leg-thigh skin side down, then note the seam, buried in the meat, that runs between the leg and the thigh; cut along and through it to release the leg from the thigh.

Removing the Breasts: Cut off the neck along with its excess skin. It is also a good idea to remove the breastbone from inside the neck cavity. Feel the keel bone, along the top center of the breast from the neck end to the tail end. Starting at the neck end, cut down along one side of the bone, pulling the meat away from the bone as you cut and always keeping your knife against the bone, not against the flesh. Remove the breast meat completely, cutting around, but not through, the wings, which you should remove separately and add to the scraps for the stockpot.

MUSCOVY DUCK BREAST WITH CHINESE SPICES

Chef Alfred's Chinese-inspired duck is a dish with many layers of complex, exotic flavors, and an interesting example of how an ingenious chef makes use of the resources of his restaurant kitchen to full advantage. Whether or not you plan to serve any of his garnitures, his duck sauce will be a glorious addition to your repertoire, as will his method of cooking the duck breast.

Manufacturing Note: Chef Portale uses Muscovy duck breasts for this recipe, but you may substitute Long Island or Peking ducks—you'll have to buy two whole ones, using the thighs for duck soup, the drumsticks for the duck salad (see box, page 133), and the carcass for stock (see page 132).

The Duck Sauce: Pour the oil into the 2-quart saucepan, and when it is hot, add the garlic, ginger, and scallions; reduce the heat to moderately low and sweat (cook slowly) the vegetables, stirring often. After about 1 minute add the chiles or chile paste. Drain the mushrooms from the soaking water, pat dry, cut out and discard the stems, and slice the mushrooms ¼ inch thick. Add them to the saucepan after the chiles have cooked a minute or so, and continue cooking slowly 6 to 8 minutes longer, until tender but not colored more than a pale yellow. Pour in the duck stock, add the remaining seasonings, and simmer until reduced by a third. The sauce should be richly flavored and lightly thickened. Taste and balance the flavors: sweet with hoisin, salt with soy, and heat with chile paste. No one flavor should be too pronounced. Set aside and warm before serving.

Ahead-of-Time Note: May be made several days in advance and refrigerated.

Browning the Napa Cabbage—while the duck breasts are cooking (next step). Cut the cabbage in half lengthwise, then cut each half into wedges approximately ¼ inch thick. Leave a piece of the core attached to each wedge to hold it together, and discard any bruised outer leaves. Set one of the frying pans over moderate heat, pour in the peanut oil, and when hot, put in one layer of cabbage and season with salt and pepper. Let brown lightly, then turn on the other side—the cabbage should remain slightly crisp. Repeat with the rest, and keep the cooked pieces warm.

Cooking the Duck: You want to keep the skin on the duck breasts, but trim off any excess skin and fat. With a very sharp knife and careful strokes, score the skin in a ⅜-inch crosshatch pattern, cutting through the skin only, not

INGREDIENTS FOR 4 SERVINGS

For the duck sauce
2 tablespoons peanut oil
6 garlic cloves, peeled and cut into ⅛-inch slices
2-inch piece of fresh ginger root, peeled and cut into ⅛-inch slices
2 scallions, trimmed and sliced into 3-inch pieces
2 Thai chiles with seeds, cut into 1-inch pieces, or 2 teaspoons red-hot chile paste (see page 113)
2 dried Chinese black mushrooms, dropped into hot water and allowed to soften for 15 minutes
1 quart duck broth (see page 132)
1 tablespoon hoisin sauce
1½ tablespoons mushroom soy sauce or plain soy sauce
1 pinch five-spice powder (available at Chinese groceries)
Salt, as needed

For the vegetables
1 head of napa cabbage
2 teaspoons peanut oil
Coarse salt

(continued)

Muscovy Duck Breast (continued)

the meat. Season the breasts liberally with salt, pepper, and the five-spice powder, pressing the seasonings onto the surface. Pour the oil into the second sauté pan, and when it is hot, add the breasts skin side down. Sauté over moderately high heat for 4 to 5 minutes, until the skin is lightly browned. Turn and cook for 4 to 5 minutes more, until the meat is medium rare. Let the breasts rest at least 10 minutes before slicing. Meanwhile, assemble the rest of the dish.

Preparing the Bok Choy and Snow Peas: Drop the bok choy into the boiling water in the 4-quart pan and maintain at the slow boil for 4 minutes. In the last 30 seconds, drop in the snow peas. Drain, and dip rapidly in and then out of the ice water, just to stop the cooking and retain the color—but not to cool the vegetables.

Assembling the Dish: Cut each duck breast on an angle into slices ½ inch wide. Lift carefully with the knife blade and place on the side of one of the 4 warm dinner plates, fanning the slices out. Form the cabbage into a circle in the center of the plate, snuggling it up to the duck. Stand the bok choy on end in the center of the cabbage, opening the leaves out slightly. Tuck the snow peas in the bok choy to create a tall and dramatic centerpiece for the duck. Scatter a few of the scallion pieces on top of the vegetables and then garnish with cilantro. Spoon the sauce around the duck and around the plate, and serve immediately.

Serving Note: This presentation is typical contemporary restaurant gymnastics, requiring impeccably clean asbestos fingers and quick dexterity. You may prefer to make a swift and beautiful arrangement of the vegetables in the center of a warm platter and surround them with the fanned-out portions of duck breast.

cook's notes

....

....

....

....

....

....

Freshly ground black pepper
4 baby bok choy
20 snow peas

For the duck
4 duck breasts, either Muscovies
*   or the smaller Long Island or*
*   Peking ducks*
Coarse salt
Freshly ground black pepper
3 tablespoons five-spice powder
*   (see above)*
1 teaspoon peanut oil

For serving
1 scallion, cut on an extreme
*   angle into very fine julienne*
*   and placed in ice water*
¼ cup beautiful sprigs of fresh
*   cilantro*

SPECIAL EQUIPMENT
SUGGESTED

A 2-quart heavy-bottomed
*   saucepan*
2 no-stick frying pans,
*   10-inch size*
Tongs
A 4-quart saucepan with
*   3 quarts of boiling salted*
*   water (for the bok choy)*
A bowl of ice and water
4 warm dinner plates or
*   a warm platter*

JACQUES TORRES

When Le Cirque's pastry chef Jacques Torres creates his towering chocolate centerpiece, he is not only a skilled pastry chef but also an inventive craftsman. Builders' tools, florist supplies, and kitchen odds and ends are all deftly employed to give birth to an exotic, edible structure. "I really try not to use special molds or anything expensive that you have to buy." To be so resourceful one has to know exactly what one is doing, and Chef Jacques knows his craft well. At twenty-six years old, he was the youngest chef ever to receive the prestigious title of "Meilleur Ouvrier de France Patissier."

Born in Provence, he did his apprenticeship in Nice, working for eight years under Jacques Maximum at the renowned Hôtel Negresco. Although his work was well received, the young chef hesitated to make a move to a

larger city. "I never worked in Paris and I didn't go right to New York. I was pretty scared to work in a big city." But eventually he met Daniel Boulud, then chef at Le Cirque, who convinced Torres to join him at the New York restaurant. The young patissier's fear of big cities disappeared.

When Chef Jacques is not creating such sumptuous desserts as the very best *crème brûlée* ever or the most unusual Chocolate Soup, he is teaching, usually at the French Culinary Institute in New York. "I love to teach. I love to know why things happen and to explain it. If you know why things happen, you know what to look and wait for." And, as rewards, perhaps he passes out to his students his lovely pralines that so remind him of his home in southern France.

CHOCOLATE SOUP

Chocolate Soup is one of Chef Jacques's creations for Le Cirque, in New York, where he is famous for his innovative desserts. Here, a chilled light chocolate sauce hides a cache of sautéed banana slices drowned in rum and sugar—a surprising pleasure indeed. He constructs his dessert either in a bowl for 6 or more, or in individual ramekins, and serves it warm, topped by tender swirls of meringue.

Manufacturing Note: In our testing for this fabulous soup, we felt the bananas needed a more serious beefing up—in a figurative way, of course. They must be fully ripe, and our flavoring proportions for them here are more ample than those shown on television. If they're not flavorful, the chocolate dominates rather than accompanies the bananas in a deliciously supportive way. The original recipe calls for 12 ounces of chocolate, which we found gave us too much; we've reduced the amount to 8 ounces.

Techniques: A discussion of chocolates and complete directions for melting chocolate are in the appendix, as are directions for beating egg whites.

Melting the Chocolate: Jacques Torres has his own way of melting chocolate, and uses his hand-held electric blender for a smooth result; always holding it so the whirling blade rests on the bottom of the bowl, he thus avoids high-flying chocolate splatters. His block of chocolate is at room temperature. First he cuts it into flakes ¼ inch thick by holding his large chef's knife at an angle to the chocolate; he presses down hard on the back of the blade so the chocolate pieces flake away. (Or you could break the bar into larger pieces and pulse it into smaller ones in your food processor.) Now turn the chocolate into a 3-quart bowl and pour the hot milk over it. Blend until beautifully smooth, either with your hand-held machine or with a portable mixer, or use a whisk and spoon. (If it cools off too much to blend smoothly, you may very carefully and briefly stir the chocolate over hot water to warm it up again.)

Preparing the Banana Garnish: Peel the bananas, quarter them lengthwise, and cut crosswise into ½-inch pieces. Transfer to a bowl, toss with the cinnamon, then pour on the rum. Set a heavy 10-inch frying pan over high heat, pour in the sugar, and cook until it turns a nice caramel-brown. Immediately swirl in the butter, and when melted, scrape in the bananas and rum—the caramel may harden, but will liquefy in a minute or so as you sauté, turning the banana slices gently with a wooden spoon. Continue

INGREDIENTS FOR 8 SERVINGS

For the chocolate soup

8 ounces best-quality "couverture" semisweet chocolate, at room temperature (for easy cutting up)

3 cups milk, brought to just under the boil

For the banana garnish

5 or 6 fully ripe bananas (just beginning to freckle, but not mushy)

1 teaspoon fragrant ground cinnamon

½ cup dark rum, plus a little more if needed

¾ cup sugar

4 tablespoons unsalted butter

For the meringue decoration

½ cup egg whites (4 "large")

1¼ cups confectioners' sugar

(continued)

Chocolate Soup (continued)

sautéing and turning the bananas for several minutes until the bananas are softened and well caramelized—add droplets more rum, if necessary, to melt the caramel.

Filling the Tureen: Spread the bananas evenly over the bottom of the soup tureen, or divide them evenly among the individual cups, and spoon on enough chocolate to cover the bananas by about ¼ inch, leaving ¼ inch free below the rim of the container. Cover with plastic wrap and chill in the refrigerator for at least an hour.

Ahead-of-Time Note: The dessert may be completed to this point a day in advance. Preheat the oven to 350° F 20 minutes before you plan to serve, and place the rack in the middle level.

Decorating: About half an hour before you plan to serve, set the soup tureen or ramekins in the baking pan and pour boiling water around them, thus allowing them to warm as you work. Whip the egg whites until they begin to foam, then, as you continue whipping, gradually sift in half the confectioners' sugar. When the whites form stiff peaks, sift and fold in the remaining sugar. Scrape the egg whites into the piping bag, and decoratively swirl 1½ to 2 inches of meringue on the top of each dessert. The chocolate should have warmed: test by poking the tip of a small knife down through the meringue into the chocolate and bananas. Leave for 5 seconds, then hold it against your palm—the knife should feel faintly warm.

Baking: Remove the tureen or ramekins from the water bath and set on a baking sheet in the middle level of the preheated 350° F oven. Bake for 6 to 8 minutes, until the meringue is lightly browned, and serve warm.

Ahead-of-Time Note: The desserts will keep warm for a good half hour in the turned-off oven with its door ajar.

SPECIAL EQUIPMENT
SUGGESTED

A hand-held electric blender or a whisk and wooden spoon

An ovenproof 8- to 10-cup shallow decorative bowl or soup tureen, or 8 ramekins holding 8 to 10 ounces each

A freestanding electric mixer with very clean bowl and whip

A fine-meshed sieve or sifter (for the confectioners' sugar and meringue)

A piping bag (a heavy-duty gallon-size plastic bag or a pastry bag) and a ⅜- to ½-inch star tip

A baking pan large enough to hold the tureen or ramekins

A kettle of boiling water

LA FAMEUSE CRÈME BRÛLÉE DU CIRQUE, AU COINTREAU
LE CIRQUE'S FAMOUS CRÈME BRÛLÉE WITH COINTREAU

How fortunate we are that Jacques Torres was able to wheedle this tender, heavenly, utterly remark-able, and beloved recipe from its creator, Francisco Gutierrez, one of Le Cirque's outstanding pastry chefs. It has been on Le Cirque's menu for twelve years, and even in these cream-endangered times it remains in constant demand. Obviously, cream is NC (i.e., nutritionally correct) in certain ex-alted circumstances, and it is the very slow, long cooking that seems to be the key to its glory.

Manufacturing Note: This is a very rich dessert, and you may well find that the following recipe will serve 10 or 12 rather than the 8 specified here.

Preheat the oven to 250° F.

Preparing the Custard: Heat the heavy cream to just below the boiling point. Add the vanilla bean and the orange peel; cover and keep warm. Stir the sugar, egg yolks, and orange liqueur together just until blended—stir, do not beat and cause bubbles. Gradually stir in the hot cream and mix well to dissolve the sugar—again, stir rather than beat. Ladle the custard through the sieve into the molds.

Baking the Custard: Slide the oven rack onto the middle level of the pre-heated oven. Arrange the molds in the baking pan, slide out the rack, and set the pan upon it. Very carefully pour enough boiling water around the molds to come halfway up the sides of them. Even more carefully—so as not to slosh water into the custards—slide the rack back into the oven. Bake about 1 hour, or until the custards are set.

When Are They Done? Test by poking the tip of a paring knife 1 inch from the side of the mold into the custard. The knife should come out clean, but the custard should still tremble slightly—showing it is not overdone. Test a second mold just to be sure. Remove the molds from their water bath and chill on a tray in the refrigerator.

To Serve Hot and Flaming:

Glazing the Custards. Shortly before serving, turn the broiler to high and place the rack so the surfaces of the custards will be about 2 inches below the heat element. Sieve the brown sugar over the tops of the custards and carefully slide them under the hot broiler element, leaving them for

(continued)

INGREDIENTS FOR 8 SERVINGS

For the custard
1 quart heavy cream or half-and-half
1 vanilla bean
1 piece of candied orange peel
¾ cup (5 ounces) sugar
8 egg yolks
3 tablespoons orange liqueur (Cointreau or Grand Marnier), plus a little more for finishing the dessert

For the glazed top
4 ounces light brown sugar

SPECIAL EQUIPMENT SUGGESTED

8 ovenproof oval molds or ramekins, ½-cup capacity, about 1 inch deep, 4 inches at the widest part and 2½ inches at the shortest
A fine-meshed sieve
A baking pan large enough to hold all the molds comfortably
A kettle of boiling water

leaving them for several minutes and watching carefully until the sugar is melted and caramelized.

Flaming. Carefully slide the custards out of the oven and remove them from their water bath. Just before serving, splash a tablespoon of orange liqueur over the hot glaze. Averting your face, ignite with a match and rapidly bring the flaming custards to the table. (Or ignite them at the table.)

To Serve Cold: Glaze the custards as described, but omit the liqueur and flames.

Ahead-of-Time Note: The custards may be cooked several days in advance; cover and refrigerate. Glaze shortly before serving.

BLOOD ORANGE ASPIC

Orange segments, mangoes, and strawberries—all suspended in a fresh orange aspic, and served with more orange segments and a fresh raspberry sauce. This is a very pretty and refreshing dessert for any time of year.

Preparing the Fruit:

The Oranges. Peel the oranges, removing all the white pith. Hold the oranges over a 4-cup measure and cut between the membranes to separate sections; drop them into a bowl. Squeeze the juices out of the remains and into the measure, then squeeze additional oranges as necessary to make 1¼ cups of juice in all.

The Berries and Mangoes. Gently fold the strawberries and mangoes together in another bowl.

Filling the Molds: Arrange a layer of orange segments in a pretty design on the bottom of each mold; cover and refrigerate the remaining segments, which will be for decoration. Fill the molds to the top with the berries and mangoes.

Preparing the Aspic: Pour the gelatin into the saucepan, stir in half the orange juice, and let the gelatin melt over the simmering water—3 to 4 minutes. When perfectly dissolved, remove from heat and pour in the remaining juice; taste, and stir in sugar to your taste. When the sugar has

INGREDIENTS FOR 6 SERVINGS

The fruit
8 blood oranges or navel oranges
⅓ cup sliced fresh strawberries
½ cup diced mango

The aspic
1 envelope (1 tablespoon) of
　plain unflavored gelatin
Sugar to taste

For serving
Chilled raspberry coulis
　(see page 154)

(continued)

Blood Orange Aspic (continued)

dissolved, pour the juice into the molds, filling them to the top. Chill for 2 hours, until well set.

Ahead-of-Time Note: May be prepared to this point not more than a few hours in advance, to preserve the fresh taste of the fruits. Cover well, and keep refrigerated until serving time.

Unmolding: To unmold the aspics, one by one run a thin sharp knife between aspic and mold, at once dip the mold briefly in hot water to loosen the aspic, and invert onto a chilled plate, giving the mold a sharp jerk and a slap on the bottom as you do so. Continue with the rest. Decorate nicely with the chilled orange segments and raspberry coulis. Serve reasonably soon.

SPECIAL EQUIPMENT SUGGESTED

8 molds or coffee cups, ½ cup (4 ounces) each
A small saucepan set over a larger pan of simmering water (for the gelatin)
Chilled dessert plates

cook's notes

JULIA'S STRAWBERRY OR RASPBERRY SAUCE OR COULIS

The sauce of many uses—to accompany ice creams, puddings, custards, and soufflés, to mention a few. Fresh berries are the most desirable, of course, but the packaged frozen ones do nicely out of season.

INGREDIENTS FOR ABOUT 2 CUPS

1 quart fresh strawberries or raspberries, or 2 10-ounce packages of frozen berries, partially defrosted
Sugar ("instant" quick-dissolving recommended) to taste— about 1 cup for fresh berries, 1 tablespoon or so for frozen berries
3 to 4 tablespoons fresh lemon juice

SPECIAL EQUIPMENT SUGGESTED

A food processor or an electric blender
A fine-meshed sieve (if needed)

Puree the berries, half the sugar called for, and 3 tablespoons of lemon juice in the machine, continuing until the sugar is completely dissolved—2 to 3 minutes. Taste carefully to be sure there are no tiny undissolved granules. Puree in more sugar by the spoonful if needed and more lemon juice by droplets. Sieve, if necessary, to remove seeds and seed residue.

Ahead-of-Time Note: Refrigerate in a covered bowl; the sauce will keep for a day or two.

From Julia Child's *The Way to Cook* (Knopf, 1991)

CHOCOLATE CENTERPIECE

Spectacular chocolate sculptures are a Jacques Torres specialty at Le Cirque, and he has been so generous as to show us how he does them. The real secret, besides using the right chocolate and your imaginative designing skills, is knowing how to temper the chocolate. Here his methods are described in detail.

Manufacturing Note about Chocolate: If you are going into fancy chocolate creations like these, do get yourself the right chocolate, which is called "couverture."

Melting the Chocolates:

Double-Boiler Method. (Complete details, including the microwave method, are in the appendix.) Place half the dark chocolate in one of the stainless steel bowls, and the white chocolate in the other. Pour 2 inches of water into each of the saucepans, then lay folded towels over the top of the pans before setting the chocolate bowls into the pans; the towels will keep water and humidity from the chocolate. Bring to the low simmer, and stir occasionally as the chocolates melt. When smooth and lump-free, in 5 to 10 minutes, remove and let the chocolates cool to tepid.

Tempering Chocolate:

Melted dark chocolate needs to be tempered—that is, brought to a certain temperature and consistency—when you wish to spread it out, shape it, and let it harden. Simple melting breaks down the fat structure; if you want to work with it, you must force the chocolate to restructure itself—by tempering. There's no difficulty here; it just takes a little time and observation. Chef Jacques suggests two methods.

The Adding-Cool-Chocolate Method. When the melted chocolate is around 100° F—about blood temperature—stir in a large handful of cold chocolate flakes, beating with the hand-held blender or a wooden spoon. (Be careful not to beat too hard and add air bubbles.) The temperature of the chocolate should gradually drop to about 80° F. To test whether or not it is ready to use, dip the back of a spoon into the chocolate and set it down, back side up. If after 1 minute the chocolate on the back of the spoon keeps its shape when you touch it, the chocolate has been tempered.

2 pounds of best-quality semisweet "couverture" chocolate, cut into flakes ¼ inch thick (as described for the Chocolate Soup on page 149)

1 pound white chocolate, also flaked

2 cups pralines (see page 158; optional)

SPECIAL EQUIPMENT SUGGESTED

Two 8-inch 3-quart stainless steel bowls set on top of 2 saucepans (for melting the chocolates)

A hand-held electric blender

An instant meat thermometer is recommended

1 or more large stiff plastic sheets (about 2 by 2 feet—available in an art supply or a florist shop)

(continued)

Chocolate Centerpiece (continued)

The Sitting Method. Set the warm melted chocolate aside in the kitchen, and when it begins to set up around the edges, stir it about to smooth and cool it, then begin testing, as described above.

Forming Chocolate Shapes:

White Chocolate Designs on Dark Chocolate.

Lay a piece of stiff plastic down on the counter. In order for the finished dark chocolate shapes to have white chocolate designs, the white chocolate pattern is applied first to the plastic, as follows. Either make polka dots of white chocolate on the plastic with your finger, or lay a piece of aluminum lattice or other cutout form down in one corner of the plastic and spread the white chocolate over it so it forms a pattern when you lift off the aluminum. Let set for several minutes.

Cover the white chocolate design with dark chocolate, spreading it evenly over the white chocolate with the offset spatula. Let it set for several minutes, then place one of the templates over the design and cut around it with a small sharp knife, going right down through the plastic. Use round-shaped templates to cut circles and half-moons. You can also cut free-form shapes like triangles and squiggles. Arrange the pieces, still on their plastic backing, on baking sheets; refrigerate for at least 10 minutes.

Bubble Wrap. Spread the melted chocolate on a piece of bubble wrap and refrigerate. Pull the bubble wrap away when set.

Actual Chocolate Mold. Pour the melted tempered chocolate into a very clean, dry mold, using a rubber spatula to spread it around. Tap the mold on your counter, or tap the sides of the mold with the back of a knife, to get rid of any bubbles. Once the mold is coated, pour off the excess chocolate, clean off the edges, and refrigerate.

Ahead-of-Time Note: May be done weeks in advance; when chilled, cover with plastic wrap.

When you are ready to work, remove the chocolate from the refrigerator. Peel the plastic away and proceed with the building of the centerpiece.

Forming the Centerpiece

Since there are no rules here, be as elaborate or as simple or as incongruous as you please. For the relatively sedate example pictured here, peel the chocolate away from the back of a large flat piece, perhaps a heart with dots

Various molds, pans, and forms of different shapes for creating templates and other designs, such as a piece of perforated aluminum lattice from the hardware store, bubble wrap (plastic wrapping material), metal cake pans, and so forth

An offset spatula—a special pastry spatula with a bent blade—desirable but not essential

(continued)

Chocolate Centerpiece (continued)

of white chocolate. Set it on a flat plate, and stand other pieces on edge upon it, cementing them in place with a brush of the melted chocolate. The chocolate works as glue. When you cut the bases of some pieces on a slant, like the triangles here, they will tilt, adding an extra element to your design.

Ahead-of-Time Note: Covered loosely with plastic wrap, the finished centerpiece will keep in a cool spot, perhaps your wine cellar, for at least a month.

PRALINES
PRALINS—PRALINES

These sweetly crunchy, sugary nuts remind Chef Jacques of his native Bandol on the Mediterranean, where vendors hawk them in the streets and on the sunny beaches. They're a very French treat to end a meal—or to garnish his elegant chocolate centerpiece on page 155.

A Note on the Name: French *pralins* are individual nuts with a plain sugar coating, in contrast to the New Orleans pralines, which are a group of nuts in a flat cake of brown and white sugars.

INGREDIENTS FOR 2 CUPS

1½ cups (about ½ pound) sugar
½ cup water
2 cups shelled almonds either blanched or not, or walnuts, pine nuts, hazelnuts, pecans, pistachios—all one kind or a mixture

Manufacturing Note: Before you begin cooking, ready your work surface, since things happen very fast when you are working with caramel. Remember, too, that any sugar syrup is burning hot—don't touch anything with your fingers until the nuts have cooled off. The whole process should take less than 10 minutes.

Blend the sugar and water in a heavy two-quart saucepan and bring to the boil. Using a heavy metal spoon, stir in the nuts and bring to the boil again. Reduce heat to moderate and continue boiling and stirring as the sugar begins to crystallize and finally turns sandy. Keep boiling and stirring a few seconds more until suddenly the nuts become coated with sandy crystallized sugar and begin to separate from each other. At once turn them out onto your prepared work surface, spread them apart, and let them cool.

Note: If you keep boiling and stirring after the nuts have separated in the pan, the sugar coating will begin to darken a sandy brown, and can turn into a clear caramel coating. You may be able to bring back the crystallized effect by continued stirring and boiling and by scraping crystallized sugar from the sides of the pan back into the nuts. When successful, your coating will then be a nice sandy brown.

Whatever happens, serve them up and don't apologize—they are quite irresistible however you present them. (Even Chef Jacques has had his troubles with the stage II—the caramel.)

Ahead-of-Time Note: If you can fend off the vandals, your *pralines* will keep for a good month or more in a covered container.

REED HEARON

His degrees in mathematics and philosophy hardly seem the ideal preparation for life in a professional kitchen. But then, considering how logical Chef Reed Hearon is about food, it may all fit. The young chef has an extraordinarily practical approach to the culinary bounty available to him: choose the finest, best-tasting ingredients and "don't get in their way." He observes with benevolent amusement young apprentices whose idea of cooking is to be wildly creative all of the time. To Reed that means making things that are rather "improbable."

"Food reflects our culture and my food is very much part of today's neo-modern minimalism." Minimal in no way means boring. Reed not only coaxes the maximum of obvious flavors from his ingredients, he also retrieves surprising "hidden" ones. His skillet mussels, for example, have no seasoning whatsoever, but when the mussels open, they release their juices into the hot skillet, creating a subtle smokiness. The dish may be the chef's idea of philosophically sound cuisine—more important, it's plainly delicious.

Reed's culinary pedigree is as impressive as his academic credentials. He began his career in an Austin, Texas, restaurant, learning the classic techniques from cookbooks. After two years he applied for a job with Jimmy Schmidt, who was about to open what would prove to be the exceedingly popular Rattlesnake Club in Denver. Reed suspected it was a long shot, but it happened that Schmidt needed someone who was familiar with southwestern food. Reed actually knew little about it, but he was used to learning from books and he plunged in. His success led to his being asked by Mark Miller to open his Sante Fe Coyote Cafe. More successes followed, which eventually culminated in Reed's opening not one but three San Francisco restaurants—Lulu, Cafe Marimba, and Lulu Bis—in the same year. He seems to revel in it. "It is obviously a business, and it is about theater and showmanship and all of that." A bustling theater is exactly the feeling at Lulu's, where dishes such as his crisp Frito Misto of Artichokes and Fennel are served family style on bright, hand-painted platters, and Iron Skillet Mussels, still sizzling and spurting, arrive at the table by the panful.

AÏOLI
THE FAMOUS MEDITERRANEAN GARLIC MAYONNAISE

A real aïoli, *such as this vigorous example from Chef Reed Hearon, is one of those uncluttered classics whose simple basics just cannot be improved upon—the best and freshest garlic pounded together with a minimum of egg yolks and the very best olive oil you can find. A little salt is all that Chef Reed adds, although he will allow pepper and drops of lemon juice for those who insist. In fact, with enough garlic, you can omit the egg yolks altogether; the object is to encourage the emulsion process. An* aïoli *is particularly good with simple fare like plain grilled fish, chicken, boiled and fried vegetables—but it really goes with almost anything, according to our chef.*

Manufacturing Note: To get the real Mediterranean feeling, you'll want to build your *aïoli* in an immense heirloom marble mortar—what a lovely experience to listen to all that slapping and swooshing. If you don't have one, you can make your *aïoli* by hand according to the directions below, but Chef Reed does not recommend a food processor or a blender since they incorporate too much air.

Techniques: For directions on mincing and pureeing garlic by hand, see the box on page 127.

Making Aïoli *by Mortar and Pestle:* Drop the egg yolks and the garlic into the mortar and pound them together with the pestle to mash the garlic into a fine paste, adding a big pinch of salt as you pound. Continue to crush and pound until the eggs are a sticky pale yellow and the garlic is completely pureed. Begin drizzling in the oil by droplets, mashing and stirring to form a thick, creamy, smooth emulsion. An *aïoli* is much thicker and stiffer than a mayonnaise—but if it is unmanageably stiff and sticky, thin it out little by little with ½-teaspoons of water. Taste, and season carefully with salt. Chef Reed uses no pepper, but you may grind some in along with droplets of lemon juice if you wish.

Making Aïoli *by Hand:* Puree the garlic as directed on page 127. Pick it up with the side of the knife and deposit it in the bowl. Whisk in the egg yolks and continue until the garlic and yolks are thick, sticky, and pale yellow. Gradually whisk in the oil by droplets, keeping the whisk against the bottom of the bowl to avoid incorporating air. Season carefully with salt, and with pepper and drops of lemon juice if you wish.

INGREDIENTS FOR ABOUT ¾ CUP

2 "large" egg yolks

2 large fresh firm unblemished garlic cloves, peeled and cut in half, visible green shoots removed

Salt

About 1 cup excellent best-quality olive oil

A few drops of fresh lemon juice (optional)

SPECIAL EQUIPMENT SUGGESTED

A mortar with large heavy pestle or a sturdy whisk and bowl

(continued)

Ahead-of-time Note: You may make an *aïoli* several hours in advance—if kept more than about half an hour, cover and refrigerate. The chef does not recommend longer storage since the garlic can lose its freshness: it is at its glorious best when freshly made and served at room temperature.

FRITO MISTO OF ARTICHOKES AND FENNEL

Chef Reed's Italian-inspired mixed fry is an inviting appetizer, with its array of baby artichokes, fennel, and lemon all cloaked in wispy shavings of Parmesan cheese. The artichokes are double deep-fried—the first frying, which may be done well in advance, cooks them tender, while the second produces that ideal combination of crisp brown exterior and meltingly creamy interior. The chef recommends that you serve this dish with a chilled Santa Ynez Valley Vin Gris in a leaf-strewn garden dappled with sunshine and cooled by soft breezes.

Frying Note: To avoid having the oil boil over the side of the pan, keep a dry utensil, such as a big kitchen spoon, nearby; if the oil threatens to erupt, dip the spoon gingerly into the surface bubbles to break them up and prevent a messy disaster.

Preparing the Artichokes:

Preliminaries. To prevent the artichokes from discoloring, prepare an acidulated water bath by squeezing the juice of the 4 lemons into the bowl of cold water, then dropping in the lemons. While you are cleaning the artichokes, dip them in and out of the acidulated water to keep them from browning.

Removing the Leaves. To remove the outside leaves, one by one bend a leaf back upon itself until it snaps, then pull the leaf off, leaving the edible bottom attached to the artichoke. Continue all around until you have exposed the tender yellow leaves near the heart, dipping the artichoke frequently into the acidulated water. Then, using a small sharp stainless steel knife, trim around the bottom to remove the tough green areas. Trim and peel the stem; holding the artichoke bottom up, trim all around the bottom to expose the tender yellow-white flesh. Slice off the green area at the top of the artichoke leaves; then cut the artichoke in half lengthwise. If a little thistle (choke) is visible, cut it out. Drop the trimmed artichokes into the acidulated water. When all are prepared, cover with a folded kitchen towel, dampening it in the water, and keep the artichokes submerged until you are ready to cook them.

INGREDIENTS FOR 4 SERVINGS

For the artichokes
4 lemons
24 baby artichokes
Peanut oil
Sea salt

The fennel and lemon
1 small fennel bulb
1 lemon
*About ½ cup all-purpose flour
   (for coating)*
Sea salt
Freshly ground black pepper

For serving
*About 1 tablespoon excellent
   top-quality olive oil*
*A 3- to 4-ounce wedge of
   Parmesan cheese*
*Aïoli (garlic mayonnaise;
   see opposite)*

(continued)

Frito Misto (continued)

First Frying or "Blanching" of the Artichokes: Drain the artichokes and spin them dry in the salad spinner. Pour the oil into the frying pan and bring to a temperature of 320° F. Test one artichoke by dropping it into the hot oil—it should sizzle—then carefully add all the artichokes. Fry until lightly golden and tender when poked with the tip of a knife, 2 to 3 minutes. Transfer with the strainer to paper towels. Reserve the oil in the pan.

Ahead-of-Time Note: The first frying may be done several hours in advance.

Preparing the Fennel and Lemon: Trim the top and the root end off the fennel. Cut the bulb in half lengthwise and remove the core with a V-shaped cut. Use the mandoline or a very sharp knife to make paper-thin slices along its cut side. Slice one end off the lemon to create a flat surface and then shave the lemon into thin slivers. Shortly before you are ready to fry, reheat the frying oil to 400° F. Pour the flour onto a flat plate and stir in salt and pepper. Toss the fennel in the flour, coating on all sides, shake off the excess, and set aside. Repeat with the lemon slices. (The artichokes are not floured.)

SPECIAL EQUIPMENT
SUGGESTED

*A bowl of cold water large
    enough to hold the
    artichokes submerged*
A salad spinner
A mandoline (vegetable slicer)
*A deep-fat fryer with basket
    or a 10- to 12-inch straight-
    sided frying pan, at least
    4 inches deep*
A wire-mesh strainer
*A baking pan or tray lined with
    paper towels*
A vegetable peeler

Ahead-of-Time Note: Although the fennel and lemon may be cut ahead, they should be coated just before frying.

Second and Final Frying: First, carefully lower the artichokes into the hot oil, then the fennel, and finally (with great care because they may spatter) the lemons. Fry just until the artichokes are browned and crisp on the outside—less than a minute. Remove all with the strainer to the paper towels to drain briefly.

Serving: Immediately transfer them to a bowl and sprinkle lightly with salt, pepper, and a dribble of the olive oil; toss the bowl to distribute the seasoning evenly, then pour the mixed fry onto a platter. Use the vegetable peeler to shave 10 to 12 long slivers of Parmesan on top and serve with lemon wedges and a bowl of *aïoli*.

IRON SKILLET MUSSELS

Chef Reed considers this dish to epitomize his style of cooking at Lulu's—it is a clean and simple dish in which the mussels do all the work. When they open and release their juices into the hot pan, the action causes a smoking that flavors the mussels, so much so that most customers think they were cooked in a wood oven. In fact, they are cooked with absolutely no seasoning whatsoever and no liquid which would dilute their own ocean flavor.

Manufacturing Note: Farm-raised mussels work particularly well for this dish since they are grown in clusters suspended in the water on ropes so they develop no grit.

Cleaning the Mussels: Scrub the mussels under water until the shells feel perfectly smooth and clean. Use your fingers or the edge of a sharp knife to pull off their beards.

The Sizzling of the Mussels: Preheat the skillet for 5 minutes over moderate heat until the pan is very hot, indeed, about 4 minutes. Spread the mussels directly on the hot skillet, adding no oil, butter, or other ingredients. The mussels will sizzle and pop. Work in batches if the skillet is too small to allow all the mussels to come in contact with the hot surface. Cook over high heat until they open, about 2 minutes.

Serving: Sprinkle the mussels with salt and pepper and serve directly from the skillet with the drawn butter, still in its melting pan, alongside for dipping.

INGREDIENTS FOR 4 SERVINGS

1 pound farm-raised mussels, such as Pen Cove or Prince Edward Island
Sea salt
Freshly ground black pepper
About 1 cup melted butter

SPECIAL EQUIPMENT SUGGESTED

A 12-inch cast-iron "fajita" skillet, or round cast-iron griddle, or round cast-iron frying pan

ROASTED SALT-ENCRUSTED COD

Encasing a fish or a whole chicken or even a loin of beef in a salt crust is a classic method of hermetically sealing foods to be roasted so that all the flavors and juices are captured inside. Here Reed Hearon takes on a whole cod and the result is a fish that maintains the essence of the sea in which it swam. There is, in addition, the high drama of bringing this browned pillar of salt to the table and breaking it open to the amazement of the multitude.

Manufacturing Note: This is a technique for whole round fish—cod- or salmon-shaped. It is not suitable for flatfish. You can mix some water with the egg whites, but the effect will not be as colorful—not recommended by our team!

Mixing the Salt for the Crust: Preheat the oven to 500° F. Measure the salt into the mixing bowl and use a large wooden spoon to stir in the egg whites, mixing vigorously until you have formed a thick white paste.

Encrusting the Fish: Using a quarter of the salt paste, make a bed in the bottom of the baking dish, covering the entire surface. Lay the fish on top of the salt, letting 3 or 4 inches of the tail drape over the edge if necessary. Pat the rest of the salt over and around the fish, sealing it in completely—except for the possible bit of overhanging tail.

Roasting the Fish: Place the pan in the preheated 500° F oven and roast for about 20 minutes.

INGREDIENTS FOR 4 SERVINGS

The salt crust and fish
5 pounds sea salt
1 quart egg whites (see box on this page)
One fine fresh whole 3½- to 4-pound cod, scaled and eviscerated, head on, gills removed

For serving
A colorful bed of tomatoes and braised baby vegetables (see box, page 168)
Aïoli (garlic mayonnaise; see page 160)

(continued)

JULIA'S CALCULATIONS FOR EGG WHITES IN SALT-ENCRUSTED FISH

This sounds like an extravagant formula: 5 pounds of sea salt and 1 quart of egg whites! However, look at it this way:

1 quart egg whites = 32 ounces

1 "large" egg white = 2 tablespoons

2 tablespoons = 1 ounce

32 ounces = 1 quart = 32 eggs

Every time you make an 8-yolk *crème anglaise* custard sauce (and we have many of them in this book), save all the whites and freeze them; after your fourth custard you will be ready for your salt-encrusted cod.

Roasted Salt-Encrusted Cod (continued)

When Is It Done? Since you can't see the fish, you have to know what to look for. The salt will have turned decidedly golden brown. Listen for the sound of boiling liquid and look for wisps of steam rising—the escaping fish juices. You should also smell the delicious aroma of roasting fish. Remove it from the oven.

Breaking the Crust and Serving the Fish: Do this either in the kitchen or at the table. The fish will be very hot, and the salt crust will hold the heat, so you have a good 10 minutes or more to make arrangements.

Breaking the Crust. Using the back of the heavy knife or the hammer, whack open the salt crust in one or more places. Then, with the knife and the spatula, lift off the crusted pieces. Switch to a large spoon and scoop out some of the soft salt underneath. Sweep salt off the top and sides of the fish with the pastry brush.

Serving. Arrange the vegetables either on the hot platter or dinner plates, and set the *aïoli* at your side. Using the tip of a clean spoon and the side of a dinner fork, carefully scrape away the skin. Lift large pieces of fish up with the spatula and place on top of the bed of vegetables. After removing all of the top fillet, lift out the bone and continue serving the bottom fillet, scooping up the juices and ladling them over the servings of fish. Nap each serving with a spoonful of *aïoli* and pass the rest of the sauce separately.

SPECIAL EQUIPMENT
SUGGESTED

*A 5- or 6-quart mixing bowl
   (for the salt)*

*An ovenproof dish, preferably
   oval, large enough to hold the
   whole fish (a bit of the tail
   may protrude)*

*A heavy knife or a hammer
   (to break the crust)*

*A large metal spatula or two,
   and a large kitchen spoon
   (for removing the fish)*

*A pastry brush (for whisking off
   excess salt)*

A hot platter or dinner plates

SAND DABS À LA PLANCHA

In Spain whole fish are often cooked à la plancha—*that is, directly on a hot griddle—and Chef Reed found the straightforward simplicity of this cooking method most appealing. He uses it for a variety of flatfish and even for fillets.*

Fish Fry Note: The fish must fit in one layer in the pan. Ideally, you cook the fish whole, heads and tails on. If your equipment cannot accommodate a whole fish, feel free to trim it to fit your requirements. Use two pans if necessary, or cook in two or even three batches.

Preparing the Fish: Using kitchen shears and working close to the body, cut the fins off the back and sides of the fish. Place the fish in a flat dish and drizzle on enough olive oil to coat them well all over. Season both sides with salt and pepper.

Frying the First Side: Heat the pan or pans until smoking hot, approximately 4 minutes. Lay the fish on the hot surface. Fry on the first side until the color begins to change around the edges and the fish may be lifted from the pan with the spatula.

Frying the Other Side: Turn the fish over to brown and cook on the other side—don't worry if some skin has adhered to the pan. As the fish cook, scatter some of the garlic and drop a nugget of butter next to each fish. Let the butter brown, and frequently turn the garlic slices over to brown them evenly; work right next to the fish so the flavors melt around it. Reduce the heat if the cooking appears to be going too fast. After a minute or so, add the peppers to the garlic and continue turning the vegetables and tucking them a little way under the side of the fish.

When Is It Done? The fish will take a total of about 5 minutes to cook. You can check by poking a thin knife through the flesh in the side and feeling for the bone; it should lift easily away from the flesh. Don't overcook; the flesh must remain quite juicy.

Finishing the Dish: Squeeze lemon juice on top of each piece of fish, turn it over briefly so the second side picks up the skillet flavors, turn it back again, and transfer to a warm platter or dinner plate. Pour or scoop the pan

(continued)

INGREDIENTS FOR 4 SERVINGS

For the fish
8 West Coast sand dabs, about
    6 ounces each, or 4 flounders
    or sole, about 1 pound each
Olive oil
Sea salt
Freshly ground black pepper

For the garnish
8 large garlic cloves, peeled and
    sliced very thin
1 stick (4 ounces) unsalted butter
8 arbol chiles or other small dried
    red chiles, left whole
1½ to 2 lemons
Italian flat-leaf parsley leaves

**SPECIAL EQUIPMENT
SUGGESTED**

Kitchen shears
A flat cast-iron griddle, "fajita"
    skillet, or frying pan—
    whatever heavy pan or pans
    you have large enough to hold
    the fish in one layer
A wide metal spatula

Sand Dabs (continued)

sauce and vegetables over the fish; garnish with parsley leaves, and serve immediately.

Variation: Rather than using butter, garlic, and peppers, you may finish the fish in a very Spanish and Portuguese way by simply drizzling on a little excellent olive oil and drops of fresh lemon juice. A parsley sprinkle will cover any skin breaks.

A BED OF VEGETABLES

At Reed Hearon's Lulu in San Francisco, they usually serve family-style platters of beautiful food garnished with or arranged on a colorful bed of vegetables. Under your salt-baked fish, for instance, may lie a collection of carefully cooked baby carrots, artichokes, yellow pattypans, and red Bliss potatoes. What these jewels are depends on the season and the day's market, and the variety changes daily.

The cooking is simple: the chef will braise a platterful of assorted vegetables together in a wide covered pan with a tablespoon of butter, a big pinch of salt, and a little water—perhaps half a cup, adding more if needed. He cooks them very slowly over very low heat for half an hour or more, until they are thoroughly tender.

Little potatoes, as an example, are left whole and scrubbed clean if really small; otherwise they are halved. Baby artichokes are trimmed down to their delicate yellow centers, while round little carrots and turnips are peeled, leaving a tuft of green stem still visible. When you are making your selection, think about similar sizes and a mix of colors.

Haricots verts, those small slim (always expensive!) green beans, are first blanched in boiling salted water until almost tender, drained, quickly "shocked" in ice water to set the color, then added to the cooked vegetables for a moment to warm through.

Some vegetables, like the small purple-tinged Italian onions (*cipolline*), diminutive Japanese eggplant, and baby zucchini, are brushed with a little olive oil and carefully grilled. Chef Reed loves to add rare species of raw tomato to his collection, and will take all sizes, shapes, and colors—from orange and yellow to zebra stripes and fuzzy-skinned peach-colored tomatoes. Living where he does, with farmer's markets and small-scale specialized growers in the area anxious to furnish him with esoterica, he is particularly blessed.

Few of us have such abundance easily at hand, but we can act imaginatively on his ideas, cutting up adult vegetables to create babies, and having fun making things beautiful.

cook's notes

LYNNE ROSSETTO KASPER

"What I set out to do was to understand how food worked," explained Lynne Rossetto Kasper. "I believed that once I understood how it worked, I could do anything." "Anything" turned out to be twenty years of consulting, lecturing, writing, and teaching about food. A decade of research led to the publication of her cookbook, *The Splendid Table: Recipes from Emilia-Romagna, the Heartland of Northern Italian Food* (William Morrow), the first book ever to win both the James Beard Cookbook of the Year and the Julia Child Best Cookbook of the Year awards.

In her book, and indeed in all her work, which includes a background in Asian and French food as well as Italian, Lynne explores her passion for artisan food traditions, agricultural history, and cultural heritage. Educating others about the connection between delicious-tasting food and responsible production is an important aspect of her work. "It *is* possible to nurture ourselves while we nurture and sustain our earth," says Lynne. She believes that organic programs that emphasize locally grown products not only teach us luscious ways of eating low on the food chain but also promote insight into and compassion for other people. "Food can be our vital and immediate link, our way of touching those 'other' than ourselves."

Lynne has serious food goals, but don't for a minute expect her work to be lacking in fun. This warm, vibrant, theatrically trained woman is a riveting storyteller whose enthusiasm is highly contagious. As she cooked in the Cambridge kitchen, pouring tiny sips of age-old balsamic vinegar, savoring olive oils before choosing the one with which to anoint her great herbed leg of lamb, and carefully tossing a bowl of intensely flavored pasta, it was easy to get caught up in her Italian passion.

GREEN BEANS WITH WALNUTS AND MORTADELLA

Mortadella is that enormous round sausage 6 to 7 inches in diameter that originated in Bologna. As Lynne explains, a fine mortadella is in fact a mousse of pork subtly flavored with herbs and spices, and Italians number it among their greatest sausages. Top-quality mortadella is a delicious treat when cut into wedges of respectable ⅜-inch thickness and passed around as recherché *cocktail finger food. Diced and lightly sautéed to release its savory essences, it mingles delightfully with fresh green beans and walnuts in the following dish.*

Steam the beans early in the day, rinsing them under cold running water to stop the cooking process and to set the color. Complete the recipe shortly before serving. (More information about green bean cookery is in the box opposite.)

About 8 to 10 minutes before serving, pour the olive oil into the pan and set over moderately high heat. Stir in the mortadella and sauté for a minute or two to warm and release its flavor without browning it. Turn in the beans, seasoning them lightly with salt and pepper; toss and turn gently together for several minutes. When well heated through, toss in the walnuts; continue tossing and turning so that all is heated. Carefully check seasoning; serve the beans at once.

cook's notes

INGREDIENTS FOR 6 TO 8 SERVINGS

1¼ to 1½ pounds fine fresh green beans, trimmed

1 teaspoon excellent olive oil

1-ounce piece of mortadella, ¼ inch thick, diced (⅓ cup)

Salt

Freshly ground black pepper to taste

½ cup broken walnut pieces, toasted 5 to 10 minutes at 350° F

SPECIAL EQUIPMENT SUGGESTED

A 12-inch sauté or frying pan
Two wooden spatulas
A warm serving bowl

JULIA'S NOTES ON COOKING GREEN BEANS

Cooked green vegetables should be beautifully green, and just cooked through. As the great Escoffier wrote, introducing green beans in his *Guide culinaire,* they are "the most exquisite of vegetables, but they must be prepared with the greatest care. They are best when a little firm to the tooth, but without exaggeration." Great care, certainly, but there is nothing difficult about cooking a bean. You may either steam green beans, which is fast and easy and works well for small quantities, or boil them—and you can cook them several hours in advance without losing their fresh quality.

To steam green beans and other green vegetables: Set a steamer basket with the vegetables into a saucepan just large enough to hold it tightly covered. Add an inch of water, bring to the boil, and cover the pan tightly. Regulate heat to moderate. Green beans will take only 3 to 5 minutes if really fresh—watch attentively that you do not overcook, and taste a sample frequently until the beans are done. If you are not serving them at once, immediately refresh the beans in iced water to stop the cooking and set the color.

The big boil: This is more cumbersome than steaming, but it is recommended for large quantities. The immense amount of boiling water means the beans will come quickly to the boil, and the rapid cooling in ice water stops the cooking and sets the color. Bring a large kettle of water to the boil—6 quarts of water for 2 pounds of beans. Provide yourself with a colander and have two trays of ice cubes available. When the water is at the rolling boil, drop in the trimmed and washed beans. Add 2 tablespoons of salt (for 6 quarts of water), and cover the kettle for a minute or two until the boil is reached again. At once remove the cover and boil uncovered; after several minutes, begin tasting as a test, and keep tasting. They are done when they are just cooked through but still have the slightest crunch. Drain immediately, and either serve at once or immediately return the beans to the kettle and run cold water over them. When half full, drain again, add the ice to the kettle and cold water to cover. Drain in 5 minutes or so, when thoroughly chilled.

The finish: Whichever method you use, the drained and cooked beans are now ready to be reheated, or to be served cold in a salad.

Ahead-of-Time Note: The beans may be cooked several hours in advance, but to keep their freshly cooked taste, I always dry them thoroughly in clean towels, then refrigerate them in a covered bowl.

ROASTED LAMB INSPIRED BY THE RENAISSANCE
AGNELLO AL FORNO

Lynne Rossetto Kasper's inspiration for this dish was a chat about the history of food in Italy, over a good meal with friends in Ferrara. As they mused over the Renaissance's strong influence on the modern cuisine of Ferrara, she realized that the once popular orange flavorings were seldom used today in that area. She decided to bring back the orange. Playing orange zest against garlic, the piquancy of anchovy, and the gentle perfume of basil, she likes the way the orange rounds out flavors while the black brine-cured olives, roasting in the pan juices, serve as a special backdrop to the meat and its seasonings. Lynne suggests that the wine to accompany her lamb be a Sangiovese di Romagna Riserva, or a Cabernet Sauvignon from the hills of Friuli or Bologna.

(continued)

Roasted Lamb (continued)

Manufacturing Note: The lamb is marinated for 24 hours before roasting.

Preliminaries—the day before:

Trimming and Trussing the Lamb. Trim the lamb with a sharp knife, removing as much of the fat and fell as you possibly and patiently can—the naked meat should be visible on all sides. Cut away any extraneous pieces of meat and reserve them for another use. Scrape the shank bone clean with the side of a sharp knife, from ankle to just below the knee. Tie the lamb with butcher's twine to secure it in a neat bundle. Pierce the meat all over on both sides at 2-inch intervals with the tip of a small knife, making incisions 1 inch deep and wide enough to accommodate the tip of your index finger.

Preparing the Marinade. Drop the orange zest into the strainer and submerge in the saucepan of boiling water for 3 minutes; drain. With the processor running, drop the garlic through the feed tube; immediately drop in the orange zest, anchovies, and basil, and when roughly mixed, pour in the olive oil. Process for just 2 to 3 seconds, only until the mixture is chopped and blended but not pureed. Turn off the machine; add the lemon juice and pepper; process only a few seconds more, until the ingredients are evenly combined and coarsely chopped.

INGREDIENTS FOR 6 TO 8 SERVINGS

For the marinade

A whole bone-in leg of lamb, about 10 pounds (shank bone left on intact; sirloin and hipbone removed and reserved for another use)

The shredded zest (colored part of peel only) of 4 large firm-skinned oranges

6 large garlic cloves, smashed and peeled

3 anchovy fillets (rinsed and boned if they are salted anchovies; for notes on anchovies, see box, page 175)

12 to 14 large leaves of fine fresh basil

3 tablespoons excellent olive oil

1 tablespoon fresh lemon juice

½ teaspoon freshly ground black pepper

Salt

For roasting the lamb

Salt

Freshly ground black pepper

1½ cups good dry red wine

1 cup unpitted brine-cured black olives, such as Ligurian or Kalamata

For the sauce

½ cup fine strong lamb, veal, or chicken stock

2 teaspoons best-quality tomato paste

(continued)

Marinating the Lamb. Using your fingers, push teaspoonfuls of the marinade into the inch-deep incisions you made in the lamb. Rub whatever doesn't fit inside the slits over the outside of the meat. Place the lamb either on a stainless steel or glass platter and cover loosely with plastic wrap, or enclose the lamb loosely in an open plastic bag and set it in a roasting pan. (Lynne likes a little air circulation around her meat!) Refrigerate overnight or up to 24 hours.

Roasting the Lamb: Preheat the oven to 350° F. Season the meat generously with salt and pepper and set it best side up in a shallow roasting pan—preferably a jelly-roll pan. Lynne wants the heat of the oven to surround the meat, but she does not use a rack. Roast for 20 minutes, then pour a cup of the red wine over the lamb and continue roasting. After another 15 to 20 minutes, rapidly (so as not to cool off the oven) strew the olives around in the pan, and baste the meat with the pan juices, adding a little more wine if the juices threaten to burn. Continue roasting, rapidly basting every 15 minutes or so—add a little water to the pan if you run out of wine and the juices are evaporating. After a total of 1¼ hours start testing just to be sure—a large leg of lamb this size should take a good 1½ hours, but much depends on the thickness of the meat, how cold it was when it went in, and how much the oven cooled off during the frequent bastings.

When Is It Done? Insert your instant-read meat thermometer into the thickest part of solid meat, not letting it touch any bone; and let the tip penetrate at least an inch. Watch the needle rise just until it stabilizes—about 5 seconds. (If the thermometer is left in longer, the temperature reading will rise about 10 degrees as the hot juices from the surface circulate back into the body of the meat.)

130° F = blood rare

135° F = rare (the meat is a good red)

140° F = medium rare ("blushed with pink," as Lynne Rossetto Kasper would say—and as she prefers it)

Finishing the Lamb: Transfer the lamb to the warm platter and slip it into the turned-off oven, leaving the door ajar—it must rest 15 to 20 minutes before carving so that the juices will be reabsorbed into the meat. If the wait is longer, tent it with foil.

(continued)

SPECIAL EQUIPMENT
SUGGESTED

Butcher's twine (unwaxed plain white cotton twine)

A zester (useful but not essential)

A strainer sitting in a saucepan just large enough to hold it submerged in boiling water

A food processor fitted with steel blade

A shallow roasting pan or a jelly-roll pan

A bulb baster or a large spoon (for basting)

A large heated platter

A warm sauce bowl

Roasted Lamb (continued)

Preparing the Sauce: Meanwhile, skim the fat from the juices in the roasting pan, set the pan over two burners on the stove top, and turn them on to high. Stir in the stock and the tomato paste, and boil over high heat to deglaze the pan, scraping up coagulated roasting juices with a wooden spatula. Let the liquid reduce by about half, to develop a deep, rich flavor. Correct seasoning and transfer the sauce and olives to the warm sauce bowl.

Serving: If the lamb is to be joined by Lynne Rossetto Kasper's green beans and mortadella, turn them out on one side of the platter. Spoon a little of the sauce over the meat and bring both to the table. Lynne likes the French carving method, where you tilt the leg up by its shank, holding the end of it with a clean napkin, and make elegant long thin slices parallel to the bone. Accompany each serving with a spoonful of sauce, a scattering of olives, and a helping of those beautiful green beans.

JULIA'S NOTES ON ANCHOVIES

Salted anchovies are a little bigger than canned anchovies and have wonderful flavor, but they are not always easy to find unless you go to an Italian market district. I had thought that because they are salted they would keep indefinitely. They'll keep, says my Italian market source, Joe Pace, whose shop is in Boston's North End, but they begin to lose quality after a can is opened. It is better to buy only as many anchovies as you need from a big can that's been freshly opened in the store, and if you don't use them all within a few days, to wash the salt off and refrigerate the anchovies in a closed jar of olive oil. But use them soon if you want to get the best flavor from them.

If you are using anchovies just for flavor, as in Lynne Rossetto Kasper's lamb marinade, simply rinse off the salt, split them open to remove the central bone, and they are ready. If, however, you want to eat them in salads and appetizers, they need more work. To prepare them, wash off the salt, then soak the anchovies in several changes of cold water until softened—this will take 30 minutes or so if they are from a fresh can—up to an hour or more if not. Test by filleting one—lay it on a board and with two forks separate one side from the central bone, then lift up and discard the bone from the fillet and remove any extraneous bits by running your fork along the length of the fillets. Taste a bit, and if still too salty, soak 5 to 10 minutes more.

To serve, you might arrange them in a dish and baste with a good vinaigrette, or with a little olive oil, pepper, oregano, and a spoonful of capers.

Ready-to-eat anchovies go off in taste within a few hours whether previously canned or salted. Open or prepare only what you plan to consume within a couple of hours. Their fragility may be the reason many people just hate anchovies—they've been eating stale ones.

SUNDAY NIGHT PASTA WITH BALSAMIC VINEGAR
PASTA DI DOMINICA CON ACETO BALSAMICO

In Italy, Sunday night suppers are usually light affairs since everyone has had a big midday meal with friends out in the country or at a family gathering. Lynne's "Sunday Night" supper is a variation on Italy's popular pasta dressed with garlic and olive oil, pasta aglio olio, *but hers goes a good step farther by blending mellow, slow-cooked garlic with the bright, fresh taste of barely cooked tomatoes, fresh green herbs—and a final anointing with sweet, rich balsamic vinegar. This is a lovely simple basic pasta, typical of the best Italian cooking, which depends on the beauty of its ingredients. There should be no waiting around when it's ready—it is to be served and eaten at once.*

Preliminaries:

Slow-Cooking the Garlic. Pour enough olive oil into the sauté pan to film the bottom lightly. Stir in the garlic, season with a sprinkling of salt and pepper, and cook slowly over low heat, stirring frequently, until the garlic is soft and barely blond, about 15 minutes. Take great care not to let it color more than a pale gold; if it browns it will lose its sweetness. (You may wish to add a little water to the pan—about ¼ cup—to keep the garlic from coloring too much.) When soft and blond, cover the pan and set aside at room temperature.

Ahead-of-Time Note: The garlic may be cooked several hours in advance.

Preparing the Sauce Ingredients. If you are using fresh tomatoes, seed and juice them but do not peel, then cut the pulp into ½-inch dice (directions are in the box on page 178). For canned tomatoes, crush them with your hands, reserve about ¼ cup for garnish, and set the rest aside in a large bowl. Chop the measured basil leaves roughly, combine with the other herbs, and set aside next to the tomatoes.

Shortly Before Serving:

Cooking the Pasta—7 to 10 minutes. Pour the salt into the rapidly boiling pasta water, and taste to be sure it is just right for you. Drop in the pasta, give it a quick stir, and cover the pan to return the water quickly back to the high boil. Then uncover the pan. Begin to test and taste the pasta as soon as it begins to bend when you lift a piece. It will be done when it is tender yet slightly firm, but not brittle to the bite—*al dente.* Undercooked pasta is

INGREDIENTS FOR 4 SERVINGS AS A MAIN COURSE

For slow-cooking the garlic

3 tablespoons excellent olive oil

12 large cloves of garlic, peeled and cut into ½-inch dice

Salt

Freshly ground black pepper

For the sauce

7 medium-size ripe red superbly flavored tomatoes (about 4 pounds) or 4 cups best-quality drained canned peeled plum tomatoes

¾ cup (firmly packed) fresh basil leaves, plus a dozen nice leaves for decoration

3 tablespoons chopped fresh mint, marjoram, and chives

For the pasta

1 pound best-quality (imported durum wheat semolina) tagliatelle or linguine

(continued)

Sunday Night Pasta (continued)

disappointing, while overcooked pasta is limp and characterless. You are the judge—get a second opinion if you have doubts. As the pasta cooks, scoop out half a cup of the pasta water, pour it into the pan with the garlic, and set the pan over moderate heat. Make sure your serving bowl and dishes are hot, and that all is ready at the table, including your guests.

Finale and Serving: The very minute that the pasta is cooked, drain it and turn it into the garlic pan along with the herbs. Proceeding rapidly, toss the pasta with salt and pepper as needed, then toss with the prepared tomatoes. Carefully correct seasoning again. Using the vegetable peeler, shave a dozen or so thin slivers of Parmesan over the pasta, transfer it to the heated bowl, scatter the reserved basil leaves and tomatoes on top, and bring to the table. Dramatically shave more cheese over the pasta, and lastly the glorious drizzle of balsamic vinegar. Toss again several times with feeling, and serve at once.

6 quarts water, rapidly boiling when you are ready to cook the pasta

1½ tablespoons salt, plus more if needed

For serving

A generous wedge of **parmigiano reggiano** *cheese, of which you will need some 25 to 30 shavings cut with a vegetable peeler*

4 to 6 tablespoons best-quality commercial balsamic vinegar

SPECIAL EQUIPMENT SUGGESTED

A heavy 12-inch sauté pan, 4 to 5 inches deep (for the garlic and final mixing of pasta)

An 8-quart kettle (for boiling the pasta)

A colander

A warm pasta bowl and serving bowls

A vegetable peeler for the cheese

A long-handled spoon and fork (for tossing and serving)

JULIA'S NOTES ON PEELING, SEEDING, AND JUICING TOMATOES

Blanching Before Peeling: One or two at a time, drop the tomatoes into a 3-quart saucepan of rapidly boiling water, bring rapidly back to the boil, and boil exactly 10 seconds. Immediately remove with a slotted spoon and drop them into a bowl of cold water. (Unless you have a caldron of boiling water, blanch no more than one or two at a time or they'll start to cook and will not peel cleanly.)

Peeling: Cut out the stem piece with a small knife, cut a ½-inch cross in the skin at the other end, and strip off the peel. (You may want to save the peels for a tomato sauce, since peel intensifies the red color as well as imparting a little flavor.)

Seeding and Juicing: You can cut a peeled tomato in half crosswise and, holding one half, cut side down, gently squeeze out juice and seeds, poking out the remaining seeds from the

interstices with your little finger. This is fine for most purposes, like the tomato sauce in Lynne Rossetto Kasper's pasta. If you need fancy decorative arrangements of tomato, however, you'll want to follow the path below.

Fancy Cutting: When you need really neat dice or matchstick-size julienne, quarter the peeled tomato through the stem end and halve the quarters lengthwise into wedges. Lay each wedge flat on your work surface and skillfully slide your knife just under the pulp and seeds to remove them, leaving you with a smooth wedge of flesh which you can then cut any way you wish.

Saucing the Remains: Except for the stem pieces, save all remains for sauce; freeze them if you are not making one at the moment.

DEAN FEARING

hat Chef Dean Fearing likes to do is to take traditional recipes and give them a twist to suit modern-day tastes. He doesn't just dabble at this—the exuberant Texas chef creates twenty-four new dishes each week for The Mansion on Turtle Creek restaurant in Dallas. His creative offerings have earned him many prestigious culinary awards as well as the praise of such notable personages as Her Majesty the Queen of England and former president George Bush.

Dean became comfortable in the kitchen at an early age. His father was an innkeeper in Louisville, Kentucky, and he and his brother would be setting up banquets, washing dishes, and "cooking off steaks while our friends were out goofing off." As a typical teenager, Dean had to be coaxed by his father to study with a retired chef, Harvey Colgin, who was teaching at Louisville Community College. "I fought my father even going to meet the man. When I did, it was one of those connections like a magnet." It was also a chance of a lifetime because Colgin had apprenticed with Escoffier himself, and he opened young Dean's eyes to the world of classic French cuisine.

Colgin taught his young pupil the basics of French cuisine—the sauces, the roasting and sauté techniques, and then helped Dean get into the Culinary Institute of America. "I would not have been able to go as far as I have today without those basics behind me. It's why I am confident and comfortable enough to make my own turns and twists on the classics."

Chef Dean's interpretations are available in his two books, *The Mansion on Turtle Creek Cookbook* (Weidenfeld & Nicolson) and *Dean Fearing's Southwest Cuisine: Blending Asia and the Americas* (Grove Weidenfeld). On his visit to Cambridge he took us through the many important steps of preparing his succulent molasses-glazed duck salad with warm sweet potato puree and his spicy shrimp dish served with tamale corn-husk canoes teeming with fresh corn puree. We are terribly glad that his father won out on that visit to Colgin.

MANSION SHRIMP DIABLO "TAMALE"

Among the Mansion on Turtle Creek's exceptional dishes is Dean Fearing's quite spectacular salad, each serving manned by a trio of shrimp in a corn husk canoe with a decoration of toasted tortilla cones, a garnish of Mexican specialties, and three different sauces. It seems like overkill but it's not, because the idea is fun. The elements are numerous, but most of them, like the Diablo Sauce, are generally useful to have on hand, and are thus listed as separate recipes. You need not include every single item, of course, when you create your own version, but Chef Dean's complete roster makes a memorable main-course luncheon.

Manufacturing Note: Because we want this recipe to make sense to the home cook, the order of battle here differs slightly in places from what you may be following on the TV. But it's all here! When you are to make this splendid dish, do go through the list of ingredients well before you begin, to be sure you have all the elements, or your own substitutes, on hand. Special ingredients like tamale husks, pumpkin seed powder, and dried corn are available in ethnic markets.

Making the Corn Husk Canoes: Drain the husks from the water and pat dry—handle carefully to keep them from shredding and splitting. You are now to form the husks into canoe shapes by spreading out the centers and tying the ends. To do so, pull a narrow ribbon of husk off the sides of each; these will tie the two ends. Gently spread and squish each husk into a canoe shape, and tie the two ends closed with the husk ribbons. Set them aside.

INGREDIENTS FOR 4 SERVINGS

For the corn husk canoes
*4 corn tamale husks, soaked 30
    minutes in cold water to soften*
*½ cup fresh corn puree (see box,
    page 183)*

For the shrimp
*12 large raw shrimp, peeled
    except for tail shells and
    deveined*
1 teaspoon salt
1 tablespoon vegetable oil
*¾ to 1 cup Diablo Sauce
    (see page 188)*

**Other ingredients including
the garnish**
Two 8-inch flour tortillas
*2 trimmed heads of romaine, cut
    into chiffonade (very narrow
    strips) 1 inch long*
*1 cup Red Jalapeño "Caesar
    Salad" Dressing (see oppostie)*

(continued)

Ahead-of-Time Note: May be made several hours in advance—cover with a damp towel and plastic so they will not dry out.

Shortly Before Serving:

The Tortillas. Brown the tortillas either by sitting them directly on a low gas burner or by toasting them on the griddle or cast-iron pan. Toast each side until lightly browned and warmed through. Remove, cut them in half at once, and roll into a cone. Place the cones on a plate and cover with an upside-down second plate to keep warm.

The Shrimp. Season the shrimp lightly with salt. Set the frying pan over high heat, add the oil, and when very hot and almost smoking, toss in the shrimp. Toss and turn for a minute, then pour in enough of the Diablo Sauce (about ¾ cup) to coat the shrimp well, and continue tossing and turning until shrimp are fully cooked, a minute or so more. Keep warm but do not overcook.

Reheat the corn puree.

Serving: Quickly toss the romaine with the Caesar dressing and arrange slightly off-center on each of the 4 plates. Fill the corn husk canoes with the warm corn puree and place in the free space left by the salad. Spoon a few tablespoons of *pico de gallo* between the salad and husk, scatter the pumpkin seed powder, dried corn, and red pepper or pomegranate seeds over the plate. Arrange three shrimp, tails pointing up, in each corn canoe. Sprinkle the cheese over the entire salad, tuck in the tortilla cone at a jaunty angle, and serve.

¼ cup Pico de Gallo (Spicy Red Salsa; see page 187)
¼ cup pumpkin seed powder
¼ cup pueblo dried corn
¼ cup diced red bell peppers or pomegranate seeds
¼ cup crumbled Mexican Cotija cheese or dried feta cheese

SPECIAL EQUIPMENT SUGGESTED

A cast-iron griddle or frying pan (if needed for the tortilla)
A heavy 10-inch no-stick frying pan
4 ample salad or dessert plates

RED JALAPEÑO "CAESAR SALAD" DRESSING

This colorful, lightly creamy dressing has nothing at all to do with Caesar salad, but our chef ... call it what he wishes since it ... so good with romaine lettuce and can even confer respectability ... Chef D... ...eens for the Mansion Shrimp Diablo "Tamale" with this dressing, and you ... ...ssed romaine with garlic-toasted croutons and crumbled Mexican-style Cotija or feta cheese.

(continued)

Red Jalapeño "Caesar Salad" Dressing (continued)

Manufacturing Note: The chef gave us directions for making 2½ cups— for a restaurant-size salad dressing with 2 or 3 egg yolks and ¾ cup each of canola and olive oils. We have cut the proportions down to make a more reasonable 1 cup of dressing.

Drop the egg yolk, garlic, shallots, anchovy, Worcestershire, pepper sauce, and vinegar into the blender, and puree until smooth—add a few droplets of water or chicken stock if the quantity is too small for the machine to do its work. Blending at moderate speed (if your machine is so equipped—if not, continue on high), very slowly drizzle in through the top, first the canola oil, then the olive oil, until the dressing has emulsified and is a creamy mayonnaise—if too thick, blend in additional droplets of water or chicken stock. Turn the sauce into a bowl and stir in the optional cilantro, lime juice, and jalapeño; taste carefully and correct seasoning.

Ahead-of-Time Note: The dressing will keep in the refrigerator for a week.

Fresh Egg Yolk Note: Made several hours ahead, this dressing contains enough acid to render bacteria harmless. However, you can leave out the egg yolk; if so, double the amount of Dijon mustard, adding it to the blender at the beginning.

DEAN FEARING'S CORN STRIPPER AND FRESH CORN PUREE

A cooked puree of fresh corn kernels makes an attractive bed for the shrimp in Dean Fearing's Mansion Shrimp Diablo "Tamale," and here's his ingenious way of getting those pesky kernels off the cob. Lay a four-sided metal grater, large holes facing up, in a baking dish. Pressing firmly, push the corn over the large holes, scraping off the kernels and juices. Rotate the cob after each push and you'll quickly remove all the kernels. Four ears of corn make about a cup of puree.

To cook the puree, Dean pours it into a skillet and bakes it for about 20 minutes in a 350° F oven, until thickened and cooked through. He seasons the puree with salt and a little lime juice, plus drops of maple syrup or honey to sweeten off-season corn.

INGREDIENTS FOR ABOUT
I CUP

For the dressing base
1 "large" egg yolk
2 cloves of smoked garlic (see page 189), or 1 medium clove of fresh garlic, peeled
1 teaspoon peeled and minced shallots
1 boneless anchovy fillet or ½ teaspoon anchovy paste
1 teaspoon Worcestershire sauce
2 teaspoons hot pepper sauce
½ teaspoon balsamic vinegar
Droplets of water or chicken stock, if needed
¼ cup canola oil
¼ cup olive oil
Salt
Freshly ground pepper to taste

Additional flavorings (optional)
1 small handful of finely chopped cilantro (2 tablespoons)
Fresh lime juice
1 smoked red or green jalapeño pepper (see page 189), seeded, peeled, and finely chopped
2 teaspoons Dijon-type prepared mustard

SPECIAL EQUIPMENT
SUGGESTED

An electric blender

MOLASSES-GLAZED DUCK SALAD

Here is a wonderfully typical Dean Fearing creation, taking a duck salad about as far as it could possibly go—and it makes great colorful eating. The recipe consists of a duck bathed during its roasting with a molasses basting sauce. When cool, the duck meat is julienned and tossed with salad greens, pecans, and julienned roasted vegetables in his special dressing, and the whole is served with a mound of Chef Dean's sweet potato puree.

With a little kitchen help it is quite do-able; but if you find it too daunting, break it down into stages or eliminate some of the components. The duck itself, roasted to a mahogany glisten, also makes a beautiful hot main course, served with the vegetables and his sweet potatoes or a modified salad on the side.

Preparing the Basting Sauce: Pour the molasses into a small bowl. Add the remaining ingredients and stir them together well. Let the sauce stand and ripen for at least 10 minutes to blend flavors. Reserve ¼ cup of the sauce for the dressing.

Ahead-of-Time Note: The basting sauce may be made several days ahead.

Preheat the oven to 450° F.

Roasting the Duck: Wash and dry the duckling. Remove the excess fat from the openings and inside the cavity. Salt and pepper extremely generously inside and out, being sure to reach all around the inside. Set the duck, breast up, in the roasting pan and place on the lower third level of the preheated oven. After 15 to 20 minutes, when the duck is beginning to brown, reduce the temperature to 350° F and continue roasting for 1 hour. Forty minutes later, when there are still about 20 minutes to go, spoon the accumulated fat out of the pan and begin basting the duck generously with the molasses basting sauce. Baste generously at 7- to 8-minute intervals—basting often and generously is important for the color and flavor of the meat. Remove the duck from the oven and let it cool to the touch. Meanwhile, degrease the roasting pan, set over heat, and deglaze with the vinegar, boiling down the liquid and pan juices to about ¼ cup; pour the liquid into a smallish saucepan and reserve for the dressing.

Carve off the two breasts, each in one piece. Remove the leg-thighs, and separate the meat from the bone. Cut the breast and leg-thigh meat into

INGREDIENTS FOR 4 SERVINGS

For the spicy molasses basting sauce

1½ cups dark unsulfured molasses

4 large garlic cloves, peeled and minced

2 large shallots, peeled and minced

2 tablespoons chopped fresh sage leaves or 1 teaspoon dried sage

2 tablespoons chopped fresh thyme leaves or 1 tablespoon dried thyme

¼ cup hot pepper sauce

1 tablespoon fresh lemon juice

For the duck

One roaster duckling, 5½ to 6 pounds

Salt

Freshly ground black pepper

(continued)

matchstick-size julienne, julienning the crisp skin also. Set aside. Chop the carcass into small pieces, and reserve for the dressing.

Ahead-of-Time Note: The duck may be roasted and the meat julienned a day in advance; cover and refrigerate.

Roasting the Vegetables: While the duck is roasting, arrange the carrots and parsnips in a single layer on the jelly-roll pan. Brush them all over with olive oil and a sprinkling of salt. If there is room in the oven, roast them along with the duck during its last ½ hour, or roast them later. They should be nicely softened, browned, and glazed, and will take a good 30 minutes.

Preparing the Dressing: Heat the oil in a medium saucepan. Stir in the onions, celery, and carrots, and sauté slowly until well browned but not burned. Add the garlic and sauté one more minute. Add the reduced vinegar-deglazing liquid from the duck-roasting pan, the black pepper, the chopped duck carcass, sage, bay leaf, and stock. Bring to a boil. Remove from heat and gradually, by driblets, blend in the cornstarch mixture. Return over heat, bring to the simmer, and maintain at the simmer for 45 minutes or so. Strain through a fine-meshed sieve, and degrease. Bring the reserved ¼ cup molasses basting sauce to the boil in its saucepan and reduce almost to a glaze. Gradually whisk in 1 cup of the strained dressing; and stir in lemon juice and salt to taste. Bring to the simmer, stir in the shallots, and taste again for seasoning—if the flavor is too intense, dilute with dribbles of the dressing, tasting until you are satisfied.

BAKED SWEET POTATO PUREE AND ITS DRUNKEN VARIATION

Sweet potatoes are definitely a southern vegetable. We have Leah Chase's New Orleans Sweet Potato Pie on page 197, and here is Chef Dean's sweet mashed recipe, which he serves with his duck salad. For about 2 cups, wash and dry 1 very large orange-skinned sweet potato (sometimes called a yam), prick in several places with a skewer, and bake in a 400° F oven for about an hour, or until thoroughly soft and the juices that flow out seem to be caramelized. Peel, and mash in a mixing bowl with a hand-held beater until broken up. Add 2 tablespoons or so of butter, a little salt to taste, and beat until smooth.

For Dean Fearing's Drunken Sweet Potatoes, follow the preceding recipe but mash in a tablespoon or two of dark rum, a teaspoon or so of grated fresh ginger, droplets of fresh lime juice, and, if you must, another tablespoon or two of butter.

½ cup malt vinegar (if not available, use red wine vinegar)

For the vegetables
7 carrots, peeled and ends trimmed
7 parsnips, peeled and ends trimmed
Olive oil
Salt

For the dressing
1 tablespoon vegetable oil
The following vegetables, cut in a rough chop:
1 cup onions
¼ cup celery
¼ cup carrots
8 large garlic cloves, peeled
1 tablespoon cracked black pepper
10 fresh sage leaves or 1½ teaspoons dried sage
1 bay leaf
1 cup chicken or veal stock
2 tablespoons cornstarch mixed with 2 tablespoons water
Fresh lemon juice to taste
Salt to taste
3 tablespoons peeled and minced shallots

For serving
1½ cups white chicory—frisée
½ cup toasted pecans (see box, page 189)

(continued)

Molasses-Glazed Duck Salad (continued)

Ahead-of-Time Note: All of the above may be prepared several hours in advance. If the elements have been refrigerated, let them come to room temperature—but the duck should be reheated briefly in the dressing to freshen it, then drained before the presentation.

The Presentation: Cut the carrots and parsnips lengthwise into 4 to 6 pieces each. Toss the frisée in a large bowl with a small handful of the pecans, the green beans, the parsnips and carrots, and lastly the duck. Then toss with half of the dressing. Scoop a mound of sweet potatoes in the center of each plate, spoon the salad over and around the potatoes, and scatter on more pecans. Drizzle the rest of the dressing over each serving, and bring to the table.

1 cup green beans (preferably
haricots verts), blanched
Sweet potato puree (see box, page
185), warmed

SPECIAL EQUIPMENT
SUGGESTED

A roasting pan large enough to
hold the duck comfortably
A jelly-roll pan (for the
vegetables)
Fine-meshed sieve
4 dinner plates

PICO DE GALLO
SPICY RED SALSA

This is one of Chef Dean Fearing's recipes for uncooked salsa known as pico de gallo, *or "cock's comb." The proportions here are a matter of your taste and of the availability of ripe red tomatoes— you may wish to use plum tomatoes, or part canned plum and fresh tomatoes; you may want more or less garlic or onions; and so forth. The jalapeño will be hot if you leave the seeds in, and quite temperate without them.*

Chop the tomato pulp and the onion into ¼-inch dice, and stir them in a mixing bowl with the remaining ingredients. Fold them together and let the salsa marinate for at least 30 minutes. Check again for seasoning.

INGREDIENTS FOR ABOUT
1 CUP

1 or 2 large firm ripe tomatoes,
peeled, cored, and seeded
(about ¾ cup)
½ small white onion
1 or 2 garlic cloves, peeled and
very finely minced
1 jalapeño pepper, with or
without seeds, finely minced
2 tablespoons finely chopped
cilantro
1 tablespoon fresh lime juice
1 tablespoon excellent olive oil
Salt to taste

JULIA'S NOTES ON FRESH VERSUS DRIED HERBS

It's not only the specialty stores that carry fresh herbs, but more and more of our regular supermarkets, and fresh herbs do give a wonderful fragrance and color to any dish. When fresh are not around, dried herbs are fine when they are freshly bottled and aromatic. Keep them tightly covered in a cool dry place and don't keep them too long—6 months to a year. Date the bottles, and smell any bottled herb before you use it to be sure it has retained its personality.

Substituting dry for fresh and fresh for dry: Substitute 1 teaspoon of fragrant dried herbs for every tablespoon of fresh herbs, and vice versa.

DIABLO SAUCE

Chef Dean anoints the shrimp for his Mansion Shrimp Diablo "Tamale" with this intriguing, mildly spicy sauce, and it is handy to have around in the refrigerator or freezer for basting hamburgers, chicken, and other grilled or broiled foods. Your own always seems far more satisfactory than any bottled job. Is that because it is, as they say now in all the advertisements, "all natural— no preservatives"?

Heat the oil in the pan, stir in the shallots, garlic, and cumin, and sauté for several minutes, until they are an even golden brown. Adding one item at a time and stirring every 10 seconds between additions, add the chiles, ginger, and red peppers; when they are all in, stir for 30 seconds more. Stir in the mango and toss briefly—15 seconds. Pour in the chicken stock and bring to the boil; reduce heat, and simmer 20 minutes to blend flavors and soften the peppers. Puree in the blender, transfer to a bowl, season with lime juice and salt, and set aside.

Ahead-of-Time Note: The sauce may be made well in advance. Refrigerate for a week in a screw-top jar, or freeze.

cook's notes

INGREDIENTS FOR ABOUT 2 CUPS

1 tablespoon canola or olive oil

3 shallots, peeled and chopped

3 garlic cloves, peeled and chopped

1 teaspoon cumin seeds

3 habanero or serrano chiles, seeds discarded, coarsely chopped

1 tablespoon finely grated fresh ginger root

2 red bell peppers, seeds and ribs removed, chopped

½ ripe mango, peeled and diced

1½ cups chicken stock (homemade or canned)

The juice of 1 to 2 limes

Salt to taste

SPECIAL EQUIPMENT SUGGESTED

A cast-iron griddle or frying pan (for the tortillas)

COLD-SMOKED GARLIC AND PEPPERS

Smoked garlic and smoked chiles give a special flavor to sauces and dressings such as Chef Dean's salad dressing on page 181. Smoke them in your own backyard grill some time when you are fired up for a meal like Michael Lomonaco's mixed grill. Or, as is easier for such a small operation, smoke them right in your kitchen using the wok setup described on page 105 for Christopher Gross's Alder-Smoked Loin of Beef. It is good to have such special edibles on hand, and they freeze perfectly—in other words, as long as you are smoking something anyway, add a bit extra. Cold-smoking like this is just for flavor; both the garlic and chiles require precooking before smoking.

Preliminary Cooking of the Garlic: Preheat the oven to 350° F. Peel the garlic cloves (for notes on fast peeling, see box, page 127). Heat 2 teaspoons of oil in the sauté pan over moderate heat and add the garlic, tossing to coat with the oil. Toss with a sprinkling of salt, and sauté until browned—3 to 5 minutes—watching carefully and turning often as they cook. Transfer the pan to the oven, and roast 8 to 10 minutes, turning occasionally, until the cloves are soft. Transfer to the perforated pan.

Preliminary Pan-Roasting of the Peppers: Heat the remaining teaspoon of oil in the cast-iron skillet over moderate heat, and when it is hot, add the peppers. Sauté them, turning often, until they are blackened and blistered on all sides. Transfer to the perforated pan.

Smoking: Set the perforated pan over whichever smoking device you have chosen, and let smoke for 15 minutes.

Ahead-of-Time Note: The smoked garlic and chiles may be kept for several days in a screw-top jar in the refrigerator or for several weeks in the freezer.

INGREDIENTS FOR A 6-OUNCE JAR

For the garlic and peppers

1 whole head of garlic with large cloves

1 tablespoon olive oil

Salt

6 whole chiles (Chef Dean uses habanero or Scotch bonnets for this recipe, but you may wish to add other varieties)

SPECIAL EQUIPMENT SUGGESTED

A 6- to 7-inch ovenproof sauté or frying pan

A heavy skillet, preferably cast-iron

A perforated pan or a colander, or heavy-duty aluminum foil shaped like a pan with a dozen or more ⅛-inch holes poked through

An outdoor wood-burning grill with lid (see page 99) or the kitchen wok-smoker suggested on page 105 plus the necessary wood chips, etc.

DEAN FEARING'S TOASTED PECANS

These spicy pecans are a treat to eat, not only as a garnish for Dean Fearing's duck salad, but served just by themselves as a cocktail snack. They're easy to make, too. Mix 2 cups of shelled pecans in a bowl with a tablespoon of vegetable oil, a large pinch of cayenne, a teaspoon of salt, and, if you wish, a tablespoon of chile powder. Spread them in a roasting pan and bake in a 325° F oven for 10 to 15 minutes, just until toasted and fragrant—watch that they don't burn. They'll keep for several days in a screw-top jar at room temperature.

LEAH CHASE

 eah Chase moves about the home kitchen with such ease that it is easy to forget that this mother of four and grandmother of sixteen runs her own New Orleans restaurant, Dooky Chase. Author of *The Dooky Chase Cookbook* (Pelican) and an ever-familiar figure on numerous boards dedicated to improving the quality of life for people in metropolitan New Orleans, she was named one of seventy-five black women who changed America in the book *I Dream a World: Portraits of Black Women Who Changed America.*

Born into a family of eleven children and raised in a small town across the lake from New Orleans, Leah would do anything to stay out of the kitchen but did manage to learn by watching her sisters and mother whip up meals. "We were poor, but my mother never had any sick children because when we were coming up, beans, cabbage, and greens from Daddy's garden were the mainstay." At eighteen, Leah moved to New Orleans and waited tables in the French Quarter—her first time inside a restaurant, for there were no restaurants that served black people. Leah fell in love with the business and knew immediately that she wanted to run her own place. "I didn't intend to do any cooking at first," Leah remembers, "but, you see, I had so many ideas in my head about food and what to serve, and I've been in the business ever since."

As she looks at the oil to check its temperature for her fried chicken, and judges the consistency of the sweet potato puree for her pie, it is apparent that this Master Chef relies on instinct rather than hard-and-fast rules. "Rules don't no more make a cook than sermons make a saint," she counsels. She does have a rule, however, for what it takes to be successful when combining the foods of the diverse New Orleans cultures into a harmonious culinary pot: "You have to be in love with that pot. You have to put all your love in that pot."

GREAT BAKING-POWDER BISCUITS

You'll never have lighter, more delicious baking-powder biscuits than these from Leah Chase. They are almost flaky, if you can call a biscuit flaky—at least they give that impression. They are excruciatingly divine baking-powder biscuits, but certainly not diet biscuits—did anyone ever expect them to be? Chef Leah's dough is very light and soft, and she handles it gently. That certainly must be one of her secrets.

Preheat the oven to 400° F and set a rack on the middle level.

Preparing the Dough: Measure the flour into a mixing bowl and stir in the baking powder and sugar. Add the shortening to the dry ingredients and cut it in with your hands or a pastry cutter until the mixture, as Leah Chase says, "is somewhat beady." It should look like a mass of small peas. Slowly pour in the milk, working it in with your hands or with a wooden spoon. The mixture should be sticky to the touch.

Forming the Biscuits: Flour your work surface and pour the dough out onto it. Knead it gently by folding it over toward you and patting it lightly; fold and pat, adding enough flour to keep the dough from sticking to the counter or your hands. Five to seven folds should be enough to work in the flour and make a smooth dough. Gently pat it into a rectangle ¾ inch thick. Cut the circles as close to each other as possible. When you pick up a circle to place it on the baking sheet, puff it up by squeezing and patting the sides as you gently rotate it. Place the circles close together on the pan, but not touching. Pat any leftover dough back into a rectangle and continue to cut out as many circles as possible, using up all the dough.

Ahead-of-Time Note: The biscuits may be loosely covered and refrigerated overnight at this point—ready to provide the family with hot biscuits for breakfast.

Baking: Place the biscuits in the preheated oven and bake for 15 to 20 minutes, until golden brown and cooked through. Serve warm or at room temperature.

Ahead-of-Time Note: Baked biscuits may be frozen—freezing preserves them better than refrigerating them, even for a short time. Never quite the same as freshly baked, of course.

INGREDIENTS FOR 12 BISCUITS, ABOUT 2½ BY 1¼ INCHES

The biscuit dough

2 cups self-rising flour, plus 1 more cup for forming the biscuits (see box, page 196)

2 heaping teaspoons double-action baking powder

1 tablespoon sugar

1 cup (8 ounces) vegetable shortening, at room temperature

1 cup milk

SPECIAL EQUIPMENT SUGGESTED

A 2½-inch round biscuit or cookie cutter

A jelly-roll pan or a cookie sheet lined with parchment paper

LEAH CHASE'S FRIED CHICKEN

This is the fried chicken that you dream about—moist and tender meat and a crunchy crust. Leah Chase has been frying her famous chicken just like this for years, ever since she started out in her New Orleans restaurant, Dooky Chase. She seasons her chicken, then lets it sit in a bath of eggs and evaporated milk; the moment before frying, she rolls it in her specially flavored flour coating.

Cutting and Seasoning the Chicken: For larger servings, separate each chicken into 8 to 10 bone-in pieces—2 wings, each with a strip of breast attached if you wish, 2 thighs, 2 drumsticks, and the breast cut in half lengthwise and, if you wish, crosswise for 4 pieces; cut off the backbone and reserve for stock (see page 87). Otherwise you can just cut the chicken into smaller pieces, including the backbone—this is finger food, and smaller pieces cook more quickly. Trim excess fat and skin off the pieces. Mix the salt and white pepper together, sprinkle it liberally over the chicken and rub it in well.

Preparing the Egg Wash: Break the eggs into a mixing bowl (a large one if you are doing it the restaurant way), whisking to break them up and to blend yolks and whites. Beat in the evaporated milk and then the water. Place the chicken pieces in the bowl or in the bag, and move them around to cover completely with the liquid. If you are in a tearing hurry, let sit for at least 5 minutes, but a refrigerated sojourn of several hours or overnight is recommended; turn and baste the chicken several times if you have bagged it.

Preparing the Frying Medium—Fat: Gradually heat the frying fat in your fryer or pan—to prevent trouble, your pan should be not more than half full. It is ready for frying at a temperature of 350° F—Leah does not use a thermometer; she sprinkles in a bit of flour, and if it bubbles up, the fat is

INGREDIENTS FOR 6 TO 8 SERVINGS

For the chicken
Two 3½-pound frying chickens (or ready-cut bone-in chicken pieces, all of one kind— such as all legs or breasts— or an assortment)
2 tablespoons salt
1 tablespoon freshly ground white pepper

For the egg wash
Either *The restaurant way, in a large bowl:*
4 "large" eggs
24 ounces (2 cans or 3 cups) evaporated milk
3 cups water
Or *The home cook's way, in a 1-gallon leakproof plastic bag:*
Half of the above ingredients

(continued)

JULIA'S WARNING FOR DEEP-FAT NEOPHYTES

Proceed with great care since hot fat can give nasty burns.

Never fill the fat fryer more than half full: fat splatters up and high sides keep it in bounds.

Always keep the pan handle turned inward so you cannot brush against it.

Heat the fat slowly in case it contains moisture which can spatter up.

Again, make it a habit to think before you act.

Fried Chicken (continued)

ready for the chicken. While you are waiting, prepare the flour and preheat the oven to 200° F.

Preparing the Flour Coating: Stir the flour, seasoning salt, and pepper together in a large roasting pan, mixing thoroughly so all is evenly distributed.

Manufacturing Note: Each chicken piece should go directly from the flour coating into the hot fat since it will brown too much if the egg wash seeps through. Please see our notes on deep-fat frying in the box opposite.

Coating and Frying the Chicken: Leah Chase coats her chicken the restaurant way: she uses one hand to pick 3 or 4 pieces of chicken out of the egg wash, shake off excess, and drop the pieces into the flour. She uses the other hand to turn the piece in the flour mixture to coat it evenly. One by one, she shakes off excess flour and lets the chicken slide quietly into the hot fat, and immediately goes on to the next piece until all are in. (You could, of course, paper-bag the seasoned flour and shake 3 or 4 pieces of chicken in it, but our team prefers tongs. You pick up the chicken one piece at a time with the tongs in one hand, shake off excess egg wash, roll the piece of chicken rapidly in the flour, and slide it into the fat.) Fry your 3 or 4 pieces of chicken for 15 to 20 minutes, turning frequently, until the chicken is browned and cooked through. It remains deliciously juicy when just cooked through—if you are not sure, you'll have to cut it open. Drain the chicken on the paper towels—keep them warm in the oven if you wish. Reheat the fat if necessary, and continue with the rest.

Serving: Serve hot or at room temperature. Leah Chase's divine biscuits go beautifully with the chicken, as does Jimmy Sneed's coleslaw (see page 254).

Re-using Fat: If the frying medium looks and smells fresh, you may wish to strain it through a fine-meshed sieve lined with several thicknesses of cheese cloth; then it may be refrigerated to be used another time. But be very fussy about your fat, since there are few edibles more depressing than foods fried in stale fat.

For the coating

3 cups all-purpose flour

2 tablespoons "seasoning salt" (Leah Chase always uses Lawry's salt, whose secret formula includes salt, sugar, paprika, turmeric, cornstarch, and garlic and onion powders)

1 tablespoon freshly ground black pepper

The frying medium

1 quart solid white vegetable shortening, lard, or vegetable oil—we shall call it all "fat" (see box opposite)

SPECIAL EQUIPMENT SUGGESTED

A deep-fat fryer or a 9- to 10-inch saucepan, 5 to 6 inches deep

A deep-fat-frying thermometer (useful but not essential)

Tongs

A baking sheet or tray lined with paper towels

JULIA'S NOTES ON DEEP-FAT FRYING—TEMPERATURES AND FATS

Temperatures

We did a great deal of fried chicken for this recipe, and have come to the conclusion that you are better off *without* a thermometer. Leah Chase has fried so many chickens she just knows by the look of things when to add the chicken, how to keep the heat right, when the chicken is done, and so forth. At first we were infinitely scientific, consulting the thermometer and adjusting the heat every minute. We tried to keep the temperature at 350° F, which turned out to be almost impossible. Our pieces of chicken went into fat that was at exactly 350° F, but they didn't cool off the fat, as we had expected, and the thermometer rose to 380° F—horrors! It stayed there for a few minutes and then rather rapidly went down to 320° F, and when we turned on the heat it rather slowly got back up to 350° F, but by that time the chicken was getting far too brown.

After several trials with precisely the same results, we decided to emulate our mentor. We observed the fat and the frying rather than the thermometer—although we left it in to see what was going on. We threw in bits of flour, and when it fizzed up as it should we slid in the chicken, which fizzed up as it should. We kept the heat moderate, and just watched the chicken as it cooked, the fat bubbling nicely but not violently. We were interested to note that the temperature went up to its usual 380° F, then gradually went down to around 280° F, where it finally remained, with the fat still bubbling and looking the way we presumed it should; and when the chicken was done and floated near the surface, it finally looked exactly the way it should—like Leah Chase's. (We did note that smaller pieces cooked more easily and nicely than larger pieces such as drumsticks.)

Fats and Oils

Lard was once the fat of choice for frying, and Leah Chase recalls the wonderful taste it gave to chicken. Now, due to the public's current fear of lard, she has resorted to vegetable oil and shortening, but see the new findings on lard in the box on page 152. In our frying experiences and tests, however, our team most definitely agrees with Pam Anderson, whose in-depth article "Rediscovering Fried Chicken" appeared in the May/June 1994 edition of *Cook's* magazine—the least smoking, and least smell-up-the-house-and-yourself frying medium is solid white vegetable shortening.

cook's notes

JULIA'S NOTES ON SELF-RISING FLOUR AND BAKING POWDERS

Self-rising flour contains salt and baking powder, but you can make your own simply by adding these two items to your regular flour. We have used the proportions given by *King Arthur Flour Cookbook.* Theirs is for 8 cups of flour, with 1 tablespoon of salt and 5 tablespoons of double-action baking powder, which translates down to:

2 cups unbleached all-purpose flour

¾ teaspoon salt

1¼ tablespoons (4 teaspoons) double-action baking powder

Baking soda is used in a batter that is very acid, such as one containing buttermilk or molasses.

Single-action baking powder consists of baking soda and cream of tartar, which act together as soon as they find themselves in a moist environment, meaning that as soon as the dough is mixed, there's no waiting around—you shove it into the oven.

Double-action baking powder is most frequently used in contemporary recipes such as Leah Chase's biscuits, where the baking powder acts both when the dough is moistened as it is made and when it goes into the oven.

Warning: Baking soda and baking powders lose their punch after a while, and so does self-rising flour. You are really better off making your own self-rising mix, according to the formula above.

PECAN DOUGH FOR SWEET PIES

This is the crust that sits so proudly under Leah Chase's sweet potato pie filling, and the touch of pecans adds a subtle hint of the South—they grow in such abundance in the area that New Orleanians can pick them up off the sidewalk. This very easily made crust will work nicely for pumpkin and squash pie, too.

Mixing the Dough: Measure the flour into a mixing bowl, thoroughly blend in the salt, then the pecans. Add the shortening and work it in with your fingers or a pastry blender until the mixture forms tiny beady lumps. Then pour in the cold water and begin to knead and squeeze the dough with your hands until it all comes together in a stiff mass—add droplets more water if it is too stiff and dry to mass. Knead and press it into a 6-inch disk. Wrap in plastic, chill for 1 hour, and it is ready to use.

Ahead-of-Time Note: The dough may be refrigerated for several days, or it may be frozen.

INGREDIENTS FOR ONE 9-INCH CRUST

1½ cups unbleached all-purpose flour

1 teaspoon salt

¼ cup pecans, finely chopped

½ cup (4 ounces) vegetable shortening

¼ cup ice water, plus droplets more if needed

NEW ORLEANS SWEET POTATO PIE

Leah Chase's sweet potato pie does New Orleans proud, and it has an easy-to-do press-in pie dough that has the unusual touch of finely chopped pecans. The sweet potato filling itself couldn't be more simple, and yet it took years of experimenting for Leah to perfect the seasoning and texture.

Preheat the oven to 375° F.

Preparing the Crusts: Divide the pecan dough in half and place one piece in each of the pie pans; pat it over the bottom and up the sides of each pan. Flute the edges by pinching 1-inch-wide pieces of dough on the outer rim between the thumb and index finger of one hand while holding the index finger of the other hand on the inside between the pinching fingers. Prick all over the bottom of the dough in each pan at 1-inch intervals with the tines of a table fork. Set the pans in the preheated oven. Be sure they don't touch the oven walls or each other. Bake for 10 to 15 minutes, or until the crusts are set and beginning to color slightly. Then remove and let crisp briefly.

Mashing the Potatoes: Meanwhile, put the potatoes into a roomy saucepan, cover by 1 inch with cold water, and bring to the boil. Boil slowly until the potatoes are very tender with absolutely no resistance at the center when pierced with a skewer or small knife. Remove them with a slotted spoon to a mixing bowl. They are now to be mashed; Chef Leah prefers the texture that hand mashing gives—and she mashes them until they are completely broken up. When mashed, stir in the sugar, cinnamon, and nutmeg; then whisk in the eggs, milk, and vanilla. Finally whisk in the butter. Taste carefully and correct seasoning.

(continued)

INGREDIENTS FOR TWO 9-INCH PIES

For the crust
A double recipe of the raw Pecan Dough (see opposite)

For the sweet potatoes
4 large sweet potatoes (about 3 pounds total), peeled
1 cup sugar
1 teaspoon ground cinnamon
¼ teaspoon freshly grated nutmeg
2 "large" eggs, lightly beaten
½ cup condensed milk
½ teaspoon pure vanilla extract
2 tablespoons unsalted butter, melted

For the garnish and serving
30 perfect unblemished pecan halves
Ground cinnamon
Lightly sweetened whipped cream or vanilla ice cream (optional but agreeable)

SPECIAL EQUIPMENT SUGGESTED

Two 9-inch pie pans
A hand-held potato masher

JULIA'S NOTES ON SWEET POTATOES VS. YAMS

Although sweet potatoes and yams often look and taste alike, they are from different plant species. Real yams are grown in South American countries but rarely here in this country, according to Sharon Tyler Herbst's *Food Lover's Tiptionary.* The sweet potatoes we find here are either the dark orange variety or the light yellow sweet potato, which is rather dry and crumbly. In contrast, the dark orange American sweet potato has vivid orange flesh, is moist and sweet, and is often called a yam.

Q: "When is a yam not a yam but a sweet potato?"

A: "When you are right here in the good old U.S. of A."

Sweet Potato Pie (continued)

Ahead-of-Time Note: If you omit the eggs and butter, you may make the filling a day or two in advance; cover and refrigerate. Shortly before you plan to bake the pies, stir the sweet potatoes over a pan of simmering water until thoroughly heated through; remove from heat and beat in the eggs, then the butter. Proceed to the next step (below).

Baking the Pies: Spoon the warm sweet potatoes into the pie shells. Lay a circle of pecan halves around the outside edges and sprinkle the tops of the pies with cinnamon. Bake for 15 minutes, or until the filling is set and the edges of the crust have browned nicely.

Serving: Serve warm, or at room temperature, or cold, accompanied by whipped cream or ice cream if you wish.

JULIAN SERRANO

W hen Julian Serrano was a teenager in Madrid, Spain, his passion was soccer and he considered making it a career. "I went to professional team tryouts and the team doctor said that my heart beat too fast. I said, 'Maybe I have to look for another career.'" He chose food and cooks with such zeal that it's hard to believe his heartbeat isn't still a little rapid. Julian admits that he was not completely sold on a culinary profession when he graduated from the hotel management school, Escuela Gastronomia P.P.O., on Spain's Costa del Sol. It was a way of making a living, which he did well in Spanish restaurants and eventually on various Caribbean cruise lines. "The boat was not what I expected. You had to feed a thousand people. The workers were not used to quality work. I stayed there to find my way to the United States."

It wasn't until 1984, when he was hired by San Francisco's popular restaurant Masa's, that Chef Julian hit his stride. "Masa gave life to me," admits Julian. "I finally realized that I could be a creative chef, that I could make beautiful things with talented people, that I could strive for perfection." To cap his finally realized passion, Chef Julian took a five-month sojourn in Europe to work with several chefs in France and Switzerland. He returned to Masa's as executive chef and is credited with taking its French cuisine to new heights by using the freshest ingredients, perfecting classic sauces, and creating work-of-art presentations.

We asked Chef Julian to prepare some of his native Spanish cuisine for us and he delighted us with a bounteous paella resplendent with lobster meat, browned chicken thighs, and whole tender clams. He also made an unusual Crème Fraîche Ice Cream garnished with Honey Lime Peaches and Almond Roasted Figs. Our hearts quickened a beat or two.

PAELLA WITH CHICKEN, CHUNKS OF LOBSTER, AND CLAMS

Chef Julian's Spanish paella is a glorious dish—and his is the real thing, full of the bright color and traditional flavors of Spain. Paella originated in Valencia, along the east coast of Spain, and was basically a dish about rice, since that is the area where it is harvested. While the Spanish workers in the rice fields made theirs with what was easily available to them—snails and rabbits—Chef Julian's modest chicken and clams are made more luxurious with lobster, but he constructs the dish with a great sense of culinary discretion.

Preheat the oven to 400° F.

Parboiling the Lobsters: Bring a large kettle of water to the boil. To keep the lobster tails from curling during their cooking, lay the spoons or pair of chopsticks along the center of the lobster tail on the stomach side, and tie in place with butcher's twine. Drop the lobsters into the boiling water, cover the pan, bring to the boil again, and boil for 30 seconds. Remove from the water and drop at once into a bowl of ice water to stop the cooking and cool the shells.

Cutting up the Lobsters: Untie the lobsters. Twist off the claws and joints, then twist the tail off the body. Using shears, cut the flippers off the ends and sides of the tails. Lay the tails on the counter, shell side up, and with a large sharp knife slice the tail into rounds, or medallions, following the natural breaks in the shell. If the intestinal vein is visible near the top of the medallions, use the toothpick or skewer to poke it out. Break the joint sections off the claws and set aside with the medallions. Break off and discard the small pointed pincers from the claws, tipping the claws up and down as you do so to let the water drain out. Then lay the claws on the counter and use the back of a heavy knife to crack the shells in several places for easy meat removal later. Crack the knuckle shells in the same manner. (Chef Julian saves the chest sections to cook up for another meal like lobster bisque or a seafood salad.)

Preparing the Chicken: Cut each thigh in half crosswise and season with salt and pepper. Film the bottom of a frying pan with olive oil, set over moderately high heat, and when hot but not smoking, lay the chicken in, skin side down. Sear the skin side until it is a beautiful golden-brown but the meat is still rare—5 to 6 minutes. Remove and set aside.

Preparing the Saffron Broth: Bring the chicken broth to the simmer in a saucepan and stir in the saffron. Keep it hot while you prepare the rice.

Preparing the Rice: Set the paella pan over moderately low heat and film the bottom with olive oil. Stir in the diced onion and cook, stirring often, until it just begins to take on color, but do not let it brown. Add the diced pepper and cook with the onion for a minute or two, then stir in the garlic. After another minute stir in the tomato. Let cook together for several minutes to evaporate accumulated juices, then stir in the rice. Sauté, stirring for several minutes, until the rice is hot and begins to turn from translucent to

INGREDIENTS FOR 6 SERVINGS

For the lobster and chicken
2 live lobsters, 1¼ pounds each
6 chicken thighs
Kosher salt
Freshly ground black pepper
Excellent olive oil

For the saffron broth
*4 to 4½ cups chicken stock
   (see page 88)*
*2 pinches of saffron (size of pinch
   depends on strength of
   saffron—too much gives a
   medicinal taste)*

For the rice
Excellent olive oil
*½ medium white onion, finely
   diced*
*1 red bell pepper, peeled, seeded,
   ribs removed, and finely diced*
*2 large garlic cloves, peeled and
   diced*
*1 medium tomato, peeled, seeded,
   and finely diced*
*2 cups Italian Arborio or
   Spanish rice*

Additional ingredients
*12 small clams (littlenecks),
   scrubbed clean*
1 cup shelled peas

For serving
*1 lemon, cut into 4 or 6
   lengthwise wedges*

(continued)

Paella (continued)

a milky color. At this point ladle in the stock, stirring to mix the ingredients together and then spreading them out evenly in the pan. The stock should just cover the rice; if it does not, add a little bit more. (Proportions are two to one or about twice as much stock as you have rice.) Bring to a boil and taste carefully, adding more salt and pepper as needed. From this point on do not stir the rice again.

The Final Arrangement: Place the chicken, skin side up, in a ring about 2 inches from the side of the pan. Tuck two clams into the rice next to each piece of chicken and then lay the lobster pieces on the other side. Overlap the claws in the center of the dish and scatter the peas over all. Place the dish in the oven and bake for 20 minutes.

When Is It Done? The rice should have completely absorbed the stock and should appear moist but not wet, and the clams should all have opened.

Serving: Remove the pan from the oven and let it rest for 2 to 3 minutes. Lay the blade of a thin, sharp knife at one end of the lemon wedges and slice between the skin and the pulp of the lemon, cutting only halfway to the other end of the wedge; slip the lemons onto the side of the pan so they stand on edge in four equidistant spots. Serve the paella from the pan.

SPECIAL EQUIPMENT
SUGGESTED

A large kettle (for boiling the lobsters)

A large pan of ice and water (to cool the lobsters)

Two small wooden spoons or 2 pairs of chopsticks the length of the lobster bodies

Butcher's twine (unwaxed plain white cotton twine)

Tongs

Kitchen shears

A toothpick or wooden skewer

A paella pan, or any 6- to 8-quart flameproof baking and serving dish or casserole 2 to 2½ inches deep, preferably a round one about 14 inches across

ALMOND ROASTED FIGS

Chef Julian remembers his days in Barcelona, where fig and almond trees are abundant, and he has created this recipe where toasted almond crunchiness blends deliciously with the warm, juicy sweetness of the figs. They are a treat served just as they are, with perhaps a helping of sour cream, and a real sensation when presented Serrano fashion with the Honey Lime Peaches and Crème Fraîche Ice Cream described at the end of this chapter.

Manufacturing Note: You can do these in two ways, each quite different in effect. If you hand chop the almonds you get a rather rough covering, which has its crunchy charms. On the other hand, when you fine-grind your nuts in the machine you get a wall-to-wall covering and a definite crust. Here we do them both ways.

Toasting and Chopping the Almonds: Preheat the oven to 375° F. Spread the almonds in one layer in a roasting or jelly-roll pan and set in the middle level of the oven. Bake 8 to 10 minutes, shaking the pan occasionally until they are a light golden-brown. Remove them from the oven, and let cool. Chop them by hand for a rough cut, or pulse them in the food processor until they are the size of coarse bread crumbs. Stir in the brown sugar and set aside.

Peeling the Figs: Black figs need not be peeled, but the thicker-skinned green figs do. Before peeling, drop them into boiling water for 5 seconds, to loosen the skin; then gingerly peel off the skin with a paring knife, leaving the stems attached. Peeled or not, cut a thin slice off the bottoms of the figs so they will stand up when baked.

Coating with Almonds: Beat the egg whites vigorously until frothy, beat in the sugar, and continue until soft peaks are formed. One at a time, hold a fig by its stem and dip into the egg whites, turning it around in the whites to coat evenly. Then roll it in the almonds and stand it up in the buttered baking dish. Continue with the rest of the figs. Preheat the oven to 400° F.

Ahead-of-Time Note: The recipe may be prepared to this point several hours in advance.

Roasting the Figs: Roast the figs in the middle level of the preheated 400° F oven for 12 to 14 minutes, until heated through and softened, but still holding their shape. Be careful not to let the nut coatings brown too much! Serve warm.

INGREDIENTS FOR 12 FIGS

For the almonds
1 cup blanched almonds
⅓ cup light brown sugar

For the figs
12 fresh firm ripe green or black figs, washed and dried
3 egg whites
2 teaspoons sugar

SPECIAL EQUIPMENT SUGGESTED

A large sharp chopping knife or a food processor
A very clean, dry, grease-free whip and bowl (for beating the egg whites)
A lightly buttered baking dish just large enough to hold the figs comfortably

JULIAN SERRANO'S SALTED ALMONDS

INGREDIENTS FOR 3 CUPS

3 cups fine fresh whole blanched almonds
1 teaspoon table salt, or to taste
Olive oil, almond oil, or flavorless vegetable oil

Preheat the oven to 325° F.

Spread the almonds out in one layer on a baking pan. Drizzle on and toss them with just enough oil to coat the nuts, then toss with a sprinkling of salt. Bake in the middle level of the preheated oven for 15 to 20 minutes, until the nuts are lightly toasted and fragrant. Turn out on paper towels and blot up excess oil. Serve warm or cool.

Ahead-of-Time Note: Store in a covered jar. These will go off in taste after a week or so. The refrigerator will delay their demise, but the freezer will keep them fresh for weeks. Bring to room temperature or warm them in the oven before serving.

Variation: Use the same system for peanuts or pecans, and see Dean Fearing's Toasted Pecans on page 189.

HONEY LIME PEACHES

Here is a sweet spark of citrus and cinnamon to make ripe summer fruits even more delectable. Chef Julian macerates his peaches in this ambrosia, or uses slices of pear or cubes of melon or any firm, perfectly ripe fruit of the season. Serve them as is, surrounded by their marinade juices, or use them as a syrupy topping for pound cake, or for ice cream, including any of those in this book.

Preparing the Marinade: Measure the honey into a small saucepan and add the cinnamon stick. Split the vanilla bean in half lengthwise and scrape the seeds into the pan; drop in the pods. Bring the honey to a boil, then turn off the heat and pour in the lime juice. Drop in the zests, cover the pan, and allow the mixture to cool completely before straining it into a medium-size bowl.

Adding the Peaches: Drop the peaches into boiling water for 15 seconds, then remove and carefully peel off the skin with a paring knife. With a very sharp small knife, cut the peaches into perfectly neat wedges, all of the same size. Marinate them at room temperature in the honey mixture for at least 3 hours, or up to 6 hours—but if left too long the fruit will start to disintegrate, especially if it was very ripe to begin with.

INGREDIENTS FOR ABOUT 2 CUPS

1 cup clover honey

4-inch stick of cinnamon

1 fragrant vanilla bean

½ cup fresh lime juice

The zests (colored part of peel only) of:

1 fine firm shiny lemon

1 small firm shiny navel orange

2 perfectly ripe firm fragrant unblemished peaches

SPECIAL EQUIPMENT SUGGESTED

A zester

A strainer

CRÈME FRAÎCHE ICE CREAM WITH FIGS AND PEACHES

*Chef Julian's ice cream is yet another example of the versatility of that good old classic, custard sauce—*crème anglaise—*as used in contemporary American cuisine, and as discussed in the box on page 207. Here the sauce is chilled and then blended with tangy* crème fraîche *before freezing. No lean cuisine here!*

Technique: A full discussion of custard sauce is in the box on page 207.

Flavoring the Cream: Heat the half-and-half in a small saucepan. Cut the vanilla beans in half lengthwise and scrape the seeds from the pods with the tip of a knife into the cream—the true vanilla flavor is in the seeds and releasing them unleashes their maximum flavor. Drop the pods into the cream, cover the pan, and set it off heat.

Making the Custard: Whisk the egg yolks in the saucepan to break them up, gradually whisk in the sugar, and continue whisking several minutes, until the mixture is thick and pale yellow. Gradually beat in the hot cream, and set over moderately low heat, stirring with a wooden spoon and watching attentively until the custard reaches 160° F. Immediately pour the custard through the sieve into the bowl set over the ice water and stir until chilled.

Finishing the Ice Cream: Blend the *crème fraîche* into the chilled custard, stirring with the wooden spoon—but not beating and causing air bubbles. When completely blended and smooth, pour it into the ice cream freezer and freeze.

Presentation: Carefully lift the peach segments out of their marinade with two forks and lay 3 or 4 of them neatly on one side of each dessert plate. Arrange the cookies in the center of the plates and cover with a scoop of the ice cream. Cut the figs in half and stand three halves on the plate opposite the peaches. Tuck a small bunch of berries next to the ice cream and press another almond wafer into the top of the ice cream. Garnish the ice cream with a sprig of mint and drizzle the peach marinade over the plate.

INGREDIENTS FOR 6 PEOPLE

For 1 quart of ice cream
2 cups half-and-half
2 vanilla beans
10 egg yolks
¾ cup sugar
2 cups crème fraîche
    (see box, page 146)

For serving
Honey Lime Peaches—or pears or melon (see preceding recipe)
Small round almond or vanilla wafers
9 Almond Roasted Figs (see page 203), still warm
1½ cups mixed berries, such as blueberries, raspberries, and blackberries
Fresh mint leaves (if available)

SPECIAL EQUIPMENT SUGGESTED

A 2-quart stainless steel saucepan (for the egg yolks)
A whisk and a wooden spoon
An instant-read thermometer
A fine-meshed sieve
A pan of ice and water
An ice cream freezer
6 dessert plates

JULIA'S CLASSIC CUSTARD SAUCE CRÈME ANGLAISE

This recipe is a standard for how to make custard sauce the careful classical way. The fast restaurant way follows.

INGREDIENTS FOR ABOUT 2 CUPS

⅔ cup sugar

6 egg yolks, in a 2-quart stainless steel saucepan

1½ cups milk, in another saucepan

1 tablespoon pure vanilla extract

3 tablespoons unsalted butter (optional)

2 tablespoons rum, Cognac, or other liqueur (optional)

SPECIAL EQUIPMENT SUGGESTED

A 2-quart stainless steel saucepan

A wire whisk

A wooden spoon

Start the custard by gradually whisking the sugar into the egg yolks, and continue whisking for several minutes, until the yolks are thick and pale yellow. A bit lifted in the wires of the whisk should fall back, creating a slowly dissolving ribbon on the surface.

Meanwhile, heat the milk almost to the simmer, then, very slowly at first, to warm them gradually and prevent them from scrambling, start whisking dribbles of the hot milk into the egg yolks. When about a cup has gone in, rapidly whisk in the rest of the milk.

Stir rather slowly with the wooden spoon over moderately low heat until just thickened enough to coat the back of the spoon—3 to 4 minutes; do not bring to the simmer or you will scramble the yolks—but you must heat the sauce enough for the yolks to poach and thicken, which occurs at 160° F. The sauce is done when it is thick enough to hold when you draw your finger across the back of the spoon as you take it out of the sauce. Stir in the butter and optional flavorings—but not so much liquid that you thin out the sauce.

Ahead-of-Time Note: May be made 2 to 3 days in advance; cover when cool and refrigerate. The sauce will thicken slightly as it cools and chills.

Chef's Restaurant Method for Custard Sauce

Restaurants don't have the time to be as careful as home cooks. Many chefs let the custard sauce come to a frank boil, then press it through a fine-meshed sieve to eliminate the lumps. The resulting sauce is perhaps not quite as delicate as the one produced according to the careful method, but it works, and it holds up under restaurant conditions—a spoonful or so of butter plus a little vanilla, rum, or chocolate will disguise the haste.

Follow the directions in the preceding recipe but have at your side a fine-meshed sieve set over a bowl, a ladle, and your portable or tabletop electric blender. Set the sauce over moderately high heat and whisk constantly as it comes to the boil. Immediately remove from heat and push it through the very fine sieve, using the bottom of your ladle. If it looks grainy—which it often does—puree it for 15 seconds or so with your electric blender, which will smooth it to a fine sheen. The sauce will thin out slightly after sieving and/or blending.

cook's notes

CAROL FIELD

A fourth-generation Californian, born in San Francisco and raised in Berkeley, Carol Field did not set out to be a "Master Chef." After graduating from Wellesley College, she began what she thought would be a journalistic career. From 1974 to 1976 she worked as a contributing, then associate, and then assistant editor at *City Magazine,* and from 1975 to 1980 as a contributing editor for *New West/California.* Carol was sent on many field assignments to write about food and notable chefs. She became captivated by Italy and its cuisine and her articles began to lean heavily toward Italian culture. "My coworkers had to keep reminding me that the name of the publication was not 'New Italian,' " recalls Carol.

Her first book, *The Hill Towns of Italy* (E. P. Dutton, 1983), was not about food, but during its preparation she became fascinated with culinary Italy. She spent the next two years traversing the country repeatedly from Como in the north to Palermo in the south working with Italian bakers. "I got involved in bread because you could understand Italy through its bread. Every region, every province, every village has its own bread." She published the results of her travels and baking experiences in 1985 in *The Italian Baker,* a thorough work on the breads of Italy that won the International Association of Culinary Professionals Tastemaker Award. It will long remain the definitive book on the subject, and Carol treated us to a display of her expertise. She showed us how to make the essential Italian yeast starter, the *biga,* and how to turn out with expertise the long, crisp breadsticks, *grissini,* plus great round rustic country loaves, and rosemary-studded olive oil rolls. Carol reworked all the breads she learned to make in Italy in an American kitchen with American ingredients so that her recipes could be faithfully reproduced.

Bread was by no means the sole object of Carol's interest. She has subsequently published *Celebrating Italy, Italy in Small Bites,* and *Focaccia: Simple Breads from the Italian Oven,* beautifully revealing the culinary heart and spirit of the people.

BIGA
CAROL FIELD'S ITALIAN-STYLE YEAST STARTER

Carol Field likes to make her rustic breads with a biga, *or yeast starter, because of the special taste and texture that dough made with a starter gives to the bread. Notes on the whys and wherefores of starters are in the box on this page. They are very easy to make, as you will see.*

Mixing the biga: Pour the warm water into a bowl or measuring cup, then sprinkle on and whisk in the yeast; let stand 5 to 10 minutes, until the mixture is creamy and the yeast has thoroughly dissolved. Pour the yeast mixture into the bowl of the mixer, stir in the rest of the water, and use the hand whisk to beat in 1 cup of the flour. Set the bowl on the machine, attach the paddle, and measure in the remaining flour. Mix at the low speed for 1 to 2

(continued)

SOME NOTES FROM JULIA ON YEAST STARTERS

A yeast starter—or *biga,* as the Italians call it—is flour and water with a small amount of yeast that is mixed to a batter consistency and allowed to ferment at room temperature for a number of hours until it has developed large, yeasty bubbles throughout. In the old days, before commercial yeast had been developed, bakers used other elements, like grapes, potatoes, and so forth, to produce their own yeast starters, from which they made their dough. They would save a portion of that day's dough to act as a starter for the next day's batch; it was a slow process but that old-fashioned bread had wonderful flavor and texture. Many contemporary bakers, like Carol Field, use a combination known as the *levain-levure* system, or starter-plus-yeast, in order to capture the texture and flavor advantages of the starter, plus the time-saving boost of fresh yeast.

Carol Field's is a fresh starter, meaning it has not been allowed to ferment to the sourdough stage. A sourdough starter is simply the same formula that has fermented to whatever degree of sourness the baker desires. Some of these starters are considered family treasures and have gone on for generations, being continually refreshed and reconstituted with loving care.

To Refresh a Starter: A fresh starter begins to sour after four or five days. To refresh a starter, such as Carol Field's *biga,* remove and discard 1½ cups of it, then blend and whisk to batter consistency 1½ cups of flour in a bowl with about ⅓ cup of water; stir this into the starter and let the starter rise again before refrigerating. You may freeze a starter.

INGREDIENTS FOR 3¾ CUPS

¼ *cup warm water (not over 105° F)*

½ *teaspoon dry-active yeast or* ⅕ *cake (a scant ½ teaspoon) fresh yeast*

1⅓ *cups water (at room temperature, about 70° F)*

3¾ *cups (scooped and leveled) unbleached all-purpose flour (see box, page 43)*

A few drops of olive oil (for the rising bowl)

SPECIAL EQUIPMENT SUGGESTED

A freestanding electric mixer with paddle attachment, or a wooden spoon and a roomy mixing bowl

A hand whisk

A large rubber band or string

A 3- to 4-quart straight-sided glass bowl or plastic container (for rising the biga*)*

A marking pen

Biga (continued)

minutes to make a sticky, batter-type dough. *Alternately:* Mix by hand first with a whisk, then with a wooden spoon (or use the food processor as suggested on page 212).

Rising: Lightly oil the rising container, and transfer the *biga* into it. Stretch the plastic tightly over the top, and secure with the rubber band or string. Mark the level of the *biga* on the outside of the container, so that you may judge the eventual amount of the rise. Set at cool room temperature (about 70° F) for 6 to 24 hours. The *biga* should triple in volume, and then fall back upon itself. It will be a sticky, big-bubbled batter when it is ready.

Ahead-of-time Note: Refrigerate the starter after 24 hours, where it will keep for several days.

GRISSINI
ITALIAN BREADSTICKS

"No one will want to make breadsticks!" declared Carol Field emphatically when we suggested that she show us how. Breadsticks, she felt, do not present a challenge to the serious baker—they're too easy to make—and stale store-bought breadsticks have so tarnished their former appeal that people have lost interest in them. But we finally persuaded her, and Carol's recipe has turned out to be one of the most popular in our series. Following her expert directions, you will find they are indeed easy to make. And what fun to have on hand a big basket of your own homemade breadsticks, fresh and crisp and brown. Set them on the table to serve with soup instead of melba toast, or for dipping into a cocktail sauce, or just to munch on for the sheer pleasure of the crunch.

Preparing the Dough: Pour the water into a small bowl or measuring cup, whisk in the yeast, and let stand until the mixture is creamy and the yeast has thoroughly dissolved—5 to 10 minutes. Pour the yeast mixture into the bowl of the electric mixer, whisk in the olive oil or lard and 1 cup of the flour. When well blended and free of lumps, attach the bowl to the machine and insert the paddle. One cup at a time, beat in most of the flour, being sure that all is well blended and free of lumps. Beat in the salt with the last of the flour and mix until a dough is formed. If any dry bits of flour remain at the bottom of the bowl, add droplets more water to incorporate them. Change to the dough hook and knead at low speed for about 3 minutes,

INGREDIENTS FOR 3 TO 5
DOZEN GRISSINI (DEPENDING
ON THE LENGTH AND
THICKNESS OF THE DOUGH)

1⅓ cups warm water (105° F to 110° F)

1½ teaspoons dry-active yeast

¼ cup excellent olive oil or lard, at room temperature

(continued)

until the dough is velvety, smooth, and elastic. Transfer the dough to a lightly floured counter, slamming it down several times and kneading vigorously for just a few turns to finish.

Shaping and Rising: Brush a 10- by 16-inch rectangle of olive oil onto the cutting board and lift the dough into the middle of it. Pat the dough gently into a rectangle, then roll it with your pin into the 10- by 16-inch shape about ¼ inch thick. Brush the top of the dough with a light film of olive oil, cover with plastic wrap, drape a kitchen towel over the plastic, and let rise in a warm spot (70° F to 75° F) until more than doubled but not tripled in volume—about 1¾ hours. (This is the only rise.)

Baking: At least 30 minutes before baking, set the baking stone, if you are using one, on the middle shelf of your oven. Heat the oven to 425° F. Lightly oil the baking sheets.

Shaping the **Grissini:** Turn the cutting board so one of the short sides of the dough rectangle is facing you. Using the pizza cutter or pastry scraper, bisect the dough lengthwise, leaving both halves in place. Trim off and discard the ragged edge from the bottom of the dough. Now, to form the *grissini,* cut a ½-inch strip—about the width of your little finger—across the bottom (or short side) of the rectangle, giving you two fingers of dough each 5 inches long. Pick one up, holding each end with the fingertips of each hand, and gently vibrate and stretch it the width of the short side of your baking sheet (10 inches), then lay it across the bottom of the sheet. Pick up, stretch, and lay the second finger of dough ½ inch above the first, leaving about 1½ inches between strips. Continue cutting, stretching, and laying down dough strips until you have filled your baking sheets. Cover the rest of the dough with plastic while you are baking the first.

(continued)

3¾ cups (500 grams or 1.1 pounds) unbleached all-purpose flour
1½ to 2 teaspoons sea salt
About ½ cup additional olive oil (for brushing on the dough and pans)

SPECIAL EQUIPMENT
SUGGESTED

A heavy-duty electric mixer with paddle and dough hook attachments (see page 212 for notes on hand kneading and the food processor)
A whisk
A 12- by 18-inch wooden cutting board (for rising the dough)
A rolling pin
2 baking sheets, about 11 by 17 inches, rimless if possible
A pizza cutter or a pastry scraper
A tape measure or a ruler
A pastry brush
A baking stone for the oven (strongly recommended by Carol Field)

Grissini (continued)

A NOTE FROM JULIA ON EQUIPMENT

Carol Field, in her televised demonstration for this series, makes her doughs in a heavy-duty electric mixer with paddle and dough hook attachments, and the recipes here follow that system. If you do not have such equipment she recommends the food processor or elbow grease. However, you will have a heavy, sticky time making her rustic dough by hand unless you have an old-fashioned hand-cranking bread bucket.

The food processor does a marvelous job for the initial kneading of dough. Always start with the dry ingredients, then add the liquids, and don't overload the machine—you can do it in batches, and unite them later by hand kneading. Do not let the dough overheat—stop and let it cool down if it feels warmer than your hand. Let the dough rest in the machine now and then, which allows the flour particles to swell as they absorb the liquid, giving you a better idea of the dough's consistency—it also makes for faster kneading. Always finish the dough by hand; this homogenizes it into a single web of interlocking strands.

Baking: Set the baking sheet directly on the heated baking stone or the oven rack, and bake until the *grissini* are crisp and golden brown—18 to 20 minutes if you are using a stone, or about 10 minutes on a plain sheet. Watch carefully the last few minutes, and if some are done before others, re-move them. (For crunchier breadsticks, set them directly on the baking stone for the last few minutes.) Cool on racks, or upright in woven baskets.

VARIATIONS

To flavor the dough itself:

- Work 4 tablespoons of finely chopped fresh sage leaves (or 3 tablespoons fresh rosemary) into the dough as you finish the kneading.

- Work 2 ounces (½ cup) of freshly grated parmigiano reggiano cheese into the dough at the end of the kneading.

To season the outside:

When the dough is still in a rectangle shape and just after making the lengthwise separation cut, lightly brush or spritz the top of the dough with water and sprinkle on ½ cup sesame seeds or poppy seeds.

Using a biga, *or yeast starter:*

For additional flavor and texture, make the dough with ⅓ cup of the *biga,* described on page 209 and as used in the rustic bread on page 216.

VARIATIONS

The same dough that makes *grissini* also makes a good *focaccia,* as noted in the box on page 215, as well as the delicious olive oil rolls described on the opposite page.

OLIVE OIL ROLLS

You can, of course, form the rolls in any shape you wish. Carol Field, however, likes to arrange hers in a circle so that they adhere to each other during baking, forming a wreath. Guests then pull it apart at the table.

The First Rise: Lightly oil the plastic container and place the just-made dough in it. Mark the level of the dough on the outside of the container so that you can judge the extent of rise. Cover tightly with plastic wrap, and let rise at 70° F to 75° F until almost slightly more than doubled in volume—2 to 3 hours.

Shaping the Rolls: Turn the risen dough out onto your lightly floured work surface and divide it into eight equal pieces. One at a time, leaving the rest of the dough covered with a towel, shape each piece into a round ball as follows: Lifting the far end, fold the dough toward you into thirds, as though folding a business letter. Give a quarter turn, and fold again, repeating the movement several times. Then, with your left hand slightly cupped, and grabbing a tiny tail of the dough under your little finger, drag the dough smoothly 6 to 8 inches across your work surface to your right. Giving the dough a quarter turn, repeat the movement with your right hand, dragging the dough across to your left. Repeat rapidly several times until you have formed a round ball. Set the ball smooth side up an inch or so from the edge of the oiled baking sheet, and rapidly continue with the rest, arranging them 1 inch apart in a circle.

The Second Rise: Brush the tops lightly with oil, cover with a towel, and let rise at 70° F to 75° F for about an hour, until the rolls have swelled enough to connect to each other, forming a wreath. Meanwhile, preheat the oven to 400° F, and set the baking stone, if you are using one, on the lower middle level.

Baking: Feel the tops of the rolls, and if a light skin seems to have formed, spritz lightly with water. (If they crust over, they will not rise in the oven.) Then brush the tops with a little olive oil, drop a nice pinch of rosemary in the center of each, and another of salt. Set the baking sheet in the preheated oven and bake for 35 to 40 minutes, or until the rolls are golden. Cool on a rack.

INGREDIENTS FOR 8 ROLLS

The preceding grissini *dough, kneaded but not risen*

Olive oil

All-purpose flour (for dusting the counter)

1 to 2 tablespoons chopped fresh rosemary, or 1 teaspoon dried rosemary

Sea salt (for sprinkling on top of the rolls)

SPECIAL EQUIPMENT SUGGESTED

A straight-sided plastic container (for dough rising), 4-quart size

A pastry brush

A baking sheet or jelly-roll pan, about 11 by 17 inches, lightly oiled

A baking stone (optional)

A plant mister (a water bottle with fine-spray nozzle attachment)

A cooling rack

CROSTINI AND BRUSCHETTA
TOPPINGS FOR TOASTED ITALIAN COUNTRY BREADS

The Italians make easy and delicious hors d'oeuvre and snacks by just grilling country bread, rubbing it with a cut garlic clove, and finishing with a dribble of olive oil and a sprinkling of salt. To be more elaborate they may include a spread or topping. Every region of Italy seems to have its own culinary vocabulary for toast with a topping, and while crostini *and* bruschetta *figure among them, I shall not attempt to sort them out further. If you are so fortunately equipped as to have a charcoal grill, it is lovely to toast the bread on it, but the broiler is always effective. Among the many ideas in Carol Field's repertoire, here are three especially fine ones. If you are using Carol's rustic loaf, she suggests that it be two days old, since freshly made bread is usually too soft for toasting and spreading.*

GARLIC AND TOMATO TOPPING

Wonderfully simple and satisfying, these need no formal recipe—just fresh ripe in-season tomatoes full of their own natural flavor. Toast ½-inch-thick slices of Carol's two-day-old rustic bread (see page 216) and cut them in halves or thirds to make them finger-food size. Rub one side with a cut clove of garlic, then cut a fine fresh tomato in half horizontally, press out the seeds, and smear the bread with the tomato. Season lightly with salt and pepper, and drizzle on a good bit of your best and fruitiest olive oil.

RED ONION AND SWEET PEPPER SPREAD

After rubbing your still warm toasted country bread with cut garlic, spread on a generous topping of the following, and serve with a drizzle of good olive oil.

Melt the butter in the pan and sweat the onions (sauté very slowly) uncovered and over very low heat, stirring frequently, until very tender and translucent but not browned. Cover and cook over very low heat for another 15 minutes, until the onions are almost creamy. Stir in the sliced peppers, thyme, balsamic vinegar, and salt, and continue to cook over low heat, without browning, and stirring occasionally, for another 15 minutes. Cool. Puree in the food processor or blender, and season to taste.

Ahead-of-Time Note: Cover and store in the refrigerator, where the spread will keep for 4 to 5 days.

INGREDIENTS FOR ABOUT I CUP

2 tablespoons unsalted butter

1½ pounds red onions, peeled and thinly sliced

3 red bell peppers, peeled, seeded, and thinly sliced

¼ teaspoon dried thyme

½ teaspoon balsamic vinegar, or to taste

½ teaspoon salt

SPECIAL EQUIPMENT SUGGESTED

A heavy 12-inch covered frying or sauté pan, preferably no-stick

A food processor or an electric blender

WALNUT AND PARSLEY SPREAD

Another unusual spread for Carol Field's toasted garlic-rubbed rustic bread, to be served warm and anointed with a drizzle of your best olive oil.

Set the slice of bread on a plate and moisten it with the vinegar. After 15 minutes, squeeze out and discard excess moisture. Puree the bread in the food processor with the rest of the ingredients listed, to make a thick paste. Taste carefully for salt and pepper. Let rest at least 2 hours, allowing the flavors to mingle and develop.

Ahead-of-Time Note: Cover and store in the refrigerator, where the spread will keep for 7 to 10 days.

INGREDIENTS FOR ABOUT 1¾ CUPS

½-inch-thick slice of Carol Field's rustic bread (see page 216), crusts off

1½ tablespoons red wine vinegar

1 medium garlic clove, peeled and minced

½ cup (firmly packed) Italian flat-leaf parsley leaves

1 tablespoon vinegar-packed capers, drained and rinsed

1 cornichon (optional)

2 tablespoons tomato paste diluted in ¼ cup warm water

⅓ cup excellent olive oil

½ cup walnut meats, toasted

Salt

A generous amount of freshly ground black pepper, ½ teaspoon at least

SPECIAL EQUIPMENT SUGGESTED

A food processor

FOCACCIA
ITALIAN-STYLE HERB BREAD WITH OLIVE OIL

The traditional garlic and herb-scented *focaccia* is a large, roughly shaped, flattish oval or rectangle of bread less than an inch thick and about 12 inches long and 8 to 10 inches wide, with a few holes like pockmarks in its surface. As usual with popular items, we now have boutique-pizza-type *focaccias* that are thicker and fancier, and covered with all kinds of things like imported olives, sun-dried tomatoes, artichoke hearts, sausages, goat cheese bits, and so on. The simple basic model here is a comfortable companion to the food at hand—a salad or cheese, broiled chicken or fish. This is the formula.

Let a batch of *grissini* dough (see page 210) rise almost to slightly more than double in volume as described for the olive oil rolls, and preheat your oven to 450° F. Turn the risen dough out onto a lightly floured work surface and cut it in half. Place each half on a lightly oiled baking sheet and push out into a rough oval with the heels of your hands. The dough will soon resist you. Let it relax a few minutes while you prepare the topping, then continue, resting several minutes, to form it into a rough, uneven, free-form oval-rectangular shape about 12 inches long and less than ½ inch thick. Now use your fingertips to make three or four uneven indentations in the dough, and proceed at once to the topping—the dough is to rise enough to be puffy but not quite doubled, 45 minutes to 1 hour.

For a simple topping, puree 2 or 3 large peeled cloves of garlic and mash to a paste with ½ teaspoon of salt, then blend with 3 tablespoons of olive oil. Paint the mixture over the surfaces of the two doughs; sprinkle on ½ tablespoon or so of chopped thyme or rosemary or a mixture of herbs, and finish with 2 to 3 tablespoons of kosher salt or crystals of sea salt.

Bake at once in the lower and upper thirds of the preheated 450° F oven, switching pans halfway through. The *focaccias* are done when lightly browned on the top and bottom—in about 20 to 25 minutes. They are at their very best when freshly made and served while still warm; however, they may be kept warm, they may be re-heated, or they may be frozen.

CAROL FIELD'S RUSTIC COUNTRY BREAD

This is that wonderful type of country bread that features the real taste of the grain, and a slightly chewy texture. When you cut off a slice, the inside is not tight-grained but rather loose with nice big holes, and the color is not dead white but somewhat yellowish in a rustic way. The dough itself is very light and soft, almost as sticky as the biga *that starts it off. Carol kneads it with her special rolling push, and if you can catch her making this recipe on TV, do watch it. Words do their best to explain, but there is no substitute for actually seeing it.*

Manufacturing Note: Since this is an especially soft dough and the kneading of it requires unusual movements, you may want to cut the recipe by two-thirds or a half, making only one or two loaves as a first try. Please note that you may adapt this recipe for the food processor, as noted in the box on page 212, and Carol suggests you use a machine of some sort since this is a very heavy, sticky, difficult dough to do by hand.

Making the Dough: Whisk the yeast into the ¼ cup of warm water in a small bowl or measuring cup and let it stand until the mixture is creamy and the yeast has thoroughly dissolved—about 10 minutes. Then pour it into the bowl of the electric mixer along with the room temperature water. Carol now likes to add the *biga,* squeezing it into the water with her hands, working it about until it is broken into small pieces and the water becomes chalky white. When the *biga* is broken up, attach the mixer paddle, pour in the flours and salt, and mix until the dough comes together in a mass. It should be very sticky and soft, and should not pull away from the bottom of the bowl—if it seems too dry, beat in more water by dribbles—up to about 2 tablespoons. On the other hand, if too wet, beat in sprinkles of flour. Just keep in mind that the dough should remain quite sticky and not pull away from the bottom of the bowl, although it should pull away from the sides of the bowl and from the paddle. Change to the dough hook and knead for 5 to 6 minutes at medium speed. The dough will still be very sticky but will have developed some elasticity—when lifted it should hold together and spring back softly.

The First Folding-Knead: Pour the dough out onto your lightly floured counter. It will be very soft, and rather than being kneaded in the usual way,

INGREDIENTS FOR 3 LOAVES

For the dough
1½ teaspoons dry-active yeast
¼ cup warm water (105° F to 110° F)
2¼ cups water, at room temperature (about 70° F)
9 ounces (about 1 cup) biga (the yeast starter), preferably 2 to 3 days old (see page 209)
4 cups unbleached all-purpose flour, plus ½ cup more for sprinkling
1⅓ cups whole wheat flour, preferably organic
1 tablespoon plus 1 teaspoon salt, preferably sea salt

Other necessities
A little olive oil (for the rising bowl)
About ½ cup cornmeal (for the baking stones)

(continued)

Rustic Country Bread (continued)

it is now to be folded over upon itself a number of times so that it will de-velop body and texture. Sprinkle the top of the dough with a small dusting of flour. Then, using the pastry scraper, fold the dough back over onto it-self. Rotate a quarter turn, dust again with flour, fold again, and repeat five or six times.

The First Rise: Lightly oil the container and lift the dough into it. Stretch a sheet of plastic closely over the top and secure with the rubber band or string. Mark the level of the dough on the outside of the container so that you may judge the extent of the rise. Let rise at room temperature (about 70° F) or cooler until tripled and full of air bubbles—3 hours or longer. It is the extent of the rise that concerns you here, not the timing.

Ahead-of-Time Note: If you wish to continue with the dough the next day, let it rise in the refrigerator overnight. Allow it to come near room temper-ature before continuing.

The Second Folding-Knead: The risen dough will still be soft and sticky as you pour it out onto your lightly floured work surface. Divide it into three equal pieces. Work on one piece at a time, keeping the rest covered with a towel. Dust the top of the dough with flour, then, using your pastry scraper, begin by folding the piece of dough over toward you two or three times as you would fold a letter; give it a quarter turn, a little sprinkle of flour, and fold again. Then knead with the pastry scraper, as you did before: Sprinkle the top of the dough with a small dusting of flour and, using the pastry scraper, fold the dough back over onto itself, give a quarter turn, and repeat several times. Although you cannot see it, you can definitely feel the dough beginning to develop a unified surface, as though a delicate sheet of rubber were holding it in shape: This is the gluten cloak that you are forming by your folding movements.

The Drag-Rolling-Knead: Shape the dough into a round by gently but firmly pulling its surface down toward your work surface with the edges of your cupped hands; repeat several times, rotating the dough a quarter turn—thus stretching the gluten cloak around the ball to shape it. Then, using the slightly cupped side of your right hand, catch a tiny tail of the dough under your little finger and smoothly drag and roll the ball of dough 6 to 8 inches to the left across your work surface. Repeat with the left hand and drag-roll to the right, and again with the right hand drag-roll to the left, and so on for several rolls until you have shaped the ball.

SPECIAL EQUIPMENT
SUGGESTED

An electric mixer with dough hook and paddle attachments
A wide-edged pastry scraper (about 6 inches across), or the side of a big spatula (for kneading)
A straight-sided plastic container, 4- to 6-quart capacity
Plastic wrap
A large rubber band or string
A marking pen
3 squares of parchment paper, 14 inches to a side
2 oven-size baking stones
A pizza peel
A plant mister (a water bottle with fine-spray nozzle attachment)

The Final Rise: Flour a square of parchment paper, and lift the round of dough upside down (seam side up) upon it. Cover with a towel and set on a baking sheet or safe flat place. Form the other two pieces of dough in the same manner, covering them with towels. Let them rise until they have roughly doubled in bulk and you can see many air bubbles under the surface—an hour or so.

Baking: At least 30 minutes before baking, set the baking stones on the bottom rung of your oven, and preheat to 450° F. Just before baking, sprinkle the stones with cornmeal. Trim the parchment paper, leaving only a ½-inch edge all around the dough. Slipping your hand under the paper, rapidly and gently invert one of the loaves onto the corner of a hot stone. At once generously spritz water into the oven, and close the door. Center a second loaf on the second stone and spritz with water, and then place the final loaf in the opposite corner of the first stone, spritzing again. The parchment paper will be peeled off the loaves in 15 minutes; although their roundness was somewhat disturbed during their transfer to the oven, the dough will spring back into shape as it bakes because you have formed it correctly.

After about 15 minutes, when the crusts have set, peel the parchment paper away from the tops of the loaves. Bake for 30 to 35 minutes in all, until you hear the familiar hollow ring when you tap the bottom of the loaves—an instant-read thermometer should register 200° F when the loaves are poked through the bottom. Transfer the loaves to a rack and let cool completely before cutting.

VARIATION—LONG LOAVES

This same dough may also be shaped into long loaves. After the dough's second rise and its shaping into three round loaves, let the loaves relax for 20 minutes. Then roll each round loaf into a fat log and place seam side up on floured parchment paper set on baking sheets or peels. Cover the loaves, and let rise until doubled in volume and filled with bubbles under the surface. Trim the parchment to within ½ inch of the edge of each loaf; then, with your hands under the parchment, gently invert them onto the hot stones and bake as you would the round loaves.

JASPER WHITE

When Jasper White talks food, people listen. Not just because this handsome chef stands well over six feet and speaks with a deep, authoritative voice but mostly because he brings such a commonsense approach to food. His dishes remind us that cooking is about food, and delicious ingredients, and enjoyment, and not about kitchen calisthenics. "There are people who really can't handle the basics and yet have an advanced way of combining ingredients that don't necessarily go together and flavors that don't traditionally taste good together and cooking techniques that don't necessarily work." He is worried about where food may be going.

Chef Jasper grew up on a farm on the Jersey shore in a family that was half Italian and "kind of fanatical about food." While studying history in college, he began to work in a restaurant "and I knew— perhaps I always knew, but I definitely knew then—that I wasn't going to study history anymore." He received his formal culinary training at the Culinary Institute of America and apprenticed in restaurants on the east and west coasts before opening his extremely successful Boston restaurant, Jasper's, in 1982. His education and apprenticeships taught him respect for the classics; his creativity is grounded in them and his food never misses.

When Jasper cooks he wants people to *remember*—to recall the exquisite taste of perfectly seasoned, delicious ingredients. "I always feel that when I wake up the next day, I should be able to remember what I ate. I mean, I have literally woken up the next day and not been able to remember what it was I ate because it was so complex it just didn't stick with me. It wasn't, 'Weren't those oysters great last night?' or 'Didn't you think that the baby bok choy was the most perfect thing you have ever eaten?' "

Not to worry. We'll all long remember the perfection of his hearty fish chowder and the succulence of his pan-roasted lobster.

KATHLEEN ANNINO'S CAPE COD COMMON CRACKERS

As any New Englander knows, you can't really enjoy a real New England chowder without toasted common crackers. These are not like pilot biscuits or saltines; they are softly crackly, layered, somewhat puffy round crackers about 1¼ inches in diameter. You split them in half, butter them, and toast them, and then you crumble them into your chowder. They are difficult to find outside the New England area, and the recipe has always been a locked-up secret. Our team decided we would break the monopoly, and our own determined Kathleen, after making thirty-eight different versions, finally, on October 25, 1994, came up with a winner. Here it is—a strange method, but a very special cracker.

Manufacturing Note: You can do all of this by hand, but Kathleen recommends a heavy-duty mixer with paddle and dough hook attachments, and a hand-cranking pasta machine.

INGREDIENTS FOR ABOUT 5½ DOZEN ROUND CRACKERS 1½ INCHES ACROSS AND ¾ INCH THICK

For the yeast starter

1½ teaspoons dry-active yeast
1 cup warm water (105° F to 110° F)
1 tablespoon light brown sugar
1½ teaspoons fresh lemon juice
½ teaspoon salt
1 cup bread flour (available in health food stores)

For the cracker dough

1 cup yeast starter
1 to 1¼ cups bread flour
6 tablespoons (3 ounces) vegetable shortening or lard
1 teaspoon salt
1 tablespoon instant potato flakes
1 tablespoon light brown sugar
½ teaspoon baking soda
3 tablespoons water
1 tablespoon fresh lemon juice
An additional 1½ to 2 cups bread flour

Making the Starter: Whisk all the ingredients together into a batter, and store in a covered container at room temperature (70° F to 75° F) for at least 24 hours or up to 60 hours. It will rise and form large bubbles, then subside and separate.

Making the Cracker Dough: Knead enough flour into 1 cup of the starter to make a firm ball of dough. Cover and let rest for 1 hour. In a separate bowl, whisk the shortening or lard, salt, potato flakes, brown sugar, and baking soda together, mixing in the water and lemon juice at the end. Knead this liquid into the ball of dough, using the paddle attachment. Gradually knead in the additional flour, changing to the dough hook as the dough stiffens. After about 5 minutes you should have a stiff, smooth ball.

Rolling Out the Dough: Cut the dough into quarters. One at a time, roll a piece of dough into a rectangle ⅜ inch thick and, starting at one of the short ends, put through the pasta rollers, fold into three like a business letter, give a quarter turn, and roll again. Repeat the process six times in all and going down to position #6 on the machine. Use as little flour as possible. The final dough should be no thicker than ¼ inch. Meanwhile, preheat the oven to 425° F.

Forming and Baking: Cut 1½-inch rounds out of the rolled dough pieces, and press the tines of a table fork through the rounds in two places. Arrange ¼ inch apart on no-stick or parchment-paper-lined baking sheets. Bake for about 8 minutes, until the crackers have risen, are a light golden-brown, and feel firm to the touch.

Drying Out and Storing: Lower the thermostat to 200° F and let the crackers dry out in the oven for 2 hours or longer—to dehydrate and crisp the inner layers.

Ahead-of-Time Note: When completely cool, store in an airtight container. If they become stale or soft, reheat for 5 minutes or so in a 400° F oven.

SWEET CORN FRITTERS

Wonderfully fresh and crisp, and wonderfully full of real corn flavor, Chef Jasper's fritters are a delight. Serve them with soups and chowders, as a first course, as an accompaniment to lobster, or as a snack. One of the secrets of their continuing popularity in his restaurant is that the oil is always fresh, which makes an enormous difference when preparing any fried food. Jasper's batter is a simple one, consisting only of the usual egg, milk, flour plus cornmeal and corn, with the additions of red bell peppers and, if you wish, country ham.

Manufacturing Notes:

The Corn. Fresh corn in season is, of course, most desirable, but we have used supermarket out-of-season December corn with enthusiastic response.

The Proportions. For family use, you will probably want to cut the proportions in half, giving 6 people at least 2 fritters apiece, depending on size.

Deep-Fat Frying. A discussion is in the box on page 195.

Preparing the Bell Pepper and the Corn: Melt the butter in the small frying pan, stir in the peppers, and sauté over moderate heat for several minutes until tender. Meanwhile, drop the husked ears of corn into the kettle of boiling water and boil just until cooked through—from 1 to 4 or 5 minutes depending upon age. Drop into cold water to cool rapidly, then remove the kernels using a corn scraper or the large holes of a grater, or cutting them off with a knife. Then scrape down the ears with the back of a knife to recuperate the milky residue, adding it to the corn kernels. You should have about 1½ cups.

Preparing the Batter: Sift or sieve the flour and cornmeal into the mixing bowl, and stir in the baking powder. Then blend in the optional ham, the scallions, corn, eggs, and milk, and scrape in the cooked peppers with their juice. Stir in seasonings to taste. Mix thoroughly, but do not overwork or the fritters will be tough. Chill for at least an hour.

Ahead-of-Time Note: The batter may be made several hours in advance and refrigerated.

INGREDIENTS FOR 2½ TO 3 DOZEN FRITTERS

The red bell pepper and the corn

3 tablespoons unsalted butter

1 small red bell pepper, cut into ⅛-inch dice

2 or 3 ears of fresh corn, husked

Dry ingredients for the batter

1½ cups all-purpose flour

½ cup yellow cornmeal

1 tablespoon fresh double-action baking powder

1 teaspoon salt

½ teaspoon freshly ground black pepper

¼ teaspoon cayenne pepper

The rest of the batter

2 or 3 ounces smoked country ham, cut into ¼-inch dice (optional)

5 scallions, green and white parts, very thinly sliced

3 eggs, lightly beaten

1 cup milk

(continued)

Sweet Corn Fritters (continued)

Getting Ready for Frying: Before beginning to fry the fritters, check the consistency of the batter—it should be firm enough to hold its shape in a spoon. Thin with droplets of milk, or thicken with sprinkles of flour. Taste, and adjust seasoning. Pour the oil into the deep-frying pan and heat slowly to a temperature of 350° F.

Frying: Using the ice cream scoop or the serving spoon, drop four or five Ping-Pong-size balls of batter into the hot oil; don't overcrowd the pan or the temperature will drop and the fritters will be greasy rather than crisp. Cook until golden brown, about a minute, turning them over and over to brown evenly. Remove them from the pan with the wire-mesh strainer and drain on the paper towels. Wait a minute or so to allow the frying oil to reheat, then continue with the remaining batter, keeping your eye on the thermometer so the temperature doesn't drop too low or go too high. Serve as soon as possible.

Ahead-of-Time Note: These are best, in our opinion, served at once, while still moist inside. When kept warm even in a slow oven, they cook more and the interior is drier and more breadlike—but you may prefer them that way!

cook's notes

Oil for frying (Jasper uses corn oil for corn fritters—you'll need 1 quart for half the recipe)

SPECIAL EQUIPMENT SUGGESTED

A small frying pan (for sautéing the peppers)

A kettle of salted boiling water (for cooking the corn)

A corn scraper, a 4-sided grater, or a sharp knife

A flour sifter or sieve

A deep-fat fryer (for a half recipe we used an 8-inch saucepan 6 inches deep)

A deep-frying thermometer (highly recommended)

A small ice cream scoop or a large serving spoon (for forming the fritters)

Tongs

A wire-mesh spoon (for removing the fritters from the frying oil)

A baking pan lined with paper towels

PAN-ROASTED LOBSTER

This is the single most popular dish at Jasper White's restaurant. He created it in 1984 after watching Chinese cooks prepare lobsters in woks, and since then has served thousands to his customers. Although the flavors are simple, the techniques employed are unusual because of the fast cooking— 6 to 8 minutes in all. An additional bonus is that the lobster is very easy to eat, and thus can appear at your most elegant dinner. Because it is a rich dish if you follow Jasper's full proportions, the rest of the meal should be very light. You might begin with a salad or cold vegetables, and although Chef Jasper accompanies his lobster with a julienne of zucchini, you really need nothing more than bread—perhaps Jasper's corn bread if you are eating at his restaurant. A fruit compote or sorbet and chocolate cookies could be your dessert.

Manufacturing Note: Cooking lobsters is not for the squeamish or faint-hearted, and if we who are carnivores are to eat lobster, we must face up to its slaughter, either by boiling or steaming it alive, or by cutting it up alive. This is one of those recipes, like *homard à l'américaine,* where the lobster cooks as it should only when cut alive and sautéed. Swiftly done Chef Jasper's way, it is killed instantly, which is not the case when it is boiled or steamed. Twitchings and movements of lobster pieces in the sauté pan, by the way, are not evidences of life—they are muscle and tendon contractions caused by the heat.

Cutting up the Lobster: Plan to cut up the lobsters just before cooking them. With one hand grip a lobster shell side up with its claws extended forward. With the other, aiming toward the front of the lobster, insert the point of your heavy knife or cleaver at the junction of chest and tail; swiftly bear down to split the chest in half lengthwise—thus killing the lobster instantly. Now reverse direction, aim toward the tail end, and split the tail section in half lengthwise. You now have a whole lobster split in half lengthwise.

Next, break off the claws with the knuckles attached.

Inside the two chest shell-halves, where the head is, locate the small, less-than-1-inch-long head sac, which you may have sliced in half—pull it out and discard.

INGREDIENTS FOR TWO 2-POUND LOBSTERS: A COPIOUS DINNER FOR 2, OR A FISH COURSE OR LUNCHEON DISH FOR 4 TO 6

For the lobsters
2 "selects" (2 pounds each) Maine or Canadian hard-shell lobsters
2 tablespoons peanut oil or clarified butter (see box, page 252)
2 large shallots, peeled and finely diced
¼ cup good quality Cognac
2 to 3 tablespoons dry white wine

For finishing the sauce
2 tablespoons finely chopped fresh chervil or 1 teaspoon fresh tarragon
2 to 3 tablespoons finely chopped fresh chives

Remove and reserve for another purpose or discard the loose black matter (which is about half the tomalley, or liver).

Whack off and discard the tip of the lobster's head (about 1 inch back from the eyes) on each half.

Pull out and discard the intestinal vein running down the length of one of the tail-meat sections.

Separate the tails from the chests.

The lobster is now ready to cook.

Removing the Claw and Joint Meat:

Blanching. Fill the sauté pan three-quarters full with water and bring to the boil. Drop in the claws with knuckles attached. Cover the pan, bring the water rapidly back to the boil, and boil for 3 minutes. Remove from the water, turn cut sides down, and drain out the cooking water, then break off the knuckles from the claws.

Shelling the Claws. You are hoping, here, to remove the meat in one piece—the large claw meat with the small, pointed pincer meat attached. Start by holding the claw bottom down, and bend the pincer not up and down but slowly and firmly back and forth across the claw shell six to eight times—to break the shell connection at that point. Then pull the pincer shell firmly but gently away from the claw, and if you have left the pincer meat attached to the claw meat inside the claw shell you have won! Then lay the claw shell on the counter and give it a strong whack with the side of the heavy knife, or cut it open with shears. Carefully pull the meat out in one piece. Crack open the knuckles and remove that meat, hopefully in one piece. Set the meat aside and discard the shells.

Manufacturing Note: Getting the meat out of a claw in a single piece may take some practice; don't worry if you don't succeed every time—all the meat is usable however it looks.

Preheat the oven to highest heat—500° F or more.

Unsalted butter, cut into ½-inch dice and chilled—the amount is up to you; Jasper uses 8 tablespoons
Freshly ground black pepper

SPECIAL EQUIPMENT SUGGESTED

A large heavy chef's knife or a Chinese cleaver
A 12-inch covered sauté pan (for blanching the lobster claws, and for sautéing the lobster later)
Kitchen shears
Tongs

(continued)

Pan-Roasted Lobster (continued)

Pan-Roasting: Set the sauté pan on a burner at highest heat for 5 minutes or more, letting it get as hot as possible. Film with oil and lay the lobster chests ʳ   ; shell side down in the pan. Use tongs to move the pieces   ...d lean them in the pan so that the shells are seared and color evenly as they turn bright red. When they have all turned color, in about a minute, turn the pieces over, flesh side down and shell sides up, and cook for 1 minute. Then set the pan in the upper third of the 500° F oven for 2 to 3 minutes, until the shells are slightly browned and even a bit charred.

Finishing the Cooking: Bearing in mind that the pan handle is burning hot, remove the pan from the oven and place it back on the burner set on highest heat. Add the shallots, dropping them into the pan juices and not on top of the lobster. Pour on the Cognac and ignite. Now add the claw and knuckle meat to the pan and, when the flames die down, pour on the wine. Stir the lobster around gently to heat the claw and knuckle meat while the chests and tails finish cooking—a minute or so. If the tail pieces look done first, turn them flesh side up to prevent overcooking—the chest pieces need slightly longer cooking.

Finishing the Sauce and Serving: Remove the lobster tails and chests with tongs and arrange them shell sides down to re-form the lobster on two warm dinner plates. Leave the claws and knuckles in the pan and reduce the heat to moderate. Add the herbs and chilled pieces of butter to the pan and swirl it around by its handle just until the butter is almost absorbed and forms a creamy emulsion with the pan juices. Place the claw meat over the chests, and the knuckle meat at strategic intervals. Taste the sauce for seasoning— it rarely needs salt, but will want some generous grinds of pepper. Spoon the sauce over the lobster, and serve at once.

MARK MILITELLO

I t took Mark Militello only one year of premed studies at Marquette University to realize that he was not heading toward the career of his dreams. He recognized cooking as his true love, so he transferred to Florida International University's School of Hospitality and Hotel Management, obtaining a culinary degree there, and one from State University of New York's Hotel and Culinary Program. It was the right choice. Within a year of opening Mark's Place in North Miami in 1988, he received the highest possible rating from both *The Miami Herald* and *South Florida* magazine. By 1990 he had been discovered nationally and was named one of the "Ten Best New Chefs in America" by *Food & Wine* magazine.

In the summer of 1994 Mark opened his second restaurant, Mark's Las Olas, in Fort Lauderdale, and it is already having the same success. "I enjoy the challenge of running two restaurants. At one time, I was a partner in three restaurants and was running back and forth to all of them." How fortunate for the food community that Mark is running between food establishments and not operating rooms!

Both his restaurants are showcases for diverse ethnic influences. The flavors of the Caribbean, South America, Cuba, Brazil, and Nicaragua are all present in a cuisine that is uniquely his own. "You see a lot of the same products in each of the cuisines, but each group prepares its food a little differently." The foods merge beautifully under Mark's expert care. He treated us to a yellowtail snapper perfectly sautéed and finished with a delicious and unpredictable combination of macadamia nuts, fresh ginger, diced fresh mango, mint, and rum; a salad made with a great fresh stalk of heart of palm and accented with the Mediterranean seasonings of basil, capers, and *picholine* olives; a spice-rich West Indian pumpkin rice and a great Jamaican "jerk"-marinated tenderloin of pork. Medicine was never this exciting.

MARK MILITELLO'S GRILLED OR BROILED TENDERLOIN OF PORK WITH JAMAICAN SPICES

Tenderloins of pork are so easy to find in our supermarkets today, and so easy to cook, that it is good to have interesting new ways to prepare them. Here's a great dish to barbecue of a summer evening, or to slip under the broiler. Chef Mark adapted his marinade and sauce from the Jamaican "jerk," the spices used in traditional Jamaican street food.

Manufacturing Note: This is such a splendid example of the tenderloin and an ideal type of recipe for the barbecue, it seems a shame to confine it to the outdoors. We find it works very well under the broiler, or on a stove-top cast-iron grill.

Readying the Pork: Trim away any fat and sinew from the meat and slice off the thin silver skin. Place the tenderloins in the baking dish in a single layer.

Preparing the Marinade:

Toasting and Grinding the Spices. Set the skillet over low heat, and when hot drop in the allspice and the nutmeg and crushed cinnamon; pan-roast for a minute or so, until the spices have released their fragrance. Grind to a fine powder, and set aside.

The Aromatics. Pulse the onions, scallions, and fresh ginger briefly in the food processor to chop roughly, then add ground spices, thyme, and chile(s), and pulse until the mixture is finely chopped.

The Liquid. With the machine running, pour in the orange juice through the feed tube. Pulse in the olive oil, soy sauce, sugar, salt, and pepper. Pour the marinade over the pork, turning the tenderloins around in it to coat them, cover the baking dish with plastic wrap, and marinate at least 4 hours but not longer than 6 hours or the marinade will overpower the meat.

Ahead-of-Time Note: The marinade itself may be made a day or two in advance and refrigerated, but it will lose its vigor if kept longer.

INGREDIENTS FOR 6 SERVINGS

The pork

Three pork tenderloins, 8 to 9 ounces each

About ½ cup olive oil (for grilling)

The marinade

1 teaspoon whole allspice

1 whole nutmeg, crushed under the side of a heavy knife

1 cinnamon stick, crushed and broken up

1½ cups roughly chopped onions

1½ cups roughly chopped scallions, white part and an inch of the tender green

1 tablespoon roughly chopped fresh ginger root

¼ cup sprigs of fresh thyme

1 Scotch bonnet chile or 2 serrano chiles, halved and seeded

1 cup juice from sour Seville oranges, or 1 cup fresh orange juice and ¼ teaspoon balsamic vinegar

2 tablespoons olive oil

(continued)

Tenderloin of Pork (continued)

Making the Sauce: Pour the vinegar and sugar into a 6-cup saucepan and bring to a boil, swirling the pan until the sugar has completely dissolved. Then boil, stirring frequently, until thickened into a syrup and reduced by half. Lower heat to a simmer, and gradually whisk in the hot stock, then the tamarind paste. Stir in the ginger and garlic, and simmer until reduced to about 1¼ cups. Strain through the sieve into a clean pan, tapping the strainer on the side of the pan to strain in the maximum without pressing the residue through the sieve and clouding the sauce. Taste carefully, and correct seasoning.

Ahead-of-Time Note: May be made a day in advance and refrigerated. Reheat before serving.

Grilling the Pork: Brush the pork with olive oil, season with salt and pepper, and place either over the outdoor coals or 5 to 6 inches under a hot broiler element. Turn the tenderloins frequently as they cook, basting with oil and the leftover marinade.

When Are They Done? When you press the meat with your finger in 15 to 18 minutes, it should have gained in texture and springiness in contrast to its squashy raw state. When you cut into it, the meat should still be a light pink—if it is rosy it is not yet done. The internal temperature should register at least 150° F.

Finishing the Dish: If you are plating the dish in the kitchen, unmold a ramekin of pumpkin rice slightly off-center on warm plates. Cut the tenderloins into bias slices about ⅜ inch thick, and overlap on one side of the mound of rice. Spoon a moderate amount of sauce around the meat and the rice. Garnish each serving with a sprig of fresh thyme.

cook's notes

1 tablespoon soy sauce
½ teaspoon sugar
½ teaspoon salt
⅛ teaspoon freshly ground black
   pepper

For the sauce
¼ cup red wine vinegar
3 tablespoons sugar
1¼ cups hot veal or meat stock
⅓ cup tamarind paste
   (see page opposite)
1 teaspoon finely chopped fresh
   ginger root
2 teaspoons peeled and minced
   garlic

For serving
*West Indian Pumpkin Rice (see
   page 236)*
6 sprigs of fresh thyme

SPECIAL EQUIPMENT
SUGGESTED

*An 8-inch heavy-bottomed skillet
   (cast-iron preferred)*
A spice mill or a coffee grinder
A food processor
*A non-aluminum baking dish
   (for marinating the pork)*
*An outdoor grill with natural
   wood charcoal*
A fine-meshed sieve
A pastry brush
Tongs

TO MAKE YOUR OWN TAMARIND PASTE

Tamarind paste, with its very special tart and sour taste, is much used in Indian and Far Eastern cooking, and we've had quite a lot of it in this book, notably with Madhur Jaffrey, whose remarks and opinions on tamarind you will find on page 22. Until Mark Militello arrived with his tamarind pods, however, all our chefs were using tamarind pulp in block form, where you cut off a piece of the block and let it soften in hot water. "Block tamarind has a tired taste," declares Chef Mark, who always make his own fresh paste since tamarind trees grow in South Florida. And indeed it's easy to do.

This beautiful tree, according to Julia Morton's "Fruits of Warm Climates" (Creative Resource Systems, Inc., Winterville, N.C.), can grow as high as 80 to 100 feet. It can have a spread of 40 feet and a massive trunk that can reach a circumference of 25 feet. It is slow-growing and sturdy, with graceful branches, and its bulging pea-pod-shaped pods grow abundantly along new branches. Pods vary in length from 2 to 7 inches, and as they mature their skins turn a dry crackly khaki color. Imbedded in the pod is a sticky brown pulpy mass in which up to a dozen baked-bean-type black seeds are imbedded. The pulp of a freshly mature tamarind is relatively flavorless, slightly tart and sour, but with an overtone of sweetness somewhere in the background.

It is this sticky pulp you are after. To separate pulp from seeds, you pry and peel the shell bits off the pulp, then you simmer the pulp for 20 minutes or so in water to cover. When softened, pour the mass through a vegetable mill set over a bowl. Grind the mass to force the pulp through the screen, leaving the seeds behind—with some difficulty but quite do-able, since the blade must rock over those seeds.

Ahead-of-Time-Note: Scrape the pulp into a covered jar and refrigerate, where it will keep nicely for several days before becoming increasingly sour. For successful longer keeping, freeze the paste in small separate portions.

WEST INDIAN PUMPKIN RICE

Rice cooked in chicken stock and a light puree of pumpkin, tossed with diced pumpkin and a bit of greenery—it's a pretty dish, and goes beautifully with Chef Mark's pork tenderloin, as it would with almost any dish that needs a rice accompaniment. West Indian pumpkins are called "calabaza" and are available in West Indian, Hispanic, and other specialty grocery stores. Their flavor is much the same as that of our pumpkin but the flesh is more compact. The best substitute is one of our winter squashes, like the butternut.

Manufacturing Note: Chef Mark uses packaged "parboiled" rice here because it holds up well for this particular dish.

Technique: Directions for pan-toasting spices and grinding them are on page 233, in Chef Mark's pork tenderloin recipe.

Preparing the Pumpkin: Cut the pumpkin into neat ⅜-inch dice. Bring the chicken stock to a boil in the large saucepan, toss in the diced pumpkin, and boil slowly until just cooked through, with the pumpkin pieces still holding their shape. Remove two-thirds of the pumpkin with the wire-mesh spoon and drop into the ice water to stop the cooking; reserve for the finished rice. Use the hand-held blender or mixer to puree the remaining pumpkin and the stock together in the saucepan. Pour the pumpkin/stock into a 4-cup measure; add more stock if needed, to make 3 cups in all. Rinse out the saucepan and set it over moderate heat.

Cooking the Rice: Melt 2 tablespoons of butter in the saucepan; stir in the onion and toasted cumin. Sweat (cook slowly) for a few minutes, stirring frequently, until the onions are tender. Stir in the rice to heat it and coat it with the butter. Pour in the hot pumpkin/stock and bring to the simmer—you may need to add a little more stock at this point; cover the pan and simmer for about 15 minutes, until the rice is almost but not quite tender and just barely damp.

Finishing the Rice: Remove from heat, and immediately use a wooden fork to toss in salt and pepper to taste, and a little more hot stock if the rice seems too compact. Then cover the pan; the rice will finish cooking as it sits.

Ahead-of-Time Note: If cooking several hours in advance, set the pan aside,

INGREDIENTS FOR 6 SERVINGS

For the pumpkin

12 ounces calabaza pumpkin (or a yellow squash, like butternut), peeled and seeded (about 2½ cups when diced)

3 cups chicken stock, plus more if needed

For the rice

2 tablespoons unsalted butter for cooking and 1 tablespoon for finishing the rice

1 medium white onion, finely diced (about 1 cup)

¼ teaspoon whole cumin seeds, toasted and ground

1½ cups (12 ounces) long-grain packaged "parboiled" rice

Salt

Freshly ground black pepper

6 scallions, green part only, sliced thin diagonally

(continued)

loosely covered. Reheat over simmering water, tossing frequently with the wooden fork.

Serving: Using the fork again, toss the reserved pumpkin, the scallions, and the last tablespoon of butter into the hot rice, and correct seasoning. If you are plating the food in the kitchen, it is attractive (as well as easy) to spoon the rice into buttered molds, and unmold directly onto the warm dinner plates; otherwise pass it in a warm vegetable dish.

SPECIAL EQUIPMENT
SUGGESTED

*A 2½-quart heavy-bottomed
    saucepan*
A wire-mesh spoon
A 2-quart bowl of ice and water
*A hand-held electric blender or
    mixer*
*A wooden fork (for tossing
    the rice)*
*A big spoon and 6 well-buttered
    metal timbales or custard cups,
    ½-cup size (for serving the
    rice)*

MANGO NOTES FROM JULIA

Mangoes are a delicious addition to our fruit supply, both alone and in fruit combinations, and our contemporary chefs use them frequently in meat and fish sauces, such as the brown butter sauce for Mark Militello's sautéed snapper. The mango's strangely misshapen, thickish oval shape conceals a strangely large, flattish oval seed that clings unwaveringly to the sweet flesh around it, making the mango difficult to cut and serve and to eat. Here are Chef Mark's ways of dealing with the mango.

When Is a Mango Ripe? Most ripe mangoes are yellow-orange with a reddish blush. When you hold a mango in your hand and gently press the flesh, it should give lightly all over, like a ripe pear or avocado. The flesh of an overripe fruit is mushy and cannot be peeled or diced.

Peeling the Mango and Removing the Seed: The large oval seed lies horizontally in the mango, and it is a messy job to remove. Work one side at a time by slicing the skin off one of the flat sides with a small sharp knife.

Then cut into the flesh at the top of the side and you will feel the seed; slice down against the seed to remove that side of the flesh (you won't get the flesh off the sides of the seed—they are for the cook to enjoy). Repeat on the other side.

The Wedge Attack Method is equally messy. One side at a time, cut down through the skin and flesh to the seed, starting in the middle of one side, and remove the flesh with skin in wedges, then slice the skin off each wedge.

The Militello Mango-Dicing Technique: Cut through the skin and flesh at the top of one of the flat sides and, slicing always against the seed, remove that side of the mango. Place the piece skin side down on your work surface and, not so deep as to pierce the skin, make long slashes ½ inch apart from edge to edge; give the piece a half turn, and slash the flesh again to make a crosshatch effect. Now turn the piece inside out and cut the diced flesh from the skin.

SAUTÉED YELLOWTAIL SNAPPER FILLETS WITH MANGO, RUM, GINGER, AND MACADAMIA NUT SAUCE

Chef Mark's unusual brown butter sauce, with its delightful mingling of flavors, makes a quick and delicious finish to a quick sauté of fish fillets—or of chicken breasts or veal scallops for that matter. When he served it to us he had brought his Florida snappers with him and used yellowtail fillets, but his technique and his sauce would work beautifully with any lean white fish, like sole, flounder, grouper, and so forth.

Purchasing Notes: Chef Mark's snappers were small ones, but his servings were large and attractively arranged—two 6-ounce fillets lying crosswise on top of each other. You'll have to buy by eye, allowing about 8 ounces per person. His fillets were carefully boned, but he left the thin delicate skin on them.

Preparing the Fish: If you are using snapper, run your fingers over the flesh of each fillet, particularly along the center, feeling for pin bones and removing them with pliers; or make a V-shaped cut in the flesh along each side of the line where the bones are attached—careful not to pierce the skin—and remove the piece with the bones embedded. If you have fillets with skin, run your hand over it and scrape off any remaining scales, then score the skin with three evenly spaced diagonal cuts about 1½ inches across and ⅛ inch deep.

Season both sides of the fish with salt and pepper. The moment before cooking, dip the fillets into the flour, coating them lightly and shaking off excess.

Sautéing the Fish: Set the pan (or pans) over moderately high heat and film the bottom with clarified butter; when very hot but not smoking, lay in as many of the fillets skin sides down as will fit comfortably—do not crowd the pan. Sear until the skin is crisp and the flesh around the edges begins to look opaque. Turn over, flipping the fillets away from you to avoid splattering, and sauté another minute, or until cooked through—when you press the flesh with your finger it should have taken on some body and should no longer feel squashy like raw fish. (If it feels firm you have overcooked it!) Transfer to a warm dinner plate or platter—if serving two per person, arrange one fillet skin side down, and the other flesh side up at an angle on

INGREDIENTS FOR 6 SERVINGS

For the fish

2½ to 3 pounds lean fish fillets,
    boned, skin left on if edible
    (see note)

Salt

Freshly ground black pepper

2 cups all-purpose flour
    (for dredging)

½ cup (2 ounces) clarified butter
    (see box, page 252)

For the sauce

1 stick (4 ounces) unsalted butter,
    cut into ½-inch slices

1 tablespoon finely julienned
    fresh ginger root

1 cup diced fresh mango
    (see notes on mangoes in the
    box on page 237)

¾ cup (loosely packed) fresh mint
    leaves, whole

⅓ cup rum

½ cup macadamia nuts, toasted
    in a 350° F oven for 8 to 10
    minutes, until lightly browned

(continued)

top of the first. Cover and keep warm while cooking the rest and making the sauce.

Making the Sauce and Serving: Meanwhile, set the saucepan over moderate heat and drop in the butter pieces, swirling the pan by its handle to melt the butter evenly. Let it boil, swirling slowly, until it has turned a light walnut-brown. Stir in the ginger, mango, and mint leaves, then the rum. Immediately tilt the pan into the burner or light with a match. When the flame subsides, swirl in the macadamia nuts, season with salt and pepper, and taste carefully for seasoning. Spoon the sauce over the fish, garnish with a couple of lime wedges, and serve immediately with the hearts-of-palm garnish.

Salt
Freshly ground black pepper

For the garnish
Lime wedges, preferably from a
key lime

For serving
Stewed Hearts of Palm
(see page 240)

SPECIAL EQUIPMENT
SUGGESTED

Small snub-nosed pliers
(if needed)
A heavy 12-inch no-stick sauté or
frying pan (a second pan
would be useful)
A 2½-quart heavy-bottomed
saucepan (for the sauce)

STEWED HEARTS OF PALM

This crunchy exotic vegetable comes from the sabal palm colloquially called swamp cabbage, which grows near the Everglades, and when you buy a can of hearts of palm, the Florida state tree is actually sitting there in that can. The heart of that tree can be as long as 3 feet and as much as 4 inches in diameter. At his Miami restaurant, Chef Mark makes this dish with fresh hearts of palm and you may find them fresh elsewhere in specialty markets. Otherwise use canned hearts of palm, which work very well in this case. Chef Mark stews his in an aromatic vegetable broth spiced with garlic, tomatoes, and that remarkably hot Florida chile, the Scotch bonnet. This recipe is a pleasantly crunchy accompaniment to his Florida snapper.

Trimming the Heart out of a Fresh Palm: Fill a 3- to 4-quart bowl with cold water and squeeze the juice of the two lemons into it; drop in the rinds also and keep the water nearby. Trim off the bottom of the palm and remove any dark bits, then stand it on end. Make a slit from the top to the bottom, going in about ¼ inch. Lay the palm down and peel away the outside leaves in layers until you are down to the heart. Cut the heart crosswise into slices ¼ inch thick. As you cut, your knife will tell you what part is tender and what part is too tough and fibrous to use. As you work, drop the slices into the bowl of acidulated water to prevent them from darkening.

Cooking the Stew: Set the pan over moderate heat, add the oil and garlic, and let toast for several minutes, stirring, until the garlic begins to color a pale golden-brown. Then stir in the celery, onion, chile, and let sweat (cook slowly) until the vegetables are tender and translucent but have not taken on any color—4 to 5 minutes. Drain the fresh heart of palm from the water and reserve ½ cup of the liquid. Blend the palm and the tomatoes in the pan with the vegetables and stir in the reserved lemon water. Season with salt and pepper and simmer until the palm is tender, 8 to 10 minutes. (If you are using canned hearts of palm, drain and cut them into ¼-inch slices. Simmer the vegetables with the tomatoes, ½ cup of water, and 2 teaspoons of real lemon juice, then add the sliced canned palm and simmer for several minutes, only until heated through and tender.) Finally, stir in the capers and olives, and simmer for a moment to blend the flavors.

Ahead-of-Time Note: The dish may be prepared several hours in advance to this point.

Serving: Reheat just before serving and stir in the fresh basil, letting it simmer for a moment to release its perfume.

cook's notes

INGREDIENTS FOR 6 SERVINGS

2 lemons

1 pound fresh heart of palm, trimmed and ready to cook, or a 17-ounce can of hearts of palm

3 tablespoons excellent olive oil

4 garlic cloves, peeled and thinly sliced

2 celery stalks, peeled and thinly sliced on the bias

1 large Spanish onion, finely diced

¼ Scotch bonnet chile, seeded and minced, or ½ serrano chile

2 or 3 large tomatoes, peeled, seeded, and diced (1 cup)

Salt

Freshly ground black pepper

2 teaspoons vinegar-packed capers, drained and rinsed

About 2 ounces **picholine** *or green Spanish olives, sliced and rinsed*

6 to 9 large fresh basil leaves, cut into chiffonade (very narrow strips)

SPECIAL EQUIPMENT SUGGESTED

A stout paring knife and a large tough sharp slicing knife, preferably saw-toothed (if you are preparing your own fresh palm)

A heavy no-stick or stainless steel 12-inch sauté or frying pan

JIMMY SNEED

Any number of factors may lead to a culinary career; in Jimmy Sneed's case it was plain old hunger. Jimmy was in France studying the language and culture, taking courses at the Sorbonne and selling newspapers café to café. "It was a great experience, but I was getting hungrier by the day. I decided to get a job where I could also get fed." The Cordon Bleu Cooking School seemed like a probable source of nourishment, and Jimmy approached the owner, Madame Brassart, who handed him a chef's coat and told him to stand in front of the class and translate for the students. When he returned to the United States and George Washington University he again needed a job and worked in a series of undistinguished establishments before deciding that if food was to be his profession he would have to apprentice with a "master."

Jimmy thought he would find a kitchen full of masters at the French embassy. "I walked unannounced into the kitchen and found a twenty-five-year-old French kid, Francis Layrle, who was chef, sous-chef, saucier, and commis." Fortunately the young man was also a friend of Jean-Louis Palladin, of Jean-Louis at the Watergate. "So I drove there for an interview with the 'greatest chef in the universe,' according to Francis. 'You, you speak French?' Jean-Louis asked. 'Oui,' I replied. 'OK, you start.'" Jean-Louis's confidence was not misplaced; Jimmy worked a total of six years with the renowned chef. "Jean-Louis made me a chef."

Jimmy absorbed the techniques of classic French cuisine and learned how to translate them into simple foods, such as his sautéed fried soft-shell crabs, his richly flavored saffron pasta, and his creamy grits. "I needed to work with a master and learn to make grand cuisine so I could apply it to simple food. If it's not fresh and well balanced, it's just common food." The thought "common" never entered our mind when we tasted Jimmy Sneed's offerings.

JIMMY SNEED'S VIRGINIA STUFFED TURKEY LEGS

Turkey legs are usually a good buy, and they can make for unexpectedly elegant eating when boned, filled with Chef Jimmy Sneed's mushroom-ham stuffing, and roasted. There's nothing daunting about boning legs since you have only two big ones to wrestle with: Just be sure your knife is sharp, and plunge in fearlessly. Getting those pesky tendons out of the drumsticks makes it worth your while.

Preparing the Stuffing:

Sautéing the Shiitake Mushrooms. Set the frying pan over moderately high heat and add ¼ inch olive oil. When it is hot enough for the sliced mushrooms to sizzle, toss them in. Season with salt and pepper as you stir and toss them for 2 minutes. Then add the garlic and shallots and continue to sauté for a minute more, tossing and stirring until they are translucent—careful not to let them burn. Pour in the chicken stock, and when absorbed by the mushrooms, in a minute or so, transfer them to a side dish and let them cool.

Pureeing the Turkey Tenderloin. Process the tenderloin in the machine with a big pinch of salt until reduced to a smooth puree. Pour in the chilled cream and puree in short spurts until it is completely incorporated—do not overdo or the cream will turn to butter; the result should be a beautifully smooth, creamy pink, having the consistency of stiffly whipped cream. Scrape down the sides of the bowl with a rubber spatula and pulse another few seconds; transfer the contents to the chilled bowl.

Finishing the Stuffing. Bring a small saucepan of water to the simmer. Meanwhile, fold the mushrooms and ham into the stuffing; then take up a spoonful, drop it into the simmering water, and let poach for 10 seconds. Remove, and taste analytically for seasoning, adding a little more salt if necessary. Stir in the chives.

Preheat the oven to 550° F.

Stuffing and Wrapping the Leg: Return the turkey legs to the work surface, cut side up. Open the legs out and season the meat with salt and pepper. Use a spoon to fill the drumstick pockets with the stuffing, pushing and packing in as much as they will hold. Then spoon the stuffing on top of the thigh meat and wrap the meat around it to re-form the legs. Lay on the counter two pieces of caul fat (or oil-soaked cheesecloth) larger than the

INGREDIENTS FOR 6 TO 8 DINNER-SIZE SERVINGS OR 12 TO 16 APPETIZER PLATES

For the turkey legs
2 turkey leg-thigh sections, about 2 pounds each, boned as described in the box on page 247
Salt
Freshly ground black pepper
Caul fat, or cheesecloth soaked in olive oil (see the box on page 247)
Olive oil (for browning and roasting the stuffed legs)

For the stuffing
The mushrooms
2 to 3 tablespoons excellent olive oil
8 ounces shiitake mushrooms, stems discarded, caps sliced ⅛ inch thick
6 ounces country ham, finely diced (about 1 cup loosely packed)
3 tablespoons finely diced chives
Sea salt
Freshly ground black pepper

(continued)

Virginia Stuffed Turkey Legs (continued)

legs, and place the legs on top. Wrap the caul fat securely around and over the legs; this will keep the stuffing inside and will serve to baste the legs as they roast. Cut away any excess caul and then, aiming to make the drumsticks and thighs of equal size, tie the circumference securely with twine so they will hold their shape and their stuffing as they cook.

Ahead-of-Time Note: The recipe may be completed several hours but not over a day in advance to this point. Cover and refrigerate.

Browning and Roasting: Film the frying pan with oil and set over high heat. When very hot and almost smoking, sear the legs on all sides to brown evenly. Transfer the pan to the preheated oven, and roast for about 25 minutes, turning once or twice for even cooking.

When Are They Done? They are done when an instant-read meat thermometer registers 162° F to 165° F.

Remove the pan from the oven and let the legs rest in it for 10 to 15 minutes. Remove the string. The caul fat will have melted away, but if you have used cheesecloth remove it with great care so as not to tear the turkey skin.

Carving and Serving: Carve the legs at a slight angle into slices approximately ¼ inch thick. Arrange them on one side of the plate, and place a serving of grits next to it, leaving room for the asparagus. If you are plating in the kitchen, nap one edge of the turkey slices lightly with rosemary sauce, being careful not to disturb the mosaic pattern embedded in the center of the turkey. Decorate with a sprig of rosemary, and serve. For family-style serving on a platter, you might mound the grits in the center, surround with the turkey, and arrange four portions of asparagus at strategic locations.

2 to 3 large garlic cloves, peeled and finely diced

1 to 2 large shallots, peeled and finely diced

2 to 3 tablespoons chicken stock or broth

The turkey forcemeat (turkey-meat mousse)

1 or 2 turkey breast tenderloins, 8 ounces total (roughly 1 cup ground)

Salt

¾ to 1 cup chilled heavy cream

For serving

Stone-Ground Grits (see page 246)

Buttered asparagus

Rosemary Sauce (see box, page 246)

SPECIAL EQUIPMENT SUGGESTED

A cleaver

A heavy 12-inch frying pan to accommodate both legs (our chef prefers cast-iron)

A food processor fitted with the metal blade

A chilled bowl sitting in pan of ice and water

Butcher's twine (unwaxed plain white cotton twine)

Tongs

An instant-read meat thermometer (useful but not essential)

JIMMY SNEED'S ROSEMARY SAUCE

Take a 6-inch sprig of fresh rosemary and blanch it in boiling water for 15 seconds to remove its bitterness. Then infuse it in 2 cups of a rich meat or poultry stock, or, even better, a veal stock, by boiling it down slowly until the stock becomes almost a syrup. Finish it off heat with a swirl of soft butter to smooth and enrich it and—voilà—you have the lovely rosemary sauce that Jimmy Sneed serves with his stuffed turkey legs.

STONE-GROUND GRITS

Just as with his pasta, Chef Jimmy likes to cook grits in chicken stock because it gives them a good rich flavor, and he prefers yellow grits to white. He also adds a nice little pat of butter for even more flavor and richness. He likes to challenge people who come to his restaurant and claim that they don't like grits with "I daresay you haven't tasted these!" After one mouthful they invariably gobble them up and ask for more.

Manufacturing Note: Feel free to increase this recipe, but remember the proportions—four times as much liquid as grits.

Bring the stock to the boil and stir in the grits. Stir in the salt and butter, reduce heat to very low so that the stock is at the barest simmer, and cover the pan. Let simmer for 20 to 25 minutes, stirring frequently, until the grits are tender and creamy.

Ahead-of-Time Note: These are at their best when served promptly, but if you prepare them in advance, set them aside and film the top with a spoonful of chicken stock. Cover and reheat over simmering water, stirring frequently, and adding droplets of chicken stock, if needed, to make them creamy again.

INGREDIENTS FOR 6 SERVINGS

For the grits
4 cups light chicken stock
1 cup yellow stone-ground grits
1 teaspoon sea salt
1 tablespoon unsalted butter

SPECIAL EQUIPMENT SUGGESTED

A 2½-quart heavy-bottomed saucepan

HOW TO BONE A TURKEY

Jimmy Sneed likes to bone his own turkeys. Thus he gets the legs cut the way he likes them, and he has the whole breasts to broil or grill, plus all of the carcass to make his splendid turkey stock.

The Leg-Thighs: He slits the skin around the knee and down to the small of the back where the thigh joins it. By bending the knee joint out and down toward the back-bone, he breaks open the thigh joint at the small of the back, cuts through it, and releases the whole leg first by scraping off the "oyster" of meat lodged on the back above the joint, and then by removing the second oyster nestled against the lower back as he scrapes against the carcass toward the tail to separate the whole leg structure from the carcass. He repeats the technique for the leg on the other side.

The Breast: Chef Jimmy starts at the ridge of the breast-bone on one side, cutting close to the bone with his very sharp knife as he moves down the carcass. He cuts around the wishbone at the front of the bird, and through the ball joint that attaches the wing to the shoulder, and thus removes the whole breast on one side. He does the same on the other side. Finally, turning the breasts skin side down, he lifts the narrow flap of loose meat—the tenderloin—from each breast and slices it off. Running down the length of the tenderloin is a thin white tendon, which he pulls and scrapes out of the meat. Having already cut through the wing joints at the shoulders, the wings themselves are easy to remove.

He now has eight turkey pieces plus a fine big carcass. For his turkey-leg recipe he will want the two leg-thighs to bone and stuff, and one tenderloin to go into the stuffing.

HOW TO BONE A TURKEY LEG

Lay on your work surface the turkey leg with thigh (second joint) attached, its inside facing up. Make a cut down the length of the thigh bone, from the exposed ball-joint end to the knee. Cutting as close as possible to the thigh bone, release the meat from the bone on each side.

Then, grabbing the exposed ball joint, start scraping the meat from the underside of the thigh bone, pulling the meat away from it as you go; scrape the bone clean, down to the knee.

Cut around the knee joint, then scrape down the drum-stick bone until there are about 2 inches of drumstick left unscraped.

Cut out of the meat as many of the tough tendons and sinews as you can, and discard them—many will remain attached to the ball joint at the knee.

Lay the leg back on the counter, lift the meat out of the way to expose the bone structure, and with your cleaver whack off the drumstick bone, leaving only the lower 2 inches of drumstick attached to the meat. Pick any bone pieces off the meat, and re-form the leg-thigh into its original shape, cut side up.

Butterfly the thickest part of the thigh meat lengthwise in order to even out its thickness and to have a piece large enough to cover the stuffing. Repeat with the second leg-thigh.

JULIA'S NOTES ON CAUL FAT

Caul fat is the lining of a pig's visceral cavity—a thin, edible membrane streaked with cobwebby lines of fat. It's wonderfully useful for wrapping up sausage patties, or for wrapping around meat or poultry to hold in a stuffing. It is also useful since it can serve to baste a turkey leg as it roasts, and after roasting, the caul disintegrates as its fat renders out into the roasting pan. You won't find pig's caul unless you live in an ethnic neighborhood or you special-order it. Many contemporary butchers have never heard of pig's caul, but Jimmy Sneed says it is always available if they ask for it.

However, there is a substitute—unglamorous though it may be, it works perfectly—a single thickness of cheese-cloth soaked in oil or melted butter, or melted turkey or chicken fat. For use here in our turkey recipe, paint the boned turkey leg generously with oil, wrap the oil-soaked cheesecloth tightly around it, and tie as described in the recipe. The meat browns as it should and the cheesecloth may be unwrapped without incident if well oiled before-hand.

CHEF JIMMY SNEED'S OWN HOMEMADE SAFFRON PASTA

Chef Jimmy Sneed's pasta is famous among his clients. "It tastes so good," they say. "I've never eaten anything like it." He makes his own, with a mixture of all-purpose and semolina flours, and a final flavoring of saffron. He cooks it in a mild chicken stock, which gives it an unusual boost of flavor. All in all, Jimmy Sneed's is a pasta well worth coming home to.

Manufacturing Note: Jimmy Sneed likes to do almost everything by hand, from the mixing to the cutting, and although one can see he would also prefer the rolling pin to the machine, he does machine roll the dough in his hand-cranking model. Our Italian experts, Nancy Verde Barr and Kathleen Annino, are enthusiastic about machine rolling but prefer machine mixing; in other words, they make their pasta doughs in the food processor following the standard directions that come with the machine.

Preparing the Dough: Measure the two flours into the mixing bowl, then work in the salt and the egg and egg yolks with your hands, squeezing and kneading to make a firm but pliable dough—adding little sprinkles of the flours if too sticky, or little dribbles of beaten egg if too dry. The completed pasta dough at this point is only flour and egg.

Adding Flavor and Color: This is a fine dough just as it is, but if you want colored pasta, you should now knead in a coloring, such as squid ink, concentrated beet juice, and so forth. Chef Jimmy Sneed suggests saffron for this recipe, to go with his sautéed crabs: Infuse a big pinch of saffron threads into 3 tablespoons of very hot water, stirring until the saffron has released its color. Then knead it in; you needn't be too thorough since it will spread itself through the pasta as you roll it out in the machine.

Resting the Dough: Dust the dough well with flour and wrap in plastic and refrigerate for an hour or more, allowing the gluten to relax.

Ahead-of-Time Note: The dough is now ready to use; it will keep in the refrigerator for a day or so but will discolor if left longer—it is safer to freeze it if the wait will be longer than 24 hours.

Rolling out the Dough: Cut the dough into four pieces and, one at a time, roll them through the widest setting of the pasta machine. Each strip is now to be folded into three even layers as follows: Fold the bottom of a short side up to cover two-thirds the length of the dough, then fold the top down to

INGREDIENTS FOR 4 TO 6 HEARTY SERVINGS

For the pasta

¾ cup each—plus more if needed, in equal amounts: unbleached all-purpose flour, and semolina (available in health food stores and Italian groceries)

A large pinch of sea salt

1 whole "large" egg and 3 egg yolks

1 cup or more additional all-purpose flour (for forming, rolling, and cutting)

For flavoring the pasta

3 tablespoons boiling water

A large pinch of saffron

For cooking and serving the pasta

4 quarts light homemade chicken stock, or canned broth diluted by a third or a half with water

6 tablespoons cold unsalted butter

Chopped scallions (white and tender green part) for garnish

(continued)

Left: Putting the dough through the pasta machine.

Below: Rolling the pasta dough into a tube.

Saffron Pasta (continued)

cover it. Flour the outside lightly. Continue rolling it through the machine, flouring lightly each time. Do this six or seven times, until the dough is a neat, smooth rectangle with even edges and a uniform color. Then, always flouring the dough, pass it through the rollers several times without folding. Now set the rollers to a thinner setting each time the dough goes through, and continue rolling out to the thinnest setting. The dough is now ready for cutting.

Cutting the Dough:

Cutting by Hand. Dust the sheet of dough liberally on both sides with flour—you are now going to roll it up upon itself and it must not stick to itself—more flour is safer than less! Starting at one of the long ends, fold an inch of the dough over upon itself, and continue folding until you can roll it up into a long tube. Using a very sharp knife, cut off the two ends of the tube, to even them. Then cut the tube into crosswise slices, and when you shake them open, you should have long strips of pasta of whichever width you want—⅛ inch is a good general size. Pick up the strips, shake them out, and drape them on the hangers; let hang for 30 minutes or so to dry out thoroughly, but if you leave them too long, the pasta strands will become brittle and may fall off the hangers onto the floor.

Cooking and Finishing the Pasta: Bring the stock to the boil and stir in the pasta, cover briefly and bring back to the boil, then uncover and boil slowly, tasting almost continually until it is just cooked through—freshly made pasta may take only a few seconds, while dried pasta can take several minutes. When ready, lift it out with the pasta fork into the wide pan, not draining it too thoroughly—you need a bit of liquid to form the sauce. Taste, and correct seasoning, then turn the heat on to high. Add the cold butter and swirl the pan around by its handle, tossing the pasta until the butter emulsifies into a creamy sauce. Serve immediately, sprinkled with the chopped scallions.

Cutting by Machine. Follow the directions that come with your pasta machine, and use the blade with the ⅛-inch separations. One at a time, flour both sides of a strip of dough and pass the narrow end of the strip through the machine. This method is easier and faster than hand cutting, but you lose that rustic look.

SPECIAL EQUIPMENT SUGGESTED

A fairly large bowl for hand mixing the dough since it can be messy—about 12 inches across and 6 or more inches deep

A hand-cranking pasta-rolling machine (the standard noodle-cutting attachment that comes with the machine may be useful)

3 or 4 plastic coat hangers (for drying the pasta)

A 6- to 8-quart saucepan or kettle (for boiling the pasta)

A wide heavy-bottomed saucepan or sauté pan (for finishing the pasta)

A wooden or plastic pasta fork

Ahead-of-Time Note: To preserve the fresh quality, you may freeze the pasta when it has dried thoroughly. Break it carefully off the coat hangers and lay it in a roasting pan. Slip the pan into a plastic bag, and freeze; then slip the pan out of the bag.

JIMMY SNEED'S NOTES ON SOFT-SHELL CRABS

Blue crabs (*Callinectes sapidus*) are native to the Chesapeake Bay, and when they shed their hard shells every season so that they can grow in size, they become known as soft-shell crabs. The shedding season begins in early May and can last through early October. Soft-shell crabs are at their most tender within 30 minutes of shedding—the so-called "velvet crab."

At this delectable point the crab is almost totally edible, and you are right there to sweep up a bushel. If the crabs remain in seawater, the new shell begins to form almost immediately. Thus they are gathered up at once, packed in straw-lined containers, and chilled. With all the careful individual surveillance they require, no wonder they are so expensive.

SAUTÉED SOFT-SHELL CRABS

Soft-shell crabs, a specialty of Jimmy Sneed's, have long been a delicacy of the Atlantic coast from Maryland on south. Now that we can buy them alive and ready to cook in many parts of the country, we asked Chef Jimmy to show us the best way to handle these toothsome creatures.

Cleaning the Crabs: Clean the crabs shortly before cooking them. To do so hold the shears in one hand and a crab in the other, its stomach resting on your palm, its claws dangling over the sides of your hand. Snip off the head and eyes in two quick cuts of the shears. Lift up a side wing of the top shell; cut off the finger-like gills attached to the body on that side, and repeat on the other. Note that the little blobs of stored fat located under the wings should be left on. Lift up the "apron," or back end, of the crab and snip it off. Squeeze the opposite side, where the eyes were, to force out the sand sac and the tomalley (greenish matter); discard. Place the cleaned crabs stomach side up on a plate, so the backs will stay moist. Proceed rapidly with the rest—Jimmy Sneed, having cleaned thousands, is very fast at this. The crabs are now ready to cook.

INGREDIENTS FOR 4 SERVINGS

The crabs
12 "velvet" soft-shell crabs (see crab notes in the box above)
About 1 cup all-purpose flour spread on a plate (for dredging)
About 3 tablespoons each:
Clarified butter (see box, page 252)
Vegetable oil—Chef Jimmy uses canola

(continued)

Sautéed Soft-Shell Crabs (continued)

Ahead-of-Time Note: Although you may clean the crabs somewhat ahead and refrigerate them, they are at their best when cooked right away.

Sautéing the Crabs: Set the frying pan or pans over moderate heat to warm. Dredge the crabs in the flour, shaking off excess—note that Chef Jimmy does not season them since they are naturally a little salty. Put ¼ inch of equal amounts of clarified butter and oil into the pan, and raise heat to high—prepare to stand back as you sauté, since the really fresh crabs tend to explode. When the butter is very hot and almost smoking, lay in as many crabs, back sides down, as will fit easily in one layer. When the back sides have browned—in about a minute—turn and sauté on the other side until golden brown—again for about a minute. You should be able to hear the crabs sizzling throughout their cooking. Remove the browned crabs to dinner plates or a platter, and keep warm while rapidly sautéing the rest, adding more butter and oil as needed.

Serving: In a small bowl, stir together 3 tablespoons each of lemon juice and clarified butter, brush it over the crabs, and sprinkle on a dusting of parsley. Serve with the saffron pasta and Richmond slaw.

For seasoning the sautéed crabs

3 tablespoons fresh lemon juice

3 tablespoons clarified butter (see box below)

1 to 3 tablespoons chopped fresh parsley

For serving

Saffron Pasta (see page 248)

Richmond Slaw (see page 254)

SPECIAL EQUIPMENT SUGGESTED

Kitchen shears

1 or 2 large heavy frying pans (Chef Jimmy recommends cast-iron)

JULIA'S NOTES ON CLARIFIED BUTTER

Plain butter contains a small percentage of milk residue, which you can see at the bottom of the pan when you melt butter. It is this residue that burns and blackens when the butter is heated. Clarified butter is the clear yellow liquid above the residue—you may spoon it off and use it as is. Or, if you want clarified butter on hand, clarify a pound of unsalted butter as follows.

Cut the butter into dice, for even melting, and set it in an 8-inch pan over moderately high heat. When melted, let it boil for just a few minutes, until it starts spluttering and crackling as the liquid in the residue evaporates. Watch it closely at this point, and when it suddenly foams up remove the pan at once from the heat—the clarification is complete. Pour the clear yellow liquid through a fine-meshed tea strainer into a preserving jar or another pan, discarding the dark brown speckles of residue remaining in the strainer. As the clarified butter cools, it will congeal and change color from yellow to cream. Cover and store in the refrigerator, or in the freezer, where it will keep for months.

JULIA'S METHOD FOR SHREDDING CABBAGE BY MACHINE

After pulling off and discarding the wilted leaves from a head of cabbage, cut the cabbage vertically (through the root) into quarters, sixths, or eighths, depending on its size. Cut out and discard the hard central core of each quarter, then cut the quarters into convenient lengths that will fit into the sleeve of your food processor. Insert a slicing disk: The 4-millimeter makes slices about ⅛ inch thick. Crowd as much as you can into the sleeve, standing the quarters cut side down (not flat-leaf side), and shred. Continue with the rest, rolling up strays together into tubes that you can stand in the sleeves. You'll probably find a few leaves in the container that didn't shred and will need cutting by hand. This is not a perfect system, but it produces a much more attractive shred than chopping with the processor's metal blade, and it is certainly much easier and usually much neater than shredding by hand.

RICHMOND SLAW

Jimmy Sneed's coleslaw is not only colorful, with bright strips of carrots and peppers, it is also seasoned just right to accompany his soft-shell crabs. The secret, he says, is in his Old Bay seasoning, which is traditional for crabs in his part of the country. However, our team made up its own formula, using the ingredients in the seasoning box on page 255, and though the various versions all differed slightly, each made a grand coleslaw to serve at any time. You may well want to double or triple the proportions here and thus have plenty for other meals, since it keeps beautifully in the refrigerator and even improves with age.

Making the Dressing: Bring the water and sugar to the boil in a 6-cup saucepan, swirling the pan by its handle until the sugar has completely dissolved. Measure in the Old Bay seasoning (or your own mixture), the pepper, and the salt. Return the liquid to the boil, set the pan aside off heat, and let it cool for 10 minutes. Stir in the celery seeds and vinegar.

Blanching and Julienning the Peppers: Quarter the peppers; remove stems, seeds, and ribs, and cut the peppers into julienne strips ⅛ inch wide and about 1½ inches long. Bring a small saucepan of water to a boil, add the salt, and when it returns to the boil, drop in the peppers. Blanch for 15 seconds, drain, and immediately drop them into the ice bath to stop the cooking and set the color. Drain again, pat dry, and put them into the bowl.

Julienning the Carrot: Rather than julienning the carrot by hand, try the mandoline with its julienne blade to make matchstick-size strips ⅛ inch

INGREDIENTS FOR 4 SERVINGS

For the dressing
¾ cup water
¼ cup sugar
1½ teaspoons Old Bay seasoning
(see box on opposite page)
¼ teaspoon freshly ground black
pepper, or to taste
1½ teaspoons salt, or to taste
¼ teaspoon celery seeds
¼ cup rice or cider vinegar

(continued)

thick—but do watch your hands since the blade is very sharp indeed. If the central core of the carrot is definitely of a different orange than the rest, do not include it. Pile several strips together, and with your knife cut them approximately the same length as the peppers. Turn them into the bowl with the peppers.

Slicing the Scallions: Slice the tender green and the white parts of the scallions into very thin rounds, and add to the other vegetables.

Shredding the Cabbage: Pull away the tough outer leaves of the cabbage, and either slice it by hand or use the food processor as described in the box on the opposite page.

Finishing the Slaw: Fold the shredded cabbage into the bowl with the other ingredients, pour on the dressing, and toss thoroughly. Taste, and toss with more salt if needed. Grate the ginger on top of the coleslaw. Cover and refrigerate for an hour or more, to let the flavors blend.

Ahead-of-Time Note: The coleslaw will keep nicely as is for a day or two. Before serving again, you may want to drain off the accumulated liquid, toss, and check the seasoning.

For the peppers
½ large red bell pepper
½ large yellow bell pepper
2 tablespoons sea salt

For the cabbage
1 large carrot, peeled
2 scallions, ends trimmed, green
   stalks left on
½ small head of green cabbage
   (2½ to 3 cups shredded)
2-inch piece of peeled fresh ginger
   root (½ teaspoon grated)

SPECIAL EQUIPMENT
SUGGESTED

A 3-quart bowl half full of cold
   water, plus a tray of ice cubes
A mandoline (vegetable slicer)
   with julienne blades (useful
   but not essential)
A ginger grater or a 4-sided metal
   grater
A food processor with 4-
   millimeter slicing disk (useful
   but not essential)
A serving bowl or a big mixing
   bowl (for the salad)

JIMMY SNEED'S FAVORITE "OLD BAY" CRAB SEASONING

According to the list of ingredients on the box label, this patented and traditional Chesapeake Bay crab seasoning contains the following ingredients. The proportions are not revealed, but the list at least gives an idea of how to wing it. I used a teaspoon of each assuming the pimiento was red pepper flakes, and I omitted the cassis, which I never found in a casual search. I ground them in my electric blender, and thought my crabs tasted just fine.

Celery salt
Laurel (bay) leaves
Ginger
Cassis (black currants)
Mustard
Cloves
Mace
Paprika
Pepper
Pimiento
Cardamom

RICK BAYLESS

With authentic Mexican cooking you are tasting many generations of flavors," explains Chef Rick Bayless. And just how did this former linguistics graduate student discover those varied layers of traditional flavors? He and his wife, Deann, packed everything into storage and ate their way through most of Mexico in a four-year grassroots exploration of the country's rich regional cooking. They explored Mexico town by town to see what people were eating in the markets, in the little restaurants, and on the streets, and they even set up housekeeping in several places in order to shop in the open-air markets and learn from the vendors. All in all, they logged thirty-five thousand miles to discover the secrets, treasures, and fundamentals of Mexican food and culture. The results are beautifully portrayed in Rick and Deann's book, *Authentic Mexican: Regional Cooking from the Heart of Mexico* (William Morrow). There, and in

their two award-winning Chicago restaurants, Frontera Grill and Topolobampo, the Baylesses go back to the originals for inspiration "because that is where the mysteries of the ages lie."

Chef Rick was not a complete stranger to the food world when he began his explorations. He grew up in his family's barbecue restaurant in Oklahoma City. He knew, however, that there was a lot more to cooking than what he could learn through his family's business, and he wanted to do something broader. His interest in Spanish and Latin American culture led first to a degree from the University of Oklahoma and then to his culinary pursuits. "I fell in love with the role that food plays in culture, and my heart drew me away from the library and into the kitchen."

Rick and Deann believe that a good meal should leave the diner with a sense of well-being. The brilliant flavors, varied textures, and beautiful colors of the dishes he prepared for us in Cambridge—his crunchy jícama and orange salad, soulful chile-glazed ribs, and satisfying black bean casserole—left us all feeling very well indeed.

RUSTIC JÍCAMA SALAD
ENSALADA DE JÍCAMA

This rustic Mexican salad should be eaten moments after it's been put together so that it maintains its fresh taste. The pieces are large because it is usually spread out on a large platter and passed family style as an appetizer. It also makes a colorful spectacle on a buffet table, and will maintain its crunchiness for a reasonable length of time.

Manufacturing Note: As with basil, the fragrance and flavor of cilantro are delicate and easily lost if the herb is mishandled. To chop, make sure it is thoroughly dry and then gently roll the leaves together, cutting through them once, as in a chiffonade, and not rapidly chopping them, as is done when mincing parsley.

Preparing the Vegetables: Peel away the buff-colored skin and fibrous layer beneath the skin of the jícama. Do this with a sharp paring knife since a vegetable peeler will not go deep enough. Cut the bulb in half crosswise. Lay each half on its cut side and cut it into slices ¼ inch wide. Stand the stack of slices on end and cut them in half diagonally. Place the jícama in the mixing bowl. Slice the cucumbers lengthwise in half, scoop out the seeds, and cut each half into diagonal slices ¼ inch thick. Add the cucumbers to the bowl along with the radishes. Pour on the lime juice and season with salt. Toss together and let marinate for 20 minutes.

Trimming the Oranges: Slice the stem and blossom ends off the oranges, stand them on the work surface, cut end down; with a very sharp knife, cut away the rind and all the white pith. Slice the oranges in half from top to bottom, then cut the halves into slices ¼ inch thick and reserve on a plate. Shortly before serving, toss the oranges and their juice into the bowl with the jícama, cucumbers, and so forth.

Serving: Pile the vegetables and fruit on the serving platter and drizzle over them the accumulated juices from the bowl. Sprinkle liberally with the ground chile, top with the pickled onions, and strew on the chopped cilantro. Serve at once.

INGREDIENTS FOR 8 SERVINGS

For the jícama
1 medium jícama (about 1½ pounds)
2 small cucumbers or 1 long English cucumber (about 1 pound total)
6 radishes, trimmed, and thinly sliced
The juice of 2 limes (about ¼ cup)
½ teaspoon salt or more, to taste
3 seedless oranges
2 teaspoons ground guajillo chile or cayenne pepper, more or less to taste
⅔ cup Pickled Red Onions (optional; see page 259)
¼ to ⅓ cup carefully chopped cilantro (see note above)

SPECIAL EQUIPMENT SUGGESTED

A large stainless steel or glass mixing bowl
A large flat platter

PICKLED RED ONIONS
ESCABECHE DE CEBOLLA

Parboiling—or, as the Mexicans say, "deflaming"—takes a lot of the bite out of onions, and when you then steep them with herbs and spices and a little vinegar you have a sprightly condiment for cold and hot dishes alike.

Parboiling the Onions: Bring 2 quarts of water to the boil in the saucepan, then add 2 teaspoons of salt and the onions. Bring back to the boil and boil a few seconds, until the onions have softened slightly and the red color has bled into the white. Drain, and turn the slices into the bowl.

Pickling the Onions: Coarsely grind the peppercorns and cumin, and fold into the onions along with the rest of the ingredients. Add just enough cold water barely to cover the onions, and fold all together. Let stand for at least 4 hours—or longer, until they take on a beautiful pink color.

Ahead-of-Time Note: Cover and store in the refrigerator, where the onions will keep for a week or more.

cook's notes

INGREDIENTS FOR ABOUT 1⅓ CUPS

2 teaspoons salt

1 large (6-ounce) red onion, peeled and sliced into rounds ⅛ inch thick

¼ teaspoon black peppercorns

¼ teaspoon cumin seeds

½ teaspoon dried Mexican oregano

2 garlic cloves, peeled and halved

¼ teaspoon salt

⅓ cup cider vinegar

SPECIAL EQUIPMENT SUGGESTED

A 2½- to 3-quart saucepan

A 1-quart glass or stainless steel bowl

A mortar and pestle or a spice grinder

CHILE-GLAZED COUNTRY RIBS
COSTILLAS ADOBADAS

Chef Rick likes country-style pork ribs for this dish because they have more meat on them, and one rib makes a generous serving per person. Besides, they have good texture, are usually reasonably priced, and look attractive on the platter. His marinade is a fine one not only for other cuts of pork but for fish and chicken as well as pork.

Making the Chile Marinade:

Roasting the Vegetables. Set the ungreased skillet or griddle over moderate heat, lay in the unpeeled garlic, and roast it, turning occasionally, until it is blackened in spots and soft, 10 to 15 minutes; cool, then slip off the papery skins and set them aside. Open the chiles out flat, and, working with one at a time, lay them in the hot skillet, press flat for a few seconds with a metal spatula until they start to crackle and even send up a faint wisp of smoke, then flip them over and press down on them to toast the other side; they are ready when they begin to change color. Transfer to a bowl, cover with boiling water, weight down with a plate to keep them submerged, and let soak for 30 minutes. Then drain and put them along with the garlic into the blender.

Adding the Liquid. Measure ½ cup of broth or water into the blender, and add the vinegar. Blend to a smooth puree, scraping and stirring every few seconds—add droplets more liquid if there is not enough for the blender to function.

Preparing the Spices. Pulverize the cumin, cloves, peppercorns, oregano, and cinnamon in the spice grinder or mortar, then transfer to the blender with the chile puree. Blend for 30 seconds more, and then, with the rubber spatula, work the puree through the strainer into a bowl. Stir in the sugar and salt.

Ahead-of-Time Note: The chile marinade may be made several weeks in advance. Refrigerate in a covered jar.

Marinating the Ribs: Place the ribs in a large glass bowl. Divide the marinade in half and smear half of it on the ribs, cover, and refrigerate for several hours (or preferably overnight). Combine the remaining chile marinade with the honey, cover, and refrigerate.

INGREDIENTS FOR 4 TO 6 SERVINGS

For the chile marinade

The roasted vegetables
4 garlic cloves, unpeeled
The following chiles, stemmed and seeded, and deveined if you wish:
3 medium-large (about 1½ ounces) ancho chiles
6 medium-large (about 1½ ounces) guajillo chiles

The liquid
½ cup meat or poultry broth or water, plus a little more if needed
2 tablespoons cider vinegar

The spices
A pinch of cumin seeds or a generous pinch of ground cumin
3 cloves or about a pinch of ground cloves
8 black peppercorns or a generous ⅛ teaspoon freshly ground black pepper

(continued)

Ahead-of-Time Note: The ribs may be marinated 2 days in advance.

Preheat the oven to 325° F.

Cooking the Ribs: Transfer the ribs to a baking dish, scraping onto them any marinade left behind in the pan. Drizzle ¼ cup water around them, cover with foil, and bake for 45 minutes, or until they are tender when pierced with a fork. Uncover and baste with the liquid in the pan. Return them to the oven uncovered for 15 minutes more to develop a nice crustiness. Pour fat and juices out of the pan or transfer the ribs to a clean roasting pan.

Ahead-of-Time Note: The recipe may be prepared a day or so in advance up to this point.

Set the oven temperature to 350° F.

Finishing and Serving: Brush the ribs heavily with the reserved marinade-honey mixture. Bake until glazed and crusty, about 15 minutes. Lay the lettuce leaves on one half of a serving platter and place the ribs over them. Scatter on the onion and radishes, and garnish with sprigs of cilantro.

CORN TORTILLAS

Chef Rick says to look for tortillas wrapped in paper bags rather than in plastic because paper usually indicates that they have been produced locally. Those in plastic could have been made "who knows where" and might contain unwanted preservatives—study the label in any case. Look for tortillas that have a good corn fragrance and soft texture—two indicators of freshness.

cook's notes

¾ *teaspoon dried oregano*
    (preferably Mexican)
½-*inch cinnamon stick or about*
    ½ *teaspoon ground cinnamon*
1 *teaspoon sugar, or more to taste*
1½ *teaspoons salt, or more to*
    taste

For the pork
6 *good-size pork country ribs,*
    about 3 pounds
2 *tablespoons honey*

For serving
6 *large romaine lettuce leaves*
¼ *large white onion, thinly sliced*
2 *radishes, trimmed and thinly*
    sliced
Sprigs of cilantro

SPECIAL EQUIPMENT
SUGGESTED

A heavy-bottomed skillet or
    griddle
A spice grinder, a mortar and
    pestle, or a coffee grinder
An electric blender
A wide rubber spatula
A medium-meshed strainer
A roasting pan (for the ribs)

BLACK BEAN TORTILLA CASSEROLE WITH SMOKY CHIPOTLE, AVOCADO, AND SOUR CREAM
CHILAQUILES DE FRÍJOL NEGRO

Chef Rick calls this dish an example of real Mexican "soul food." Anytime tortillas are fried and then simmered in a sauce, they become chilaquiles, *and that's soul food. This is probably the most soulful of all because the sauce is made not from tomatoes or tomatillos but from earthy, simple black beans. In addition, it is wonderful for parties because you may cook the bean sauce several days ahead, fry the tortillas the morning of the day, and all you have to do is assemble it at the last minute. You might serve* chilaquiles *with breakfast, or at lunch with a salad, or alongside a pork or beef dish.*

Manufacturing Note: Special Mexican ingredients may be found in Mexican grocery stores.

Cooking the Beans: Pour the beans into the colander, and pick them over, discarding any that are defective and any pieces of stone or earth. Rinse them well under running water, and transfer them to the kettle. Measure in the broth or water, and add the onion and garlic. Make a slit down the side of each chipotle chile, and scrape out the seeds, touching them as little as possible to avoid irritating your fingers. Add one of the chiles to the beans and set the other two aside. Add the 2 teaspoons of sauce from the chile can, and the branch of epazote, and bring the beans to the simmer. Simmer, partially covered, until the beans are thoroughly tender—about 2 hours—and taste carefully to be sure they are properly cooked. You may need to add a little broth or water during cooking, to keep the beans submerged at all times.

Preparing the Bean Puree: When done, ladle out batches of beans and their cooking liquid and drop into the processor or blender. (If using a blender, cover the top loosely; otherwise the beans, expanding as they become pureed, could blow the top off the container.) Puree the beans and their liquid and pour into the 12-inch skillet. Stir in enough broth or water (it may take an extra cup or so) to bring the bean sauce to the consistency of a thin cream soup. Season with salt.

Frying the Tortillas: Heat the oil in the deep-fat-frying pan or second skillet to 375° F and plan to fry the tortilla strips in four or five batches. Each batch will take about a minute to crisp, and most of the bubbling will have

INGREDIENTS FOR 4 TO 6 SERVINGS

For the beans
1¼ cups dry black beans
5 cups poultry or meat broth, or water, plus more if needed
½ medium onion, roughly chopped
4 large garlic cloves, peeled and roughly chopped
3 canned chiles chipotles en adobo *(canned chile peppers) plus 2 teaspoons of the tomato-flavored* adobo *(flavored can juices)*
1 branch of epazote (see box, page 53)
Salt to taste

For the tortillas
1½ cups corn oil
Twelve 5- to 6-inch corn tortillas, sliced into ½-inch strips
8 good-size leaves of epazote

(continued)

Black Bean Tortilla Casserole (continued)

subsided when they are browned and ready. Bring the oil temperature back to 375° F before each new batch goes in. Drain on paper towels.

Preparing the **Chilaquiles:** Fold the tortilla strips into the bean sauce and bring to the simmer over moderate heat. Add the reserved second chile, another spoonful or two of the sauce from the can, and the epazote leaves. Stir gently every half minute or so for 2 or 3 minutes until the tortillas have softened but are not falling apart; they will have absorbed a good amount of the sauce.

Serving: Scoop the *chilaquiles* onto the warm serving platter. Drizzle with *crème fraîche* or cream, and sprinkle with cheese and the remaining chile sliced into strips. Dot with the avocado and serve.

For the garnish

½ cup homemade thick cream (crème fraîche; *see box, page 146*), or store-bought sour cream thinned with a little heavy cream

¼ cup finely grated aged Mexican cheese, **queso añejo,** *or other aged cheese such as dried feta, aged Monterey Jack, or mild Parmesan*

1 small ripe avocado, peeled, pitted, and cut into ½-inch cubes

SPECIAL EQUIPMENT SUGGESTED

A colander

A 4- to 5-quart kettle (for simmering the beans)

A ladle

A food processor or an electric blender

A 12-inch skillet or saucepan 3 to 4 inches deep (for simmering the puree)

A deep-fat-frying pan or another 12- by 4-inch pan

A deep-fat-frying thermometer (useful but not essential)

A 10-inch deep-dish pie plate or other deep platter for serving

RICK BAYLESS'S REFRIED BEANS
FRIJOLES REFRITOS

When Chef Rick made his great bean casserole, chilaquiles de fríjol negro, *I said that I would just love to know how to do refried beans his way. He generously complied, offering the following recipe. Lard, he told us, gives this dish its authentic, rich, meaty Mexican flavor—if just the mention of the word gives you the heebies, please see our up-to-date findings on page 43.*

Sautéing the Onion and Garlic: Warm the pan, then sauté the diced onion in the lard over moderate heat, stirring, until tender; raise heat to moderately high and continue sautéing, stirring frequently, until the onion is nicely browned—the browning is necessary to give the proper roasted flavor. Stir the garlic into the pan and sauté a minute or two to brown very lightly.

Adding and Mashing the Beans: Remove and discard the epazote from the beans if you have used it. Reserving the cooking liquid, and, using the slotted spoon, transfer the beans to the pan with the onion and garlic. Stir the beans about in the pan to mix all together, then mash into a coarse puree with the back of the wooden spoon or potato masher, adding a little of the cooking liquid if too thick. Simmer, stirring, until the beans have the consistency of thin mashed potatoes—they will thicken a little more when you remove them from heat. Taste, adding salt as needed.

Ahead-of-Time Note: May be made several days in advance; cover and refrigerate. Reheat over simmering water, stirring frequently and adding bean-cooking juices or water if too thick.

Serving: The beans are ready when they are heated through. Spoon out onto the warm platter and garnish with grated Mexican cheese and fried tortillas or tortilla chips.

INGREDIENTS FOR 6 SERVINGS

The beans

1¼ cups dry black beans, cooked according to the directions in the black bean casserole recipe on page 263 (you may omit the epazote and chipotle chile)

The flavoring

½ medium white onion, diced

2 tablespoons lard, preferably home-rendered (see box, page 43)

2 large garlic cloves, peeled and finely minced

1 teaspoon salt

SPECIAL EQUIPMENT SUGGESTED

A 10-inch heavy-bottomed sauté pan or saucepan

A slotted spoon

A wooden spoon or a potato masher

MONIQUE BARBEAU

Although she is a mere twenty-nine years old as of this writing, Vancouver native Monique Barbeau has already had a first-class background. She graduated from the Culinary Institute of America in 1987 and in 1991 received a bachelor of science degree in hospitality and management from Florida International University. Without a whit of experience in the restaurant industry she was hired by Barry Wine at his prestigious New York restaurant The Quilted Giraffe. "I was lucky. I learned so many great things there," recalls Chef Monique. Equally lucky, but justly deserved, were the positions that followed at New York's Le Bernardin and Chanterelle.

"I wanted to return to the Northwest," she recalls, and once again fate was on her side. She was chosen from more than two hundred applicants to be the chef at Fullers in the Sheraton Seattle Hotel and Towers. By the time she was nominated a James Beard "Rising Star Chef" in 1993, this vibrant young woman had already made her mark in the culinary industry by giving a global touch to products indigenous to the Northwest. Her enthusiasm keeps her open to new ideas and new foods, and her training allows her to execute them with finesse. She expertly cured a side of salmon for us, flavoring it with tequila and citrus. Her trip to Israel in 1994 as part of "Chefs Salute Peace" was the inspiration for her Eggplant Falafel with homemade pita bread. "Although my food is based in the Northwest, I feel that it could limit me, so when I have the opportunity to travel I feel it is my responsibility to show people a bit of my travels and I grab things from wherever I go and bring them back."

In the six years since her graduation, Chef Monique has already accomplished a lot, but she is in no way sitting back and resting. "It's endless. There's always so much more."

TEQUILA AND LIME CURED GRAVLAX

Dill-cured salmon is almost as popular nowadays as smoked salmon, and Chef Monique has come up with a new version of her own—she uses not only dill but a sprightly bouquet of flavors including orange, lime, and coriander, and tequila rather than Cognac. What a pride and pleasure to have your own homemade salmon in your refrigerator! It makes such an easy and very special appetizer or luncheon treat.

Manufacturing Note: The gravlax needs 3 to 5 days of daily attention to cure.

Readying the Salmon: Lay the salmon skin side down on your cutting board, and run your fingers searchingly along the length and width of the flesh to find any regular bones, and especially the thin, flexible pin bones which are located near the center of the upper end. Remove the bones with the pliers, pulling them out in the direction in which they are pointing. Check again with your finger to be sure you got them all, since bones will tear the flesh when you are slicing, later.

Day One—The First Dry Cure: Mix the salt and sugar together and reserve a third of it for Day Two. Next to the salmon place a plastic-wrapped pan and, forming a bed ¼ inch thick along the length and width of the salmon, spread on the cure. Turn the salmon over and lay it flesh side down on the cure. Scatter leftover cure along the sides and ends of the fish, and then pull the plastic up so it wraps around the fish securely and will capture extruding juices. Place the board (or another pan) on top of the fish, and set 5 pounds of cans or other heavy objects on the board to weight down the salmon. Refrigerate for 24 hours.

Day Two—The Liquid Cure: Pour the tequila and the lime juice into a bowl, and stir in the zests. Place the coriander seeds in a plastic bag, lay it on your work surface, and crush the seeds with a rolling pin or the bottom of a heavy pan; pour them into the bowl, then chop the herbs roughly and stir them in. Pour the tequila marinade into the second plastic-lined pan, spreading the zests and the herbs out so they are evenly distributed on what will be the length and width of the fish. Sprinkle the reserved dry cure over the liquid, again reserving a bit for the ends and the sides. Remove the salmon from the refrigerator, and lay it flesh side down on top of the cure,

INGREDIENTS FOR I SIDE OF SALMON

For the dry cure
1½-pound side of salmon, unsliced, skin on
1½ cups kosher salt
3 cups light brown sugar

For the liquid cure
½ cup tequila
½ cup fresh lime juice
Zest of 1 lemon (colored part of peel only)
Zest of 1 orange (colored part of peel only)
2 teaspoons whole coriander seeds
3 sprigs of fresh dill, with stems
3 sprigs of fresh mint, with stems
3 sprigs of fresh basil, with stems

(continued)

Tequila and Lime Cured Gravlax (continued)

scattering the dry ingredients along the sides and the ends of the fish. Wrap the plastic around it, replace the board and weights, and refrigerate for another 24 hours.

Day Three—The Finished Cured Salmon: Remove the salmon from the refrigerator and unwrap it. Feel it carefully from one end to the other: If the curing is complete, the flesh will have turned a deep red color and will feel decidedly firm from one end to the other. If it is not, return it to the refrigerator for another day or two—when it feels evenly firm it is ready to be sliced and served. If your salmon still has a somewhat fatty uneven half-inch strip of belly running almost the length of the fillet on one side, cut it off and save it for the cook since it makes good eating but interferes with slicing.

Slicing the Salmon: The slicing of a salmon into thin, long, wide, handsome pieces is a very special art form that we shall not attempt to describe, except to say that you start at the tail end, using smooth, long strokes with your very sharp, long knife, and that you leave the skin on the cutting board. Cut only as much as you plan to eat.

Ahead-of-Time Note: Store the salmon in its cure, but it need not be weighted down. Cured salmon will keep at least 10 days in the refrigerator.

SPECIAL EQUIPMENT
SUGGESTED

Two jelly-roll pans covered with plastic wrap
Needle-nose pliers
A flat board and heavy cans of food (for weighting the salmon)
A zester
A long, thin, very sharp knife (for slicing the salmon)

DEEP-FRIED CAPERS

Capers take on a new taste when deep-fried, and this is one of Chef Monique's creative innovations. As they hit the hot oil, the tiny caper buds open up like black flowers, making a crisp, salty, and attractively sourish garnish. Monique serves them with her cured salmon, and they would also do well on smoked or poached salmon, sole meunière, veal scallopini, egg dishes, and salads.

Pour enough vegetable oil into the saucepan to come to a depth of 2 inches, and bring to a frying temperature, 350° F. Pat the capers dry on paper towels and stand back from the oil since the capers will pop and splatter. Drop one into the oil, and when the oil is hot enough the caper will sizzle. Then carefully lower in the remaining capers. Fry for about 30 seconds as they rise to the surface and the blossoms open. Remove with the wire-mesh strainer and drain on paper towels.

Ahead-of-Time Note: The capers will stay crisp for about a day. Cover loosely and store at room temperature.

INGREDIENTS FOR ¼ CUP

Vegetable oil (for deep-frying)
About ¼ cup brine-cured capers, drained but unrinsed

SPECIAL EQUIPMENT SUGGESTED

A 6-cup heavy-bottomed saucepan
A wire-mesh strainer
Paper towels

MONIQUE BARBEAU'S DUKKA SPICE

Chef Monique brought back this intriguing spice mixture from her trip to Israel. She sprinkles the tops of her pita breads with *dukka* before baking. She uses it to flavor meats and vegetables, too, and always has a jar on hand.

INGREDIENTS FOR 3 CUPS

1 cup sesame seeds
¾ cup (3 ounces) hazelnuts
1 cup coriander seeds
¼ cup cumin seeds
½ teaspoon Tellicherry peppercorns
1 teaspoon salt

Preheat the oven to 350° F. Pour the sesame seeds into a small baking pan, and the hazelnuts into another. Toast the sesame seeds for 3 to 5 minutes, until golden, and the hazelnuts for about 10 minutes, until lightly browned and fragrant. When slightly cooled, rub the hazelnuts in a towel to remove as much of their skins as will come off.

Meanwhile, one at a time, pulverize the coriander seeds, the cumin seeds, and the peppercorns in the grinder, then pour them into the bowl. Finally, grind the hazelnuts. Mix the ground spices and nuts in the bowl together with the toasted sesame seeds and the salt, and set aside.

Ahead-of-Time Note: Stored in a screw-top jar, the *dukka* will keep about a week in the refrigerator, or may be frozen.

WATERCRESS OIL

Chef Monique uses watercress oil as a seasoning for her salmon gravlax appetizers. It is much like a vinaigrette dressing and may be used in many of the same creative ways. Charlie Trotter, incidentally, has a more elaborate version in the box on page 59—it's good to have several paths to follow.

Manufacturing Note: The electric blender produces less watercress juice than the juice extractor; thus if you are using the blender, either double the watercress or cut down on the oil and lemon juice. Extract the juice, in any case, then complete the recipe at once to preserve all the fine green cress color.

Run the watercress leaves through the juice extractor and pour the resulting juice into the bowl sitting over ice—you should have about ¼ cup of beautiful bright green liquid. Alternately, put the watercress into a blender, process it as fine as possible, then strain the resulting puree through the cheesecloth into the chilled bowl—you will have about 2 tablespoons. Squeeze in the lemon juice and, continuing to work over ice, slowly and steadily drizzle in the olive oil, whisking all the while in order to form an emulsion. Whisk in the salt and pepper, and refrigerate in a covered container until ready to use.

Ahead-of-Time Note: The oil should keep nicely in the refrigerator for several days.

INGREDIENTS FOR ABOUT
½ TO ¾ CUP

1 bunch of watercress leaves
1 tablespoon fresh lemon juice
½ cup excellent olive oil
Salt
Freshly ground black pepper

SPECIAL EQUIPMENT
SUGGESTED

*A vegetable juicer or a blender
  (see note above)*
*A strainer lined with washed
  cheesecloth (if needed)*
*A small bowl sitting in a larger
  bowl of ice and water to cover*
A whisk

cook's notes

SAVORY DILL PANCAKES

Chef Monique layers these appetizer-size pancakes with her Tequila and Lime Cured Gravlax for a most impressive and delicious first course. The pancakes are equally fine as an hors d'oeuvre with a dab of caviar or even with just a bit of her tomato crème fraîche. *Use any herb and seasoning you like.*

Manufacturing Note: As do many of today's chefs, Monique uses plastic squeeze bottles for her decorative dabs of sauces and herb oils.

Mixing the Batter: Measure the dry ingredients into a bowl and stir them together to blend. Gradually pour in 1 cup of the milk, whisking to blend thoroughly. Gradually add more milk if necessary, to make a thick, pourable batter. Stir in the vegetables and check the consistency again, adding more milk if necessary. Season carefully with salt and pepper; be particularly careful with the salt if the pancakes are to be served with the salmon, which is itself salty. Refrigerate the batter for at least 6 hours.

Ahead-of-Time Note: The batter may be made the day before and refrigerated.

Frying the Pancakes: Pour a few teaspoons of the olive oil into the no-stick pan just to film the bottom. When the pan is hot, spoon in the batter to make pancakes about 2 inches in diameter—approximately 2 tablespoons of batter per pancake. Cook about 2 minutes, or until the bottom is golden brown and bubbles begin to appear on top. Turn and cook a minute or two on the second side. Place the pancakes on paper toweling and continue with the rest of the batter, adding more oil if necessary.

Ahead-of-Time Note: The pancakes may be kept warm in a 150° F or 200° F oven on a cookie sheet for a brief time while you finish cooking the rest of them.

The Assemblage: Place one pancake in the center of each of four appetizer-size plates. Scatter a few of the greens in the center of a pancake, letting them drape over the edge. Position a slice of gravlax on top of the greens, and drizzle or squirt a few teaspoons each of tomato *crème fraîche* and watercress oil on top of the salmon. Cover with a pancake and repeat the layers a second time, ending with a pancake. Decorate the plate with drizzles of *crème fraîche* and watercress oil, scatter the capers over the pancake and the plate, and garnish with dill sprigs.

INGREDIENTS FOR 2 CUPS OF BATTER MAKING SIXTEEN 2-INCH PANCAKES

For the pancake batter
1¼ cups all-purpose flour
1 teaspoon ground cumin
2 teaspoons baking powder
1 to 1¼ cups milk

The vegetable additions
½ cup peeled, seeded, and finely diced cucumbers
½ cup minced red onion
½ cup scallions, green and white parts, thinly sliced on the bias
¼ cup finely chopped fresh dill
¼ to ½ teaspoon salt
About 6 good grindings of pepper

For frying the pancakes
About 3 tablespoons olive oil

(continued)

Savory Dill Pancakes (continued)

For serving

1 cup mixed fresh greens (frisée, red oak, etc.), dressed with olive oil and lemon juice

Thin slices of gravlax (see page 267), 2 per pancake

Tomato Crème Fraîche *(see page 273)*

Watercress Oil (see page 270)

Deep-Fried Capers (see page 269)

Sprigs of fresh dill

SPECIAL EQUIPMENT SUGGESTED

A whisk

A no-stick frying pan or griddle

A metal spatula

Plastic squeeze bottles (for the crème fraîche *and the watercress oil)*

TOMATO CRÈME FRAÎCHE

Chef Monique has some splendid tips for making ingredients such as tomato paste and crème fraîche *at home, and this tomato cream is one of her favorites. It's a useful garnish for hard-boiled eggs and cold dishes, and is beautiful with her salmon and spiced pancake recipe on page 271.*

Manufacturing Note: You may substitute sour cream for the *crème fraîche,* and if you want just a small amount for decorative dabs, just take a few tablespoons of the tomato paste and stir in just a few tablespoons of the cream.

Making Crème Fraîche: Stir the buttermilk into the heavy cream, cover with plastic wrap, and leave at room temperature until it has thickened (24 hours). Then place in the refrigerator, where it will keep for a week or so; it will thicken more as it ages. (Another method is in the box on page 146.)

Making the Tomato Paste: Pour the olive oil into the sauté pan and add the shallots and garlic; sweat (cook slowly) the vegetables until they are softened but take on no color, about 2 minutes. Stir in the tomatoes and cook them down slowly over moderately high heat until most of the juices have evaporated, about 5 minutes. Add the vinegar and boil to reduce the liquid until the tomatoes are dry and paste-like, about 3 more minutes. Strain through the sieve and let cool.

Putting It Together: The tomato cream should remain decidedly red and have a nice tomato taste. The best way to judge the amount of *crème fraîche* to add to the tomato paste is by color and taste. Start by stirring in a cup of the cream, adding more and tasting until you are satisfied.

Ahead-of-Time Note: Covered airtight, tomato *crème fraîche* will keep in the refrigerator for several days.

INGREDIENTS FOR 1½ CUPS

For the *crème fraîche*
2 tablespoons buttermilk
1 to 1½ cups heavy cream

For the homemade tomato paste
2 tablespoons olive oil
1 large shallot, peeled and finely chopped
1 large garlic clove, peeled and minced
1¾ to 2 pounds ripe red tomatoes (about 3 large regulars or 6 to 8 plum tomatoes), peeled, seeded, and coarsely chopped (about 3 cups)
¼ cup red wine vinegar

SPECIAL EQUIPMENT SUGGESTED

A medium-size sauté pan
A fine-meshed sieve or a **chinois**

MONIQUE BARBEAU'S PITA BREAD

Chef Monique is enthusiastic about Israeli cuisine and likes to make her own pita bread, which she often tops with a sprinkling of the Israeli spice combination dukka. *Pitas are fun to make, especially when you have a glass window in your oven door and can watch them ballooning up as they bake.*

Manufacturing Notes: Chef Monique's recipe calls for forming the dough and baking it immediately—no rise at all. It worked, and, to my surprise, the freshly baked little breads had a good taste. However, a rise to almost triple in volume gave a slightly more interesting taste and tenderer texture, as well as longer keeping qualities. Nevertheless it is good to know that you can make, bake, and eat a pita bread in so short a time.

The Oven: Slide the rack into the lower middle level of the oven, and preheat it to 500° F 20 minutes before you plan to bake—which would be now, first thing, if you do not plan to let the dough rise.

Mixing the Pita Dough: Measure the ½ cup of warm water into a small bowl or glass measure, sprinkle on the yeast and stir it up, then let it dissolve completely—5 minutes or so.

In the Electric Mixer: Meanwhile, measure the flour and salt into the bowl of the mixer, and attach the dough hook. With the machine running at slow speed, blend the water into the fully dissolved yeast, and pour the yeast-water mixture into the machine. Knead for several minutes until well incorporated; increase speed to medium until you have formed a soft dough 2 to 3 minutes. Turn the dough out onto a lightly floured board, cover loosely with a towel, and let rest 5 minutes, then knead vigorously by hand for about 3 minutes, until the dough is smooth and elastic.

Or Make the Dough in the Food Processor: as described in the box on page 212. Either plan to form and bake the pitas at once or place the dough in a covered container and let rise at around 75° F until almost tripled in volume—about 2 hours.

Rolling and Cutting the Dough: Roll the dough out ¼ inch thick—if it resists you or shrinks back, cover loosely with a towel and let it relax for 5 minutes, then continue. Cut it into 3-inch circles. Place them on the cookie sheet, brush them lightly with melted butter, and sprinkle with a dusting of the *dukka* spice.

INGREDIENTS FOR ABOUT TWO DOZEN 3-INCH PITA BREADS

1 tablespoon dry-active yeast
½ cup warm water (not over 105° F)
3 cups all-purpose flour
½ teaspoon salt
¾ cup water
Melted unsalted butter
Dukka spice (see box, page 269)

SPECIAL EQUIPMENT SUGGESTED

An electric mixer fitted with dough hook (or a food processor with plastic blade)
A rolling pin
A 3-inch-round dough cutter
A cookie sheet, no-stick suggested
A pastry brush

Ahead-of-Time Note: Formed, unbaked pita may be frozen and baked fresh as needed.

Baking: Place the pan in the lower middle level of the preheated 500° F oven and bake for about 2 minutes in all—the pitas will begin to puff up in a minute because of the intense heat and will need another minute or so to finish cooking. They are not to brown or crisp. (Some of the breads will not puff dramatically for easy separation, but you will be able to cut and peel them apart while still warm.)

TAHINI DRESSING
SESAME DRESSING

Sesame seed paste (a.k.a. tahini) is classic with falafel, and also with eggplant, and tahini dressing is so addictive you will want to eat it just by itself, or serve it as a dip with potato chips or tortillas.

Measure the tahini paste into a small mixing bowl. Stir and whisk to loosen it, then whisk in the lemon juice and garlic. As it thickens, start whisking in the water to smooth and loosen it. The mixture should be soft but not runny and have enough body to hold its shape on a plate. Stir in the salt and taste carefully for seasoning, adding more lemon juice if you think it is needed.

Ahead-of-Time Note: Refrigerate in a covered container, where it will keep for several days at least.

INGREDIENTS FOR ABOUT 2 CUPS

1 cup tahini paste (sesame seed paste)
½ cup or more fresh lemon juice
3 large garlic cloves, peeled and minced
¼ cup or more water
½ teaspoon salt

cook's notes

EGGPLANT FALAFEL WITH TAHINI DRESSING

Chef Monique was inspired to make this recipe after her visit to Israel, where she fell in love with the flavors in that part of the world. Falafel, an Israeli specialty, look like little meatballs, and indeed have a meaty taste, but they are a high-class vegetarian food containing only chickpeas and eggplant, richly flavored with cilantro, onions, and a variety of spices. Monique serves them with her own pita bread, crisp salad greens, and colorful vegetables to make an especially appealing dish.

Manufacturing Note: Although 60 patties may be more than you would wish to serve at one sitting, the falafel mixture freezes nicely for another meal. Or cut down the recipe by half or two-thirds. Please note that the TV recipe called for one large eggplant weighing 1½ pounds, which took us an hour to cook; here we've suggested two smaller ones and a 30-minute baking time.

Roasting the Eggplant: Preheat the oven to 350° F. Cut the eggplants in half lengthwise and place flesh side down in the roasting pan. Pour water into the pan to the depth of ¼ inch, cover tightly with foil, and roast in the oven for 20 to 30 minutes, until the flesh is very soft. Remove from the pan and let cool.

Preparing the Falafel: Scoop the flesh of the eggplant out of the skin and into the bowl of the food processor. The soaked, raw chickpeas will have swelled and should be crisp to the bite; add them to the eggplant. Break the cilantro bunch in half lengthwise and drop it in, along with the red onion, the garlic, cumin, coriander, cayenne, and baking soda. Process until the ingredients are finely minced and form a rough paste. Remove the cover and sprinkle on ¼ cup of the flour; pulse and then feel the mixture; it should not be wet. If it is, pulse in more flour. Refrigerate for at least 4 hours or overnight to blend the flavors.

Preheat the oven to 300° F.

Deep-Frying the Falafel: Pour 4 inches of oil into the deep-fat fryer or saucepan, and heat it to 350° F. If the falafel is loose and damp, beat in a little more flour—it should just hold its shape. Taste it, and correct seasoning. Planning to fry only four or five balls at a time, either use one of the soup spoons to scoop up a heaping tablespoon of the mixture and use the second spoon to round the mound out and push it into the hot oil, or dip out a ball

INGREDIENTS FOR 50 TO 60 PATTIES

For the falafel

2 firm shiny perfect eggplants, about ¾ pound each

2 cups chickpeas, soaked 5 to 6 hours or overnight, and drained

1 bunch (2 large handfuls) of fresh cilantro

1 large red onion, roughly chopped

3 large garlic cloves, peeled

1 teaspoon cumin

1 teaspoon ground coriander

¼ teaspoon cayenne pepper

½ teaspoon baking soda

¼ to ½ cup flour, plus more if needed

About 2 teaspoons salt

Freshly ground black pepper

Vegetable oil (for deep-frying)

For serving

Homemade pita bread (see page 274) or small store-bought pitas

Tahini Dressing (see page 275)

(continued)

Eggplant Falafel with Tahini Dressing (continued)

of falafel with the ice cream scoop and drop it into the oil. The balls will immediately sink to the bottom and gradually float to the top of the oil. Let them fry for about 3 minutes, until they are cooked through and golden-brown. Transfer with the slotted spoon to the paper towels. When all are fried, set the pan in the preheated oven for about 5 minutes, for the falafel to finish cooking.

Serving: Place a heaping tablespoon of the tahini dressing in the center of each plate and lay a couple of salad greens on top of it. Scatter the diced tomatoes on the plate around the tahini dressing. Scatter the scallions, then the radishes, and then the cucumber over and among the tomatoes. Cut the pita breads in half or quarters and place three pieces on top of the greens. Arrange three falafel on top, and scatter with the fresh mint or parsley leaves.

THE MISE EN PLACE
SETTING EVERYTHING OUT THE CHEF'S WAY

Before she begins to do any of the cooking for any of her recipes, Monique Barbeau, like all well-trained chefs, prepares her *mise en place,* the professional culinary term for setting all the food and equipment needed out on the work space and prepping them before beginning to cook. It is absolutely necessary in the fast and hectic atmosphere of a restaurant kitchen. Cooking authority Dione Lucas, the famous and popular teacher of French cookery in the 1940s until her death in 1971, was one of the first I know of to urge that home cooks adopt the *mise en place* habit. When everything is there, it makes cooking so much faster and easier—and you won't forget to add any special ingredients.

For the garnish

About 1 cup salad greens

1 large ripe red tomato, seeded, juiced, and diced

1 large yellow tomato, seeded, juiced, and diced

3 scallions, white part and tender green, trimmed and thinly sliced on the bias

6 radishes, trimmed and thinly sliced

⅓ large unwaxed and unpeeled cucumber, halved lengthwise and thinly sliced

A handful of fresh mint leaves or Italian flat-leaf parsley, chopped

SPECIAL EQUIPMENT
SUGGESTED

A roasting pan

Aluminum foil

An electric food processor

A deep-fat fryer or an 8-inch saucepan about 6 inches deep

A deep-fat-frying thermometer (useful but not essential)

2 kitchen soup spoons or a ½-inch ice cream scoop

A slotted spoon or a wire-mesh strainer

A cookie sheet covered with paper towels

JOACHIM SPLICHAL

When Chef Joachim Splichal enters a kitchen and ties on his work apron, one has the sense that something wonderful is about to happen. Within minutes, this talented chef is exhibiting the care and efficiency which have won him numerous international awards. "I think that to do a perfect dish, to get a final product that is really excellent, you need to take care of each ingredient," says Joachim as he scrutinizes each potato that will be sliced for his potato lasagna and as he runs his fingers through the barley and sniffs the Parmesan that will go into his barley risotto. He swiftly turns carrots and leeks into fine, perfect dice while attending to both a fragrant white *nage* and a rich braise of lamb shanks, the meat of which is soon meltingly tender. It is obvious that his efficient care is grounded in thorough classical training.

Born and raised in Spaichingen, West Germany, Joachim graduated from the Hotel and Management School in Montreux, Switzerland. Before opening his own Los Angeles restaurant, Patina, in 1989 and his enormously successful California/French bistro, Pinot, in 1992, Chef Joachim accumulated more than sixteen years of experience in the restaurant and hotel business—four particularly valuable years working as sous-chef for Jacques Maximin at the Chantecler Restaurant at the Hôtel Negresco in Nice. "There is so much to learn. It took me ten years to get a good base. Some guys work with two good chefs and then they open a restaurant. It is better to stay longer in good restaurants and learn more."

Perhaps the best proof that Chef Joachim has developed a broad, firm base is that he is continually called upon as a teacher and consultant by large international concerns. He was responsible for developing the food concepts for such diverse establishments as the deluxe Peabody Hotel in Orlando, Florida, the Cheeca Lodge in the Florida Keys, the Hay-Adams in Washington, D.C., and the popular Canyon Ranch spa resorts in Tucson, Arizona, and Lenox, Massachusetts. We were delighted he could take the time to share some of his unique dishes and his expertise with us.

JOACHIM SPLICHAL'S POTATO LASAGNA OF CHANTERELLE MUSHROOMS

Chef Joachim loves potatoes and he creates a great number of dishes from them at his California restaurants—he even hosts entire potato dinners. There are too many Italian and pasta restaurants in Los Angeles, he says, and he enjoys playing around with Italian ideas, such as substituting barley for rice in his risotto on page 287, and potatoes for pasta in his lasagna here.

This concoction of paper-thin potato slices layered between sautéed wild mushrooms could also be called Potato Napoleons, since you are going to produce four of them, each constructed with a cooked potato slice on which you mound a spoonful of mushrooms, topped by another slice, more mushrooms, a third potato slice, and a third spread of mushrooms, ending with the final and fourth potato. You could continue on to dizzying heights, but more than three layers and four potato slices make difficult and precarious eating. Each portion is bathed in a beautiful white butter sauce garnished with parsley and diced tomato.

Manufacturing Notes: To produce the large, very thin, perfect slices of potato for this dish you could try slicing by hand, but Chef Joachim uses a vegetable slicer, the efficient little Japanese mandoline; he easily cut sixteen perfect slices from one large baking potato. The base for his heavenly white butter sauce is a strongly reduced vegetable broth, called a *nage,* and it starts out the recipe.

Preparing the **Nage:** Melt the butter in the saucepan, add the vegetables and garlic. Sweat them (cook slowly, stirring frequently) for about 10 minutes, until they are translucent and limp but have colored no more than a pale yellow—the final sauce is to be white. Add the thyme and then pour on the wine; increase the heat slightly and simmer gently until the wine is reduced by half. Pour in enough warm water to cover the vegetables, and simmer, stirring occasionally, for 20 minutes, or until the vegetables are completely translucent and have almost broken down. Strain the *nage* through the sieve into a smaller saucepan, pressing down hard on the vegetables with the back of the ladle to be sure you extract all the juices from them. You will have 1¼ to 1½ cups of broth—more than you will need for 4 servings. Reserve half for another occasion.

INGREDIENTS FOR 4 SERVINGS

For the sauce base—the *nage*

1 tablespoon unsalted butter

The following vegetables, coarsely sliced or chopped:

1 leek, white and tender green parts, slit lengthwise and well washed

3 celery stalks, trimmed and washed

1 medium white onion, peeled

2 large shallots, peeled

1 large garlic clove, peeled and cut in half

2 sprigs of fresh thyme

1 cup dry white wine

Ahead-of-Time Note: May be made up to 3 days in advance and refrigerated in a covered jar; or it will keep for weeks in the freezer.

Preheat the oven to 350° F.

Preparing the Potatoes: Line one of the jelly-roll pans with a sheet of parchment paper, brush it with a film of clarified butter, and sprinkle lightly with salt and pepper. With a sharp knife cut off all four sides of the potato to form a neat rectangular block about 2½ inches long and 2 inches wide. Using the mandoline, slice the potato into lengthwise rectangles no more than ⅟₁₆ inch thick. You will need sixteen perfect slices of the same size. Arrange them in one layer in four rows of four on the parchment and brush them well with more clarified butter. Season with salt and pepper, and cover with another sheet of parchment paper. Place the second jelly-roll pan on top to keep the potatoes from curling, and bake in the middle level of the oven for 5 to 7 minutes, or until the potatoes are tender—be sure they are fully cooked. Set aside in the pan with the parchment covering them, and reduce the oven to 200° F.

Ahead-of-Time Note: The potatoes may be cooked in advance and refrigerated, but they will never taste as fresh and fine—better to do them several hours in advance and keep them warm in a low oven.

Sautéing the Mushrooms: Melt the butter in the large sauté pan over moderately high heat, and when it is just beginning to brown, toss in the mushrooms, season with salt and pepper, and sauté for 5 to 6 minutes, until their liquid is released and then evaporates. Add the shallots and sauté together for a minute or two. Remove from heat.

Assembling the Lasagna: Gently and carefully peel the top layer of parchment paper off the potatoes, leaving the sixteen potato slices in place. You are now to make four rectangular piles consisting of three layers of mushrooms layered between four slices of cooked potato. Form them one at a time on the baking sheet, as follows: Top a slice of potato with a heaping tablespoon of mushrooms. Very carefully, using the wide spatula, cover the mushrooms with a second slice of potato, and continue with another layer of mushrooms, a third slice of potato, a final spoon-

For the potatoes
¼ cup clarified butter (see box,
    page 252)
Coarse salt
Freshly ground black pepper
1 or 2 large fine baking potatoes,
    12 ounces each

For the mushrooms
3 tablespoons unsalted butter
10 ounces mushrooms (small
    chanterelles if available),
    brushed clean, stems scraped,
    thinly sliced (or shiitakes, stems
    removed)
1 or 2 large shallots, peeled and
    minced (about 2 tablespoons)

(continued)

Potato Lasagna of Chanterelle Mushrooms (continued)

ful of mushrooms, and topping that with its fourth and final slice of potato. You now have the first serving. Rapidly repeat with the rest of the potatoes and mushrooms, completing four rectangular piles in all. Keep them warm in the 200° F oven while making the sauce.

Finishing the Sauce: Shortly before you are planning to serve, bring the half portion of *nage* back to the boil. Add half the butter and whisk it in until it is slightly melted, then pour it immediately into the blender. Blend at high speed, adding the remaining butter by pieces through the sleeve, and blend just a few seconds, until creamy and emulsified. Pour back into the saucepan and place over lowest heat, to keep the sauce barely warm—more heat will break the emulsion and the sauce will thin out. Stir in the parsley, the tomatoes, several good grinds of pepper, and a big pinch of salt, tasting carefully as you go.

Serving: Remove the layered potato lasagnas from the oven and use the flat metal spatula to transfer the four lasagnas to the four warm plates. Ladle the sauce over and around each one, and serve immediately.

cook's notes

For finishing the sauce

4 ounces (1 stick) unsalted butter, at room temperature

2 tablespoons coarsely chopped Italian flat-leaf parsley

2 plum tomatoes, peeled, seeded, ribs removed, and finely julienned, then diced

Freshly ground white pepper

SPECIAL EQUIPMENT
SUGGESTED

A 4-quart heavy-bottomed stainless steel saucepan (for the nage*)*

A sturdy sieve (Chef Joachim prefers his chinois*)*

A ladle

A mandoline (vegetable slicer)

2 jelly-roll pans, or a jelly-roll pan and a flat pan that will fit inside it

Parchment paper

A pastry brush

A 10- to 12-inch frying pan (for the mushrooms)

A wide metal spatula

An electric blender (for the sauce)

4 warm appetizer plates

BRAISED LAMB SHANKS

Lamb shanks, slowly and carefully braised in a flavorful broth, make a marvelously hearty meal. Since all braises and stews are made in much the same fashion, this is an especially fine model to have in your repertoire.

Preheat the oven to 350° F.

Browning the Lamb: Salt and pepper the lamb shanks on all sides, dredge in the flour, and pat off excess. Set the casserole over moderately high heat, and when hot, swirl in just enough butter to film the bottom. As the butter foam subsides, lay in the lamb shanks and sauté, turning often with tongs, until all the pieces are quite evenly browned on all sides—this will take a good 10 minutes of careful work. Remove the casserole from heat, set the shanks on a side dish, and with paper towels pat up excess fat from the bottom of the casserole, but leave a film of fat for the vegetables to come. Return it to the burner over moderate heat.

Browning the Aromatic Vegetables: Stir the onion, leek, carrots, celery, shallot, and garlic into the casserole, and add another tablespoon of butter if there is not enough fat to coat them. Sauté, stirring frequently, for several minutes, until they are lightly browned; then stir in the tomatoes. Raise heat to moderately high, add the thyme and bay leaf, and cook for 3 to 4 minutes more, stirring frequently, until all the vegetables are softened and the tomatoes have rendered their juices. Return the browned shanks to the casserole.

Braising the Shanks: Pour on the chicken stock, veal stock, and wine, adding a little more stock if the liquid does not quite cover the ingredients. Bring to the simmer on the top of the stove, then cover and set in the preheated 350° F oven. Smaller pieces will take a little less time to cook, while the meatier ones may take almost 2 hours. Check occasionally—the liquid should be simmering slowly throughout the cooking.

When Is It Done? The shanks are done when the meat is tender if pierced with a fork, and it can be pulled cleanly away from the bone.

Degreasing the Braising Liquid: Remove the lamb shanks to their side dish, cover with foil and keep warm. Strain the contents of the casserole into a clean saucepan, pressing hard on the ingredients to extract every drop of

INGREDIENTS FOR 4 TO 6
SERVINGS

For the lamb
*3 hind shanks of lamb, cut in
    half crosswise (3¼ to 3½
    pounds total)*
Salt
Freshly ground black pepper
*All-purpose flour (for dredging
    the lamb)*
1 to 2 tablespoons unsalted butter

**The aromatics for flavoring the
    braise**
*The following vegetables coarsely
    chopped:*
1 medium yellow onion
*1 medium leek, trimmed,
    quartered, and washed, white
    and tender green parts*
2 medium carrots
1 large celery stalk
*1 extra-large shallot or 2
    medium-size shallots, peeled*
*4 large garlic cloves, unpeeled,
    crushed*
*A little more unsalted butter,
    if needed*

(continued)

liquid; discard the solids. Using a ladle or a large spoon, skim any visible fat off the surface of the liquid, which will be the basis for the sauce.

Ahead-of-Time Note: The recipe may be completed a day or two in advance to this point. Return the lamb shanks and skimmed braising liquid to the casserole, and when cool, cover and refrigerate. Before continuing, cover the casserole and simmer slowly for 5 minutes or so, until the meat is thoroughly warmed, then remove the lamb shanks, and keep warm; pour the sauce into its pan.

Finishing the Dish and Serving: Set the braising liquid over high heat to reduce it by half, frequently skimming any accumulated fat off the surface. Taste carefully, and adjust seasoning as needed. Just before serving, remove from heat and swirl in the butter, which will smooth and lightly thicken the sauce. Mound the risotto in the center of the warm platter, arrange the lamb shanks on top, and ladle the sauce over the meat. Scatter on the parsley leaves, and serve.

cook's notes

5 or 6 ripe plum tomatoes (or several regular tomatoes), unpeeled, halved, and quartered
2 sprigs of fresh thyme
1 bay leaf

The braising liquid
5 cups chicken stock, plus more as needed
1 cup veal stock or an additional cup of chicken stock
½ cup dry white wine or dry white French vermouth

For finishing the sauce
2 tablespoons unsalted butter, at room temperature

For serving
Barley Risotto (see page 287)
Sprigs of fresh parsley leaves

SPECIAL EQUIPMENT SUGGESTED

A heavy 7- to 8-quart covered casserole, such as an oval one 12 by 9 by 5 inches, or a heavy, wide 8-quart ovenproof saucepan with cover
Tongs
A strainer
A 2½-quart saucepan (for the final sauce)
A warm platter (preferably an oval one)

BARLEY RISOTTO

Barley, probably the world's oldest grain, is seldom seen on the American table as a cooked vegetable, but it's likely we'll be eating more of it when this recipe of Chef Joachim's becomes known. He bases his technique on Italian risotto, simmering his barley in a good stock and aromatic vegetables. The effect is that of a risotto, but the barley kernel is sturdier than the rice kernel, giving you more of a chew and a quite different flavor.

Manufacturing Note: This recipe uses "pearled" barley, meaning the kernel has been husked and thus cooks in about 20 minutes—certainly a reasonable amount of time. More ideas for barley and two other grains are in the box on page 288.

Cooking the Barley: Melt 1 tablespoon of butter in the saucepan over moderately high heat. Stir in the onion and sauté, stirring frequently, for 4 to 6 minutes, or until it is nicely browned—caramelized, as our contemporary chefs would say. Deglaze the pan by pouring in the wine and stirring all around the bottom and sides to loosen and incorporate the flavorful brown bits. Simmer the wine for a moment until it is reduced by half, then stir in the barley and continue stirring slowly for 2 minutes. Pour in enough chicken stock just to cover the barley, and bring to the simmer. Maintain uncovered and at the simmer for 22 to 25 minutes, stirring every 2 to 3 minutes, until the barley is tender and fully cooked. Add more stock as the liquid evaporates.

Sautéing the Aromatic Vegetables: Meanwhile, melt 2 tablespoons of the butter in the frying pan and stir in the finely diced shallots, leeks, and carrots. Sauté over moderately high heat for a minute or two, until just cooked through, then stir them into the barley and let them simmer together for just a moment to blend the flavors.

Ahead-of-Time Note: May be cooked as much as a day in advance to this point. When cool, cover and refrigerate. Reheat, still covered, over simmering water, stirring frequently.

INGREDIENTS FOR 4 SERVINGS

For the barley

3 to 8 tablespoons (1½ to 4 ounces) unsalted butter (1 tablespoon for the initial cooking, 2 tablespoons for the aromatic vegetables, plus up to 5 tablespoons more for finishing the risotto)

¼ cup finely diced onion

1 cup dry white wine or dry white French vermouth

1½ cups (12 ounces) "pearled" barley (available in health food stores)

1 quart hot chicken stock, plus more as needed

The aromatic vegetable flavoring

2 large shallots, peeled and finely chopped (¼ cup)

1 medium leek, white and tender green parts, finely diced (½ cup)

1 medium carrot, finely diced (½ cup)

(continued)

Barley Risotto (continued)

Finishing the Risotto: Remove the pan from heat and immediately stir in the Parmesan cheese, then, tablespoon by tablespoon, the final butter—the amount is up to you; Chef Joachim folds it all in. Taste carefully for seasoning, and fold in the parsley.

For finishing

1½ ounces freshly grated Parmesan cheese (about ½ cup)

Salt

Freshly ground white pepper

2 tablespoons finely chopped fresh curly parsley

SPECIAL EQUIPMENT SUGGESTED

A 5- to 6-quart heavy-bottomed saucepan with lid

A 10-inch frying pan

JULIA'S IDEAS FOR BARLEY AND OTHER KERNELS

Barley Soup—Scotch Broth: The recipe for this nourishing soup always used to appear on the box of barley. Make a good meat stock, preferably a lamb stock, or use a beef broth diluted with a little water. For 2 quarts to serve 6 people, cut into small neat dice less than ⅜-inch size: ½ cup each of onions, white or yellow turnips, and carrots. Stir them along with ⅓ cup pearled barley into the broth and simmer for 15 to 20 minutes, or until the barley is tender. Just before serving, stir in 1 cup of neatly diced tomato pulp, either fresh or canned, correct seasoning, and fold in several tablespoons of chopped fresh parsley.

The Three Kernels: A combination of barley, brown rice, and wheat berries—what could be healthier? With a prudent addition of butter before dishing them out, they make very good eating besides. However, you'll need a pressure cooker for the wheat berries since open-pot cookery can be endless if not futile, while under pressure they cook in less than 15 minutes. After picking over and

washing 1 cup of the berries, cook them under 15 pounds' pressure in 3 cups of water, then let the pressure go down by itself—about 10 minutes. Remove the pressure valve, uncover the pan, and pour in 1 cup of chicken broth, ½ cup of pearled barley kernels, ½ cup of brown rice, and a little sprinkle of salt. Simmer with the pan partially covered for 15 to 20 minutes, or until the kernels are as tender as you wish them to be. (May be cooked in advance to this point.) Shortly before serving, uncover the pan and rapidly boil off excess liquid, stirring frequently to prevent scorching. Carefully season to taste, and finish the dish with a toss of softened butter.

Variations: You could toss the cooked kernels with five or six strips of crisp crumbled bacon or diced sautéed ham. You could also use the cooked kernels as a stuffing for baked tomatoes or zucchini or bell peppers, topping the stuffing with grated mozzarella.

APPENDIX

CHOCOLATE—MELTING

The Stove-top Method over a Hot Water Bath: Break 8 ounces to 1 pound of chocolate into ½-inch pieces and set aside in a perfectly dry 4- to 8-cup saucepan. Pour 2 to 3 inches of water into a roomy larger pan and bring to the simmer. Remove the pan from heat and let cool 15 seconds; then cover the chocolate pan tightly, and set it in the pan of hot water. In 5 minutes or so stir up the chocolate, which should be smoothly melted and glistening. If not, remove the chocolate pan and reheat the water in the larger pan to below the simmer, remove from heat, return the chocolate pan to it, and stir until the chocolate is smooth and glistening.

The Microwave Chocolate Melt: (Microwave strengths vary, and if yours is top-of-the-line powerful, use the shorter amounts of time indicated.) Spread the chocolate pieces in an open glass bowl, and set uncovered in the microwave oven. Microwave on "high" for 45 seconds to 1 minute. The chocolate should be soft and glistening, and still hold some of its broken shapes. Stir it up to let it melt completely, but if has not quite melted, try another 10 to 15 seconds, and if necessary another, and another. I'm always on the conservative side here as to timing, since too many seconds and the chocolate will burn.

How to Melt Chocolate with Liquid Flavoring: When a recipe calls for chocolate melted in a small amount of liquid flavoring, such as coffee or rum, the minimum amount of liquid is 1 tablespoon per 2 ounces of chocolate. You can add more but not less or the chocolate will stiffen. As an example, break 8 ounces of chocolate into a saucepan and add ¼ cup of strong coffee or rum. Cover the pan tightly and let it melt over hot water as in the stove-top method. (Note: I prefer the water bath method over the microwave when it is a question of chocolate and liquid—it works better for me.)

A Remedy for Stiffened Chocolate: If you have mistreated your chocolate and it has "seized" (stiffened), you can usually smooth it out by beating in a tablespoon of hot water, setting the pan in hot water, and stirring it about. It will rarely smooth out enough to glisten as a frosting should, but it will be suitable for use in cakes or sauces.

Note: See also Jacques Torres's very special method of melting and tempering chocolate for decorations on page 155.

EGG WHITE—BEATING

A good number of egg whites are beaten in this book, some by machine and some by hand. The goal is perfectly beaten whites that rise to some seven times their original volume and hold themselves in stiff, shining peaks. Here's what to watch for:

A Clean Separation: Be sure there is no speck of yolk in the egg whites, since that can hinder the rise.

A Clean Bowl and Beater: Be absolutely sure there is no oil or grease on either the bowl or the beater. Wash and dry both, then put a teaspoon of salt and a tablespoon of vinegar in the bowl and rub all over with paper towels, rubbing the beater also. Wipe both clean but do not wash them, since the faint vinegar residue will help to stabilize the egg whites.

Room Temperature: Set the bowl for a minute or so in a larger bowl of hot water to take off the chill and your egg whites will mount higher and faster.

The Relation of Bowl to Beater: You want the whole mass of egg whites to be involved—in other words, use a large beater in a small bowl. The balloon whip and copper bowl are ideal. A heavy-duty tabletop electric mixer with large whip that rotates around itself as it rotates around the bowl is also ideal. Otherwise you can use a portable electric mixer with double whisks, and rotate it around the bowl as though you yourself were the aforementioned tabletop model.

The Method: Whether you are beating by hand or machine, start fast for a few seconds, to break up the globular mass of the egg whites, then slow down, until the whites have begun to foam. Gradually increase speed, until the whites form stiff, shining peaks.

Be careful and watchful with a fast machine—don't overbeat or the egg whites will break down, begin to look grainy, and lose both their staying power and their puffing ability. (If this does happen, however, beat in another white, which will bring them back to usable form.)

HERB BOUQUET

This is a combination of herbs tied in a bundle so they will stay together during cooking, and can be lifted out easily afterward. The traditional small bouquet consists of a small sprig of thyme or ¼ teaspoon dried, a medium-size Turkish bay leaf, and 4 sprigs of fresh parsley with their stems. At times other items are called for, such as tarragon, or a clove of garlic, or celery leaves. You tie them all together with white butcher's twine, or fold them around the parsley and tie, or make a bundle in washed cheesecloth.

OLIVE OIL

It is trendy for contemporary recipes to call exclusively for "extra-virgin" olive oil, as though that were a definitive definition of great taste. The reality is that all virgins are not alike. When a label states that the oil is "extra-virgin," it is telling you only that it is made from the first cold pressing of the olives and that its oleic acid content amounts to no more than 1 percent. Although this does suggest that the oil will indeed taste of olives, it in no way guarantees a delicious taste or, more importantly, a taste you will like. The flavor will vary from country to country, from region to region, and depending on the care given to the picking and pressing of the olives.

The prices of extra-virgin olive oils vary greatly and you will pay more, presumably, for the better ones. But don't buy by the look of the bottle, or the reputation of the bottler, or the price—buy by the taste. Therefore, in this book we have called for "excellent olive oil"—and we mean "excellent" according to your taste.

SUGAR SYRUPS AND CARAMEL

Boiling sugar and making sugar syrups and caramel are essential to any good cook's repertoire—you should never have trouble when you follow the few basic directions here.

SUGAR SYRUPS

Sugar syrups are made up of sugar and water—⅓ to 1 cup of water per cup of sugar—boiled to various stages of sugar concentration, beginning with the "simple syrup," where the sugar and water are heated just until the sugar is dissolved. Often flavored with vanilla or liqueur, they are used to imbibe the layers of a cake, or to poach fruit, or wherever a sweetened liquid is wanted.

Warning: Unless you are used to syrups, remove the pan from heat when you are testing, since once the "thread" stage is reached, a boiling syrup thickens quickly—you might be testing for "soft ball" and while you are doing so the still boiling syrup can be reaching the "crack" stage, and you will be in serious trouble. Work quickly, in other words.

The Thread Stage: Boiled a little longer, the last drops to fall from the tip of a spoon into a cup of cold water will form threads. This is the sugar syrup that is used for fruit glazes, or beaten into egg yolks for the wonderfully rich butter cream frostings of the classic cuisine.

The Soft Ball Stage: As the water continues to evaporate, the syrup quite rapidly reaches the soft ball stage—a bit dropped off the spoon into the water will form a soft mass in your fingers. It is ready to be beaten into egg whites for a meringue frosting.

The Hard Ball and the Hard Crack: You then go through the hard ball and hard crack and finally the syrup begins to turn into caramel. Here's how to go about serious sugar boiling:

First, provide yourself with a moderately heavy pan that has a tight-fitting cover, so that the steam condensing on its lid will wash down the sides of the pan and prevent sugar crystals from forming.

Second, be sure, at the outset, that the sugar has completely dissolved and the syrup is perfectly, limpidly clear before you start in on your serious boiling.

Third, once you start boiling, never stir the syrup; however, you may swish it, holding the pan by its handle.

Cleaning the Pan and Utensils: Fill the pan with water, add any utensils, and simmer a few minutes to melt the hardened syrup or caramel.

CARAMEL

The Syrup Method: Proceed as for any sugar syrup, in a tightly covered pan, and when the surface bubbles are thick, uncover the pan. The syrup will begin to color. Continue boiling and swirling a few seconds more, until it is a light caramel-brown, then remove from heat and continue swirling—it will darken more. Set the bottom of the pan in the cold water to cool it and stop the cooking. This is a good method when you want to pour the caramel into a mold to line it, or you want a caramel syrup or sauce.

The Direct Method: Pour the sugar into a heavy pan, such as a cast-iron skillet, set over moderately high heat, and stir the sugar around as it gradually turns a caramel brown. This method is easy and practical when you are making a sauce in that same pan, or you wish to caramelize onions or apples, and so forth.

INDEX

A NOTE ON THE TYPE

The text of this book was set on the Macintosh in Adobe Garamond. Designed for the Adobe Corporation by Robert Slimbach, the fonts are based on modern renderings of the type first cut by Claude Garamond (c. 1480–1561). Garamond was a pupil of Geoffroy Tory and is believed to have followed the Venetian models, although he introduced a number of important differences, and it is to him we owe the letter which we know as "old style." He gave to his letters a certain elegance and a feeling of movement that won their creator an immediate reputation and the patronage of Francis I of France.

Color separations by Professional Graphics, Rockford, Illinois
Printed and bound by R. R. Donnelley & Sons, Willard, Ohio
*Designed by Emily & Scott Santoro/*WORKSIGHT